THE BROKEN WORLD

OTHER BOOKS BY LINDSEY KLINGELE

The Marked Girl

THE BROKEN WORLD

Lindsey Klingele

An Imprint of HarperCollins*Publishers*

HarperTeen is an imprint of HarperCollins Publishers.

The Broken World
Copyright © 2017 by Lindsey Klingele
All rights reserved. Printed in the United States of America.
No part of this book may be used or reproduced in any manner whatsoever without
written permission except in the case of brief quotations embodied in critical articles
and reviews. For information address HarperCollins Children's Books, a division of
HarperCollins Publishers, 195 Broadway, New York, NY 10007.
www.epicreads.com
Library of Congress Control Number: 2016949960
ISBN 978-0-06-238036-4 (trade bdg.)
Typography by Kate J. Engbring
17 18 19 20 21 PC/LSCH 10 9 8 7 6 5 4 3 2 1
❖
First Edition

For Phil,
my home

APOCALYPSE NOW

Los Angeles was going to hell.

People from everywhere else in the country had been saying that for years, of course. They gasped in fear at the helter-skelter sixties, raised their eyebrows when teased hair, pleather, and loud music took over the Sunset Strip in the eighties, and shook their heads at the nineties riots. And that was all *before* reality TV. They said too much sunshine soaked into people's brains and addled them. Or maybe it was the Botox. Or the traffic. The city was home to gangs, vegan cleanses, Lindsay Lohan. One day the whole place would break away and sink right into the Pacific Ocean, and good riddance—it was all falling apart, anyway.

Shannon Mei had heard all that and more her whole life, but never had any reason to take it seriously.

Until now.

Shannon's best friend, Liv Phillips, had been gone for twenty-four hours, and in that time, their hometown had taken a serious left turn into the crazy. For a solid chunk of those twenty-four hours, Shannon had been holed up at the West Los Angeles Medical Center, staking out the room of a strange, mostly unpleasant boy and watching the city outside turn to chaos.

For the twentieth time that day, Shannon parted the blinds in the tiny hospital room and looked out the window. In late August in Los Angeles, the sky should have been a deep, clear—but still familiar and unremarkable—blue, maybe dotted here and there with wispy white clouds.

But this sky wasn't the one Shannon knew.

For one thing, it was orange. And not the bright, Technicolor orange of sunrises and sunsets, but a sickly, brownish orange, thick with rust-colored clouds. It looked *angry*. And the people in the city sprawled out beneath it gazed up, helplessly, at a sky that had turned on them like a loyal dog suddenly gone feral. What else could they do? Run? How could you run from the sky?

And that wasn't the only thing going wrong. After a large earthquake the day before (one Shannon knew had been caused by Liv *traveling to another world*), the ground continued to rumble every couple of hours. It was getting warmer, too. Los Angeles was always hot in August, but temperatures didn't usually climb quite this fast during the day. Even in the air-conditioned hospital, the fabric of Shannon's slinky T-shirt clung to her back.

She closed the blinds again.

Inside the small room, it was dark and quiet. Merek lay still on the hospital bed, his thin, lanky frame nearly edging off the small cot. The top of his head was wrapped in gauze, and the right side of his face was a dark bruise. Merek was being treated for smoke inhalation, a concussion, and a gash on his collarbone that needed twelve stitches. But that bruise on his face was maybe the worst—a nasty gift from when Cedric, Merek's friend, enemy, and leader, had smashed Merek's face into the ground repeatedly for what turned out to be no reason at all.

Merek was still unconscious, leaving Shannon alone to parse through everything that had happened in the past day while the world outside fell apart. That her best friend, Liv—calm, steady, annoyingly organized Liv—was secretly some kind of scroll who had the ability to open *portals* to another world through the power of a back tattoo, of all things, was ridiculous enough. That Liv had befriended a group of runaway royals from said other world, and was also on the run from monsters and knights and who knew what else—it was a lot for Shannon to keep track of.

Like, a whole lot.

It was almost too much to be believed, if Shannon hadn't been an actual witness to all of it. She still felt like maybe she was insane, or dreaming. But all she had to do was part the blinds of the hospital room to see the sky and know that the craziness was real. And far from over.

Whatever was going on outside, it had something to do with the portals—and with Liv. But Liv wasn't around to fix things right now, and Shannon couldn't follow or even call her—she doubted the magical "other world," whose name she could barely pronounce, had Verizon cell towers. Liv had left her behind, left her to deal with this whole mess.

Not that Shannon had any idea what to do. She'd stayed with Merek the day before, like she promised Liv she would. But right after she'd gone home for a much-needed nap and shower, everything went to hell.

It was like the whole city had ground to a halt. Even Shannon's rational, left-brained parents, who never raised their voices at her even when she stole the car, wore miniskirts to church, or dropped out of advanced calculus to take drama, had genuine panic in their eyes. They sat with Shannon as the freaky orange sky turned darker—but not completely black—that night, and the three of them hardly slept at all. The next morning, they decided to skip *work*, which scared Shannon more than anything else. But Shannon had promised to look after Merek, and she couldn't shake the urge to do *something*, so that morning she'd left her parents a letter explaining that she went to check on Liv (a lie) and would be back soon (hopefully true).

So now, here she was. A TV on the wall across from Merek's bed was on, but muted. Shannon reached for the remote and turned up the volume.

A pore-free news anchor with a helmet of shiny blond hair had her Very Serious News Face on. She was talking via satellite to a balding man who looked like he'd had maybe three too many cups of coffee and a stern-looking man with thick eyebrows and a buzz cut. The ticker at the bottom of the screen read, "ENVIRONMENTAL CATASTROPHE IN LA?" And then, below that, "GOVERNMENT CONSIDERING FEMA RESPONSE."

"So are you definitely saying this is an effect of climate change?" the news anchor asked, a tiny furrow appearing in the skin between her perfectly plucked brows.

Buzz Cut Man scoffed, while Balding Man put his jittery hands in front of him.

"No, no, I'm not *definitely* saying anything," Balding Man replied. "At this juncture, it would be irresponsible to ascribe any one cause."

"But you're not ruling out climate change."

"I don't think we can rule out anything. But it seems unlikely that global warming would cause such radical changes overnight, or even in an instant, as many reports indicate—"

"But what else *could* cause such abnormalities in the sky and weather?"

"Well, uh . . . it could be many things. . . ."

Beads of sweat dripped down into the Balding Man's collar. Shannon felt a jolt of sympathy for him. Buzz Cut man took his cue to cut in. "While the scientists are dithering back and forth, Amy, what we should be focusing on is how to contain a worsening situation in Los Angeles. A military presence is needed to stem the panic—"

"Loud girl?"

Shannon muted the television again and spun toward the scratchy voice. Merek was awake, his eyes on her. She scooted her plastic chair closer to the edge of his bed.

"Welcome back."

"Where am I?" Merek asked, struggling to rise. "It's so . . . white."

"You're at a hospital on Wilshire. The doctors have been treating you for smoke inhalation."

Merek's hand slowly rose to the bandages around his head. He winced.

"And a head wound."

When Merek brought his hand back down, he saw the small tube sticking out of his right arm, just above the elbow. The tubing led from his arm to a small fluid sack hanging from a stand by his bed. His eyes widened, and he reached to pull the tubing from his skin. Shannon moved quickly to stop him, grabbing his free hand with her own.

"Stop. That's making you better."

"Is that going *inside* of me?"

"Pretty sure, yeah."

"Why?!"

"I don't know, I'm not a doctor. But they know what they're doing here. This is where Zac Efron had his appendectomy."

Merek's eyes stayed on the tubing. "This is barbaric. How long have I been here?"

"About a day."

Merek pushed himself up to a sitting position and looked to the door. "Are the others outside?"

"Uh . . ." Shannon bit her lip and looked down. In the past few hours that she'd been watching Merek sleep, she'd wondered how she would tell him his friends had split. Tact had never been her strong suit. But honesty was.

"No, they're not here. They're gone."

"Gone where?"

"Back to your home planet."

"*What?*"

Shannon drew a big breath. "Joe said that Cedric had to get out of the hospital because the police want him on account of how he's always around when police officers get beat up. Which, fair enough. And Joe couldn't tell the cops the truth, because talking about portals and monsters and knights would get us all locked up. Again, fair."

Merek gave a quick, exasperated sigh, which Shannon just took as a cue to continue.

"So Cedric, Kat, Liv, and her brother and sister went to Daisy's house in Malibu to wait for you to get better. Oh yeah, and Cedric's sneaky little sister went, too. Then that same sneaky little sister stole Liv's brother in the middle of the night and made him open a portal to your home world. Or maybe he went willingly, that part's less clear. Joe told me all this on the phone. Anyway, the others decided to go after Liv's brother. Well, Liv, Cedric, and Kat did, anyway. So. That's the short version."

Merek leaned back against his pillows, and for a moment Shannon saw what might have been a glimmer of hurt in his eyes. But it disappeared so quickly she wondered if she'd ever seen it at all. When he spoke, his voice was cold.

"They left me here."

"Yeah, looks that way," Shannon said. "If it helps, they left me here, too."

"Pardon me if I do not find that of particular comfort."

"Hey," Shannon said, meeting his eyes. "You want to talk about comfort? *I'm* the one who's been sitting in this tiny room for hours and hours, waiting for you to wake up. And does this chair *look* comfortable to you?"

She gestured to her plastic chair. Merek just raised an eyebrow. Which was clearly a mistake, because he immediately winced in pain.

"Serves you right for being so ungrateful," Shannon said.

"I never asked you to sit on a chair for me."

"Yeah, well, I never asked for my best friend to be able to jump to another world and leave me behind with Captain Sarcastic. I never asked to have to lie to my parents, or watch the city fall into an apocalypse—"

"What?"

"Oh yeah, did I forget to mention that?"

Shannon stood up and walked to the window. She pulled open the blinds, revealing the orange nightmare of a sky. "The world is falling apart."

From the doorway, someone cleared his throat. Shannon looked up to see Joe, Liv's social worker. He nodded toward the window. "There might be something we can do about that."

"Joe!" Shannon couldn't keep the joy out of her voice. She'd only met Joe once or twice during the past few years, usually when he was helping Liv find a new foster home after one flamed out. And even though it turned out Joe had the same back tattoo—marking, whatever—as Liv, and the same ability to open portals to another world, he'd still become a point of sanity and comfort over the past few days. When your best friend starts making out with princes and jumping through portals, it can be good to have an adult-type figure around.

Joe smiled at Shannon and then quickly and quietly closed the door behind him, shutting the three of them away from the busy hospital hallway.

"Any news?" Shannon asked.

Joe gave his head a small shake, and Shannon tried not to be disappointed. She knew it was asking a lot to expect Liv to come home in less than a day, but she still hoped her best friend made it back sooner rather than later.

"What about Daisy?"

Joe sighed. "I've been in touch with her parents. They're trying to catch a flight back to LA, but all flights to and from the city have been canceled for the time being. For now, I'm keeping Daisy with me. She's at the vending machines in the hall." Joe looked to Merek. "I'm glad to see you're awake. How are you feeling?"

"Like I've been stabbed, battered, and left to die," Merek responded.

"Cedric didn't want to leave you behind," Joe said.

Merek rolled his eyes. "I doubt that very much. If anything, I am sure he was glad at the chance to finally be rid of me."

"All right with the self-pity already, we get it," Shannon said. "Nobody likes you, everybody hates you, blah, blah, blah." She turned to Joe. "You said there's something we might be able to do? About the sky?"

"Hopefully," Joe said, and sighed. "It's a long shot. But the sky began to change the minute Liv went through that portal. We have to assume the two are connected. Maybe opening that large portal with three scrolls had something to do with it, or maybe it was just the final portal that broke the Earth's back, so to speak. What we need is more information."

"Where do we get that kind of information? I'm guessing there's not a helpful blog somewhere?"

Joe blew air through his mouth and crossed his arms. "Doubtful. I think I'll need to go right to the source this time."

"The source?"

"The Knights of Valere," Joe said.

Shannon raised her eyebrows, but said nothing. She hadn't been present the first time the ancient sect of nut jobs who called themselves the Knights of Valere had attacked Liv, but she'd been there the second time. She'd seen their leader, a man Liv referred to as the professor, try to shoot Liv to prevent her from opening a portal.

The Knights were not Shannon's favorite people.

"But aren't the Knights the bad guys?" Shannon asked. "I mean, you're like Liv, Joe. A scroll. Won't they just try to kill you?"

Joe cocked his head. "Maybe. But they're the only ones who know anything about the portals. They may have the answers we need."

Joe's eyes went to the window, and Shannon's followed. "Desperate times . . . ," she whispered.

"But before we can even think about getting to the Knights, we first have to figure out a way to get out of the hospital."

"Sounds like a fine idea to me," Merek put in. He reached for the tubing in his arm again. And again, Shannon stopped him.

"It won't be that easy," Joe went on. "Merek, the doctors have to clear you. And after that, the police will have questions for you. They'll want to know how this happened, who you were with . . . We'll have to come up with a story, a good one they can't poke holes in. I'll tell the police you're a minor so that I can take you into my care and there's less chance they'll want you to go down to the station . . . but for that to work, you need to be convincing."

"Convincing?" Merek asked.

"Yes," Joe said. "We don't have time to deal with the cops and child services right now. We need to find the Knights and figure out how to fix whatever's happening out there in the city, before things get worse and people start getting killed."

Merek shook his head in confusion. "Who's getting killed?"

"Los Angeles is a big city with millions of people," Joe said. "The kind of panic this will cause, the earthquakes alone . . . we *need* to get out of here and find the Knights as soon as possible. So, Merek, your first interaction with the police has to be completely believable. You have to be sincere, polite, and willing to cooperate if we have even a chance of pulling this off."

"Oh man," Shannon said, shaking her head at Merek's anything-but-polite expression. "We are so screwed."

THE LOST WORLD

Liv Phillips was standing on a cliff, literally overlooking a whole new world, and all she could think about were cheeseburgers. Greasy take-out burgers that left drippings trailing down your palm, fancy LA bistro burgers you had to cut with a knife and fork, straight-from-the-grill backyard burgers slapped onto a paper plate . . .

Liv's stomach rumbled.

Standing next to her, Cedric West, an honest-to-God, full-on prince who also happened to be full-on icing her out, gave Liv a quick side-eye.

"I can't help it!" she said, putting one hand over her noisy stomach.

"We will eat as soon as we make camp. First, we have to get as close to the castle as possible before night falls again."

"I know, I know," Liv replied helplessly. "*I'm* aware of the plan. It's just that my stomach isn't."

Cedric didn't respond, but looked out again over the landscape in front of them.

The cliff they were standing on was large. Which was fitting, considering that everything in this world was large. The whole of Caelum appeared to Liv like someone had taken a picture of a European forest and enlarged the image one and a half times. Everything was just a little too big to be completely believable, from the rock she stood on to the tall evergreen trees that loomed up behind her and cast their small group into shadow.

They'd been walking through this world for hours, only stopping once to sleep for a bit and twice more to eat. They'd gone through their provisions quickly—their provisions being a couple of water bottles and granola bars found in the bottom of the earthquake kit backpack Daisy had pressed into Liv's hands the day before, when she'd still been standing on a normal California beach about to jump through a portal. Now the black backpack carried nothing but a flashlight, some walkie-talkies, and the empty water bottles.

For breakfast, Liv, Cedric, and Kat had made a meal of mushroom tops that were larger than Liv's hand. Since then, she'd passed flowers that came up to her knees and tree trunks as thick as cars. At her back was a mountain peak that reached for the sky, and although she'd been walking away from it for the better part of a day, when she turned around, it always appeared to be the same distance behind her. But though everything in this world was large, it also seemed oddly flat, as though drained of some color, some dimension. Like she was looking at an old painting where the perspective was slightly off. When she'd tried to explain this to Cedric, his eyes had narrowed, but he hadn't said a word in response. Then again, he wasn't saying much of anything to Liv.

So she'd spent the day trudging on behind him and Kat, trying not to slow them down with her wide-eyed wonder and questions. Both the royal teens seemed to be changed now that they were back in their home world. Cedric was full of purpose. It was as if there were an invisible string between him and the castle, and it was pulling tighter with every second.

Kat, meanwhile, was a different person altogether. Back in Los Angeles, the beautiful, dark-haired warrior had been wary and caustic, unable to trust Liv or anything else she saw around her. But now she moved with an actual *bounce* in her step. Her brown eyes lit up, and she seemed to almost float at Cedric's side as she walked through the world that was hers. She was home.

Liv tried not to think about how at ease Kat and Cedric looked walking side by side in this never-ending forest. They communicated in shorthand, sometimes using a single word or even just a look that Liv could barely decipher. They were two people who had known each other since the cradle and would go on knowing each other until the end. They were betrothed, meant for each other. Sure of their place together and in their world.

The term *third wheel* didn't even begin to cut it.

All Liv could do was try to push aside the part of her that was still stinging after Cedric rejected her on the Santa Monica Pier. It wasn't easy, but at least she had a plan. Or more of an objective, really. Find Peter. Then get the hell out of here. It would be much easier to get over Cedric once he was a whole world away.

She hoped.

After several hours of walking, Cedric and Kat stopped suddenly at the cliff edge. Liv looked down and saw that the cliff dropped more than a hundred feet to the dark forest floor below, where a thick, white-gray mist swirled around the tree trunks. She felt, not for the first time, that nothing around her was quite *real*. Almost like she was in a dream, or a movie adaptation of one of Grimm's fairy tales.

"We should move back from the edge." Kat's voice cut into Liv's thoughts. For the first time since they'd crashed through a portal and onto Caelum's leafy floor, Kat sounded uneasy.

"What is it?" Cedric asked, immediately on alert.

Kat nodded toward a group of thick trees in the forest below the cliff. At first, Liv couldn't see anything. But then she noticed a slight movement—not so much in the trees themselves, but in the dense shadows around them.

"Get down," Cedric said, his voice low. He dropped to his stomach on the cliff top, and Kat and Liv followed suit on either side of him.

With her chin pressed against the hard rock, Liv watched as the movement grew closer and closer, pushing through the forest below in a slow but purposeful trail.

"What is it?" she whispered.

Cedric put a finger to his lips.

And then the first creature burst through the trees.

Liv had to bite down on her lower lip to keep from screaming.

The being—the *thing*—below was unlike anything she'd ever seen in real life. It stood upright like a man, but was covered in the thick, gray skin of an elephant. And it had two horns that curled up on each side of its head and ended in fine points. In one hand, the creature held a sword and, in the other, a mace. It looked like a movie monster come to life, and Liv had to remind herself she wasn't on a set. That wasn't makeup and a costume, dreamed up in storyboards and brought to life by human hands.

There was nothing human about it.

The thing was joined by a second creature, and then a third. They kept coming, walking in a straight line just at the base of the cliff, pushing aside saplings and bushes in their way. Their heads swiveled to look around them, but, mercifully, they never looked up. Liv's muscles felt tight with the strain of staying still when they wanted so badly to get her far, far away.

Finally, the creatures moved out of sight. The forest swallowed them back up until they were shadows cutting through the mist, and then nothing.

Liv saw the tension leave Cedric's shoulders, which was her own cue to finally exhale.

"Wraths," Cedric said, answering her earlier question.

"*That's* what wraths really look like?"

Cedric just gave a quick nod and jumped to his feet.

Liv stared at the direction in which the wraths had disappeared. She'd been close to wraths before—much too close for comfort, in fact—but that had been back in Los Angeles. There, the wraths were affected by quelling, which was the Earth's way of covering up any magic that crossed its borders. To human beings, wraths looked like any other man or woman you might pass on the street. But Liv, who had her own bit of magic on the very skin of her back, could see snippets of the truth behind the human facade—the all-black eyes, the too-many teeth, the pointed nails. Remnants of the wraths' true, unrepressed form.

Which, apparently, included horns.

Kat also stood up and put her hand to her hip, where Liv knew a knife was hidden in the lining of her pants.

"I have never seen wraths this close to the city before . . . aside from our last night in the castle."

Cedric's eyes were still in the direction of the retreating wraths. "Is it possible they already have free rein over our lands this far from the castle? There must have been some sort of resistance after the takeover of Westing."

"Westing?" Liv asked.

"The main city surrounding the palace."

"Wait, Westing as in . . . West? Like your last name?"

Cedric nodded, his eyes still scanning the distance. Kat just rolled her eyes, like Liv's questions were too dumb to merit a verbal response.

"Those wraths looked as though they were scouting. But for what?" Kat said, turning to Cedric.

"I do not know."

"I would feel much more comfortable if we had silver weapons before advancing after them," Kat said, once again gripping the knife hilt at her hip. "It is no use cutting down wraths with this single steel blade only to have them rise up again moments later."

Liv shuddered at the image. "Like Freddy Krueger."

Unsurprisingly, both Cedric and Kat ignored her.

"The largest cache of silver weapons is in the castle," Cedric finally said.

Kat shook her head. "But it will be impossible to get *to* the castle if we do not know how far out from Westing the wraths have spread. We have no idea how many lie in wait between here and there, or even how many are still within the city walls. It makes more sense to first find any Guardians who made it out of the city. Maybe we can gather more information, more fighters. . . . We should head south toward the villages, and prepare to launch a full assault from there."

Cedric seemed to consider this.

This time, Liv stepped forward. "Wait. That's the opposite direction of where we've been going. You said that Peter was most likely at the castle. *That's* where we need to go."

Cedric turned to Liv. When he spoke, he didn't meet her eyes. He looked at her forehead, her ears. "I can only guess that is where Emme took your brother. I do not know for sure."

"All we know for sure is there are more wraths outside Westing than we anticipated," Kat said. "We will need better weapons and more men to cut through them."

"But . . ." Liv felt panic creeping over her as she imagined what might have happened to Peter, what might be happening to him at this very moment. "My brother went through that portal alone, and he might not have known how to do it right. If he went through like Malquin did the first time, without wrath blood on him, he could be hurt. He could be *dying*."

Liv's thoughts lingered on Malquin, once just Joe's brother and a scroll, like her. But he'd gone through the portal incorrectly years before and been twisted up by it. His arm was permanently withered . . . not to mention his mind. Liv wouldn't risk that with her own brother.

"I need to find Peter as soon as possible. It's the whole reason I'm here."

"Yes, I am aware," Cedric said, voice cold.

Of course he was. And of course he was mad about it. After learning that Malquin wanted to use Liv, Peter, and Daisy to open up a giant portal between their worlds, Cedric had wanted to keep them out of Malquin's hands at all costs. And instead here she was, playing right into them. Liv knew she was probably walking right into a trap set by Malquin, but this was her *brother*. She'd only just gotten him back after years of being apart—and she wouldn't lose him again. She would run into a trap for him if she had to. She would sprint.

Only, she needed Cedric at her side. She'd threatened to come through the portal alone, but a part of her knew that he wouldn't let that happen. He'd abandoned his own plans to come with her—she'd left him with no choice. And he'd barely looked at her since.

She missed the Cedric she'd first met in Los Angeles. The one who'd spooned maple syrup right into his mouth, the one she'd been able to open up to about her parents, the one who used to look right at her, just look and look and not turn away. . . .

"I know you're angry with me," Liv said, choosing her words

carefully. "But if Peter is at the castle, that's where I need to go."

Kat responded first. "You cannot find it without us."

Cedric looked off into the forest and said nothing. As if sensing his weakening resolve, Kat moved toward him and put one hand on his shoulder. "Remember, we must make the choice we know to be right, no matter what . . . *else* . . . gets in the way."

Cedric took a deep breath and was quiet for a moment. Then he lifted his head, and his voice was clear. "I still believe Emme would take Peter straight to the castle, as that's the most likely place for Malquin to be as well. But you are right, Kat. We need to know more about the movements of the wraths before we get too close." Cedric paused. "We will follow them. The wraths are heading in the direction of the castle already, so it will not send us too far off track. If we get close enough, we may be able to hear them speaking. We might find out for sure that Peter is there, and we might gain information enough to launch an attack, if necessary. Is that acceptable to everyone?"

Liv and Kat both gave tentative nods. When they noticed their mirrored movements, they each quickly looked away.

"Wonderful," Cedric said. "Now, to get down from this cliff."

⊱┼┼┼⊰

Growing up in the city, Liv had sometimes wondered if she was secretly an outdoorsy person, the kind who might like camping or even horseback riding, if given a chance. Now she knew the answer was a definitive *no*. Unfortunately, Caelum was pretty much *only* outdoors. They hadn't passed a single home, shop, castle, or even another person on the way from the portal. They weren't even following an established trail. After making their way down the side of the cliff, Kat and Cedric began looking for signs in the dense woods to point which direction the wraths had gone. Liv followed a few paces behind, mostly trying not to trip on the rocks and roots in her way.

Kat reached out to a tree with thick, green-gray leaves. She touched a branch that was snapped clean in half. "They are not exactly hiding their tracks."

Cedric shook his head, his expression troubled.

"Isn't that a good thing?" Liv asked.

Kat and Cedric just exchanged a look and said nothing. Liv fought not to roll her eyes and instead forged ahead, one foot after another. Every step she took would bring her closer to Peter. Of course, she didn't know what would even happen once they got back to LA. Would they have to go into hiding? Or leave the city she loved and start a whole new life?

She sifted through her enemies in her head. The Knights wanted her dead because she was a scroll. Malquin wanted her and one of her siblings to help him open a highway portal between Earth and Caelum. One that was powerful enough to stay open on both ends and provide passage for his monster army. Earth's quelling prevented portals from staying open on that side, while in Caelum they remained forever, a gash torn in the sky. But even though Malquin had forced Liv and Daisy to help him open a portal in the warehouse, it hadn't stayed open for very long. They'd been interrupted, and the portal had closed, bringing down a whole Venice block with it.

Was the other end of that portal still open somewhere here

on Caelum? And could Malquin still use it to bring his wrath army through to Earth, even if it would now be a one-way trip? Liv didn't know, but she shuddered at the thought of those monsters filing through the portal, landing less than a mile from the bodybuilders, stoners, and smiling tourists of Venice Beach.

Though if Malquin could still use that portal to get back to LA, he might not need Peter and Liv at all anymore. He might even let them go. . . .

Liv heard a sharp snapping sound on her right.

She whirled her head around, but saw nothing. Well, nothing aside from leaves the size of her face and tree trunks that might have broken a chainsaw in two.

Up ahead, Cedric and Kat were talking in low voices. Liv ran to catch up.

"It does not make any sense," Kat said, trailing her fingers over the top of a bush that looked like it had been recently trampled. "They did not veer from this trail."

Cedric shook his head. "Wraths are slow, particularly when they move in groups. We should have reached them by now."

Liv heard another snapping noise, this one directly behind her. She forced herself to turn her head slowly. Again, she saw nothing. Green and shadows, shadows and green. Close to the ground, the grayish mist thickened over massive tree roots.

"We should be right on top of them," Kat said.

"Unless . . ."

Another snap.

"Um, guys?" Liv said. Her voice sounded muted, as though

it were being choked by the denseness of the surrounding trees.

Snap. This time, the noise came from Liv's left.

"Unless . . . ," Kat echoed, her eyes wide.

"They are on top of us."

The words had barely left Cedric's mouth before the forest erupted with noise—breaking, growling, snapping, yelling. The wraths came from every direction. They pushed themselves forward from behind trees, sprang up from positions near the ground, knocked over smaller saplings and bushes.

Up close, the wraths were so terrifying, so *alien*, that Liv momentarily forgot how to breathe. The creatures were tall, some nearing at least seven feet, and many of them had horns that were longer than her arms. Their eyes were flat, black circles tucked deep behind mounds of gray flesh that was pocked, bunched, and stretched over squarish faces. And their mouths . . . their mouths were wide, with cracking lips that spread apart to reveal overcrowded rows of teeth.

Liv forced herself to move toward Kat and Cedric until their backs were to one another. They looked out onto the ring of monsters that surrounded them. There were nine . . . ten . . . eleven? They kept coming.

The wrath nearest to Liv moved forward on its thick legs, which were covered in a rough-looking brown fabric. In LA, the quelling had disguised some wraths as human women and some as men, but here the distinction wasn't at all clear. As the creature approached Liv, she saw a belt strapped to its waist, and secured to the belt was an axe. The sharp edge of the axe was a disturbing brown-red color.

The wrath stopped, six inches from her. Half of its mouth stretched upward in a sneer. Or was it a smile?

Liv screamed.

That's when the wrath's arm shot out. Its thick, coarse hand wrapped around her throat. And squeezed.

THE FAST AND THE FURIOUS

Liv couldn't breathe.

The thick fingers wrapped around each side of her neck were like two sides of a vise, moving closer and closer together. Her vision started to go black around the edges. She could barely see as Kat struck out at the wrath before she was knocked to the ground by another one of the creatures.

Through the escalating ringing in her ears, Liv heard a single, muffled sound: "Stop!"

The hand kept squeezing.

"Malquin has been looking for her. He will want her alive!"

The hand stilled.

"She is a child of the scrolls, the one Malquin has been searching for. If she dies, he will surely kill you," Cedric said, his voice strained.

"You know nothing of Malquin or what he will surely do," the wrath said in a low, inhuman growl. If boulders could split open and speak, Liv thought they might sound like this creature. But after a few seconds, the wrath's hand loosened on her neck. Just a fraction of an inch, but enough for her to take a breath of air.

"You can easily determine if what I say is true," Cedric replied. "Check to see if she is a scroll."

One beat passed, then two. Liv's breath was still raggedy, but at least her vision was returning.

The wrath spun her around so she was facing Cedric and Kat, who now both stood in defensive positions. But despite their fierce expressions, they looked small, tiny even, surrounded by the circle of monsters. Kat held up one small knife, while Cedric had no weapon at all.

The wrath who held Liv tossed her backpack aside and lifted the back of her shirt. She struggled, but it held her firm. The wrath's eyes combed over her back for a few seconds before it threw her to the ground.

"She comes with us," the wrath said. It nodded to Cedric. "And you, are you a scroll as well?"

Cedric hesitated, his jaw tightening. It was clear the wrath didn't know who he was. Would it be more or less likely to kill him if it knew he was the prince? Cedric seemed to be thinking over the same question. But he thought for just a beat too long.

"Evidently not," the wrath said. It made a small motion with its rock-like head. "Kill them."

"No!" Liv tried to scream, but her voice was raspy and thin coming from her bruised throat.

Kat and Cedric had already sprung into action. Cedric whirled around to the wrath closest to him, one with a sword that dangled from its belt. Cedric kicked out at the wrath's knee, and when it connected, Liv heard a snapping sound, followed by the creature's bellow. Cedric gripped the handle of the wrath's sword and pulled it out in one sure motion. He barely had it pointed outward before another wrath was upon him.

Cedric swung out at the second wrath, and the blade connected. Thick blackish blood ran from the creature's neck as it sank to its knees. But two more wraths were already charging Cedric, and he had to duck to avoid their fists.

While Cedric bent low, Kat jumped high over a swinging mace that was aimed at her legs. The tops of her toes barely grazed the weapon. But before she touched the ground, she was burying the tip of her knife into the shoulder of the wrath who held the mace. It screamed, with a voice like metal dragging across concrete.

Liv watched helplessly as Kat and Cedric dodged each blow, all while more wraths closed in. She had no weapon, and she searched the ground for something to grab . . . a rock, a stick, anything. Her hand closed around something cool and thick. It was a knife attached to the waist belt of the wrath Cedric had knocked down. The creature was still gripping its knee and yelling; it didn't notice Liv creeping up at its side. She closed her hand around the hilt of the knife and pulled it free. For a second she just stared at the knife, unsure what to do with it. Then she spun on her knees and thrust it into the foot of the wrath closest to her.

The creature roared and kicked Liv in the gut with its free leg. She went flying backward, landing on rough ground and unable to pull in a breath. Above, she could see a circle of whitish sky, the tips of the trees. Kat appeared in her line of sight, stepping backward as she dodged a wrath's claws. But Kat didn't see the second wrath, the one who came up behind her.

Liv tried to scream Kat's name, but she still couldn't pull enough air into her lungs. She only got out a *nnnhhh* sound before the wrath behind Kat took another step forward and thrust a knife into her side.

Kat's eyes widened in surprise. Her mouth dropped open. In the moment that she put together what had happened to her, the wrath in front of her kicked her to the ground. Kat went down hard, landing nearly on top of Liv.

Cedric turned, screaming Kat's name.

But he couldn't get to her, because two wraths caught him by the arms and held him. He struggled against them, his arms straining, his eyes fixed on Kat and the spot on the lower right of her shirt that was quickly turning red. He didn't see as a third wrath came up from behind him. He didn't turn his head as it lifted up a sword.

Liv tried to scream as the sword swooped down toward the skin of Cedric's neck, but she was too late, it was too late . . .

The sword froze in midair, and the wrath gripping it froze also. A thin arrow stuck out from the creature's neck, its silver tip dark with blood. The wrath fell backward. When its body hit the ground, Liv could feel the vibrations ringing in her own head.

There was just a second of silent confusion as the wraths looked to their fallen companion. Then everything turned to chaos.

Arrows came from everywhere and nowhere, traveling silently through the air and landing in the wraths, who yelled and turned their attention outside the circle, trying to locate the source of the arrows.

Through the dense tangle of limbs and fallen bodies, Liv could see only the darkness of the forest. Cedric took advantage of the interruption and broke free from the wraths who held him. He pulled the first arrow from the neck of the fallen wrath, spun around, and jabbed it into the shoulder of the nearest creature.

The group of wraths began to thin out. Some had fallen, while others disappeared back into the trees. The wraths who'd been struck with arrows didn't get up again.

Liv pushed past the ache in her abdomen and lifted herself off the ground. She crawled over to Kat, who was breathing heavily. Liv gently rolled her over to get a better look at the stab wound.

"Is it bad?" Kat asked, her voice catching.

The gash was just above Kat's right hip. Liv couldn't tell how deep it was, but the area of T-shirt around the wound was dark with blood.

"Barely nicked you," Liv said, struggling to keep her voice light.

Liv caught Cedric's eye just after the wraths he was facing retreated back into the woods. He raced over to where Kat lay on the ground and dropped to his knees.

"I am all right," Kat said before Cedric could even get a word out.

"Kat—"

"I said I am *all right*," Kat responded. Slowly, teeth gritted, she sat up, one hand to the wound on her hip. "Make sure they are truly gone."

As the last of the wraths scattered into the trees, the forest went still. It was just the three of them, surrounded by a few wrath bodies, each with one or more arrows sunk into their thickened skin.

Cedric's eyes stayed on the tree line. He tilted his head upward, and Liv followed his gaze to the cluster of branches in the nearest tree. The branches moved slightly, and Liv put one protective arm over Kat, who brushed it away with a grimace.

Then something dropped down from the trees and landed on the ground with a grunt. The something stood, and Liv could see it was a young man. He was tall, with light-brown hair that fell past his ears. He wore what looked like a silver breastplate tied over green-and-brown clothes that had been patched over more than a few times. His face and nose were long and thin, and something about him looked familiar to Liv, but she couldn't quite place how or why. In his right hand, he clutched a bow.

The young man locked eyes with Cedric, and both of them went very still. Cedric still clutched his sword, and the young man's face was impassive. The seconds dragged by until, at the same time, Cedric and the young man both dropped their weapons to the ground. They ran at each other, and for a moment Liv thought they were going to start throwing punches.

Instead, they hugged.

"You're alive," the young man rasped. He laughed then, an incredulous laugh. "Our prince—alive!"

"Thanks in no small part to you," Cedric said, then motioned to Kat. "Though I think we will need more of your help."

"I told you—" Kat started.

"Yes, yes, you are *all right*," Cedric said. "Still, some bandages and a chance to rest would not hurt."

"We can certainly be of assistance there," the young man said. He put out a hand to help Liv off the ground.

"Sorry, but . . . who are you?" Liv asked.

"You can trust him," Cedric said, slowly helping Kat to her feet. "Liv, meet Rafe Maxillion Harcourt, first son of Duke Harcourt and master both of the bow and of excellent timing, thankfully. He is Merek's brother."

Liv's eyebrows shot up. "Oh."

Rafe winked. "Pleased to meet you." He turned to Cedric. "Forgive me, but I was under the belief you were either locked up in a dungeon or dead. But clearly that's not true, so—where in hell have you been?"

Kat snorted in response before Cedric could reply. "Funny you should ask."

RED DAWN

It turned out an apocalypse did little to help LA's traffic problem.

Shannon's head was swimming in exhaust fumes as she gazed out at the slowest-moving jam-up of cars she'd ever seen in her life. And worse, she was stuck in the passenger seat and couldn't even express her frustration by pounding on the horn. At the wheel of his decade-old Jeep, Joe was too cautious and levelheaded to honk at the hundreds of cars in front of them on the 134 (though no one else on the road seemed to share his stance on honking).

"Another breakdown," Joe said, pointing to a stalled-out car on the roadway up ahead.

Shannon groaned. "Seriously, Joe, if you stop and pull a Good Samaritan with every car we pass, we'll never get to Pasadena."

Joe sighed. "This one looks abandoned anyway."

She felt a stab of guilt as they inched past the car, which was not only empty, but also had its windows smashed in. A pile of blankets and debris was littered outside the car's doors, and Shannon could only guess what had happened to the people inside. She tore her gaze away.

Even if she wanted to, she couldn't help every single person who was currently trying to evacuate the city. What she *could* do was try to stop things from getting worse. Which was why she'd persuaded Joe to take her with him as he went to track down a lead on one of the Knights of Valere. Daisy and Merek had come along as well—Daisy because she was still waiting for her parents to come and get her, and Merek because, well, he had nowhere else to go after being released from the hospital.

Shannon's phone buzzed in her lap. She sighed, but knew better than to ignore it.

"Hey, Mom, what's—?"

"Where the hell are you?"

Shannon's mom had never sworn at her before, not once in her life. Not even when she'd "borrowed" the van at fifteen, before she technically had her license, and it accidentally got towed from the beach.

"I'm safe, Mom. Don't worry."

"Don't worry? I'm beyond worry. How could you just leave? Do you even know what's happening out there?"

"I've got an idea—"

"Shannon Ning Mei, this is not a game. What could possibly have possessed you to leave the house at a time like this?"

"I had to, Mom. I had to check on Liv and make sure she's all right." The lie came out smoothly, but Shannon's hand that held her phone twitched a little, and she was glad her mom couldn't see her.

"I am sure Liv is perfectly fine."

"She doesn't have a family like I do, Mom. She doesn't have anyone."

A pause. "I understand why you'd want to make sure your friend is okay." Her mom's voice was slightly softer. "But you're my daughter, and I need to know that *you're* okay. I need you here."

"I told you, Mom, I'm safe."

"Where are you? I'm coming to get you."

"No! Mom, I'll leave soon. I mean right away. I'll leave right away."

"You better, Shannon. I want you home before dark, or I'm calling the police."

"I think they've got other things to worry about—"

"Shannon Ning—"

"Okay, okay. No need to keep middle-naming me. I'll be home before dark."

They said good-bye and Shannon hung up, then let out a huge breath.

"I don't feel comfortable with you lying to your parents," Joe said, his eyes on the road.

"Would you rather I told them we were on the hunt for former members of an ancient sect bent on keeping magic portals from opening on Earth?"

Joe sighed again, and Shannon looked out the window as they moved toward an off-ramp at a glacial pace. The truth was, she hated lying to her parents, too. It felt different now than it ever had before, which was funny, because trying to save the city was a much better reason to disobey her parents than cutting class to get tickets for a Taylor Swift concert.

But then again, she'd never seen her parents this upset before. Her mom, an environmental scientist who gave lectures on American wastefulness and had never set foot in a Costco, had already bought out several shelves' worth of canned goods, bottled water, and toilet paper from the local store. Shannon's dad, meanwhile, had started obsessively watching the news, his eyes bouncing between the CNN talking heads on TV and the CNN app on his tablet.

Not that the news had any more . . . well, *news* on what was causing the "abnormalities" in the atmosphere. But there was plenty of information on the results. People were getting out of the city as fast as their hybrid cars could take them.

Shannon felt restless and stuck. And worse—she felt powerless to help her parents. Just like everyone else in Los Angeles, they were desperately trying to understand *why* all this was happening, why their lives had turned upside down in an instant. Unlike everyone else, Shannon had a good idea what was going on. But she couldn't tell her parents about Liv's tattoo, or portals, or any of it—not without sounding crazy. And even if she did tell them the truth, and they believed her, what exactly could they do with that knowledge? They weren't scholars on arcane magic or whatever energy worked the portal stuff. There was nothing they could do to fix things.

But the same wasn't true for Shannon. She *could* do something—she could help Joe. Even if it meant being stuck in traffic for hours on end in a car that was honestly starting to smell.

"This world has far too many people," Merek said from the

backseat. A bicyclist moved quickly past his window, and he flinched backward. "Do you not feel cramped all the time?"

"I do right now," Daisy responded, squirming away from him. "Seriously, Joe, how small is this car? You could have at least gotten an SUV."

"I don't think social workers make SUV-level salary," Shannon responded.

"Hey," Joe replied. "You're right, but still. Hey."

"Are we there yet?" Merek asked, completely oblivious to how annoying that question was during a long car ride. Daisy snorted, and even Joe managed a small smile.

"Now, now, don't make Joe turn this car around," Shannon said, grinning.

Merek looked between them, confused at their smiles. "I do not understand half the things you say, let alone why you dragged me along on this ridiculous mission."

"It was this or stay in the hospital," Joe replied.

"With *the tubes*," Shannon added.

Merek made a face like he didn't care, but Shannon could see him half shudder as he turned to face the window, ignoring them once again.

Eventually, Joe turned onto a small side street on the outskirts of Pasadena. The houses had mostly dirt lawns, and the few palm trees wilted in the hot, still air. Joe parked in front of an adobe house with faded Spanish tile on the roof.

"This is it," he said.

Shannon reached for her door handle, but Joe stopped her.

"I think it would be best for the three of you to wait in the car, at least until I make sure it's safe."

"I thought you said there was only, like, a twenty percent chance a Knight actually lives here," Shannon said. Even though Joe had spent years trying to keep Liv, Daisy, and Peter safe from the Knights who'd killed their parents, he said he'd only picked up on their actual trail a few times. And he'd never gone *looking* for them before.

"That means there's a twenty percent possibility it's dangerous."

"So you drove us all this way just so we could sit in the car?"

"You're the one who begged to come, Shannon. If you want to help, this is how you can do it. By listening to me and keeping an eye on these two."

"Hey!" Daisy and Merek both said in unison from the backseat.

"Sorry, guys, but Daisy, you're only thirteen. And Merek, you could still pull your stitches out at any moment."

"Wait—what?" Merek asked, eyes wide. "That could happen?"

"Fine, I'll stay and watch over the backseat misfits." Shannon sighed and lifted her hand from the door handle. "But at least leave the air on. It's a hundred degrees outside."

"A hundred and two, according to my phone," Daisy piped in from the backseat.

Joe shook his head, but left the keys in the ignition as he got out of the car and headed up the dusty front walk toward the house.

Merek shifted over to look at Daisy's phone. "That thing

can tell you the current weather?"

"Current, future, whatever."

"Can I see?"

Daisy shrugged and handed her phone over to Merek. He took it cautiously, as though it were a hot cup of coffee that might spill and burn him.

"This world has so . . . much," he murmured. And for once, he didn't sound snide.

Shannon wondered, not for the first time, what Merek's home world was like, and how Liv was doing there. What would it be like to leave behind everything you knew and travel to a place so different? Personally, she'd never wanted to live anywhere *but* Los Angeles. She'd known what she wanted to be ever since the first time she'd seen *Hannah Montana*: famous. She already lived in LA, so she figured she was half-way there. She and Liv planned to go to USC or UCLA; she'd study theater and Liv would study film, they'd get an apartment together, and then they'd take over the world. One of them leaving Los Angeles—let alone their whole world—had never been part of the plan.

Shannon watched Merek, wondering if he'd had any sort of life plan before coming to LA. He glanced up from the phone screen to see her staring at him and grinned, lifting one cocky eyebrow as if to say *caught you*. Shannon opened her mouth to put him in his place when, suddenly, the Jeep started shaking.

It wasn't a gentle shake, either. The Jeep lurched quickly to the right, then back again. Daisy yelped, and Merek put his hands on the back of the seat in front of him to steady himself, eyes wild. Shannon gripped the armrest and waited for the earth-quake to be over. They'd been happening every few hours for the past couple of days, but they were jarring every single time.

After a minute or two, the shaking tapered off.

"It feels like they're getting stronger," Daisy said, her voice low.

Shannon thought she was right, but didn't want to say so. The idea that things were getting worse made her feel restless. The air in the car felt sticky and oppressive, even with the AC on. She squirmed in her seat.

"I can't wait in this cramped car anymore. I have to go check on Joe."

"But he said—"

"I know what he said. But if this guy is dangerous, Joe might need backup. And if he's not, then we have just as much right to hear what he has to say. You more than anyone, Daisy."

Daisy shifted awkwardly, and Shannon thought of the dark marking on her back. It was identical to Liv's, and it had the same power to open up a gateway to another world. Daisy might look like just another thirteen-year-old girl (well, a thirteen-year-old girl with a $500 Coach bag), but she had a big role in whatever was happening to their city.

Shannon hopped out of the car and a second later heard the other car doors open and shut behind her. Merek moved quickly to her side.

"Well, aren't you the rash one," he asked.

"You can always get back in the car if you want," Shannon snapped.

Shannon felt just a little nervous as she walked toward the front door of the house, but there was no way she was turning back now. It felt too good to be outside the car, to be doing something.

She opened the front door, pushing her way inside. After a few steps she stopped, suddenly finding it hard to move, or think, or breathe.

She'd walked out of an apocalypse and into a horror show.

A man—what used to be a man—was lying on the living room floor. The carpeting underneath him was stained dark brown, and similar dark brown stains spotted the nearby couch, chair, coffee table, wall. Shannon covered her face with her hands to block out the smell, the sight of the blood, but she couldn't. There was too much of it. Her knees buckled.

Merek put a gentle hand on Shannon's back to keep her upright. She had just enough foresight to throw out an arm behind her, stopping Daisy from coming inside.

For Shannon, it was already too late to unsee any of it.

Behind the body, Joe stood with one hand on his knee, one hand clutching his cell phone to his ear. His face was a shade of white-green. He looked up at Shannon and Merek with watery eyes.

"Someone else got here first."

WARGAMES

"This changes everything."

Rafe split off a piece of bread from the chunk he was holding and passed it over to Cedric, who quickly put it in his mouth. He left it on his tongue for a few moments, even though he was so hungry his stomach felt like a hollow pit. The bread tasted—well, not *good*, necessarily, but familiar. Whole, and thick, and just a bit hard. It had obviously been made by hand, wrapped in cloth, and carried around in a pack for days.

It tasted like home.

"The fact that a whole other world exists?" Cedric spoke around the bread in his mouth. "I'd say it changes more than a little."

"Not that," Rafe said, waving his hand. He'd seemed mostly skeptical at Cedric's tale of escaping from Malquin and surviving in Los Angeles for months. "I meant that you are *alive*. So few Guardians made it out of the wrath attack on Westing, and none who knew what had happened in the palace. After all this time . . . we assumed the worst."

Cedric shook his head. "Our families were alive when we left, and we have reason to believe they are alive still."

"All of them?" Rafe asked, his voice thick.

"Yes, all."

Rafe sagged back a bit, his eyes closed in what looked to Cedric like relief. The four of his men who also sat in the circle around the fire exchanged glances, as though they weren't sure they believed Cedric's claims. But at the moment, Cedric didn't care.

They had food, and some herbs and poultices to treat Kat's wound.

Although Cedric had begged her to get some rest, Kat had refused, instead staying wide-awake as the gash in her lower back was wrapped. She sat now next to a bundle of weapons, fighting to keep her eyes open.

"It is true," Kat said, her voice sluggish but still forceful as she looked around the men at the fire. "Our parents—all the royals—live."

Rafe narrowed his eyes. "But my brother went with you? Where is he now?"

Cedric hesitated, then forced himself to look Rafe squarely in the face. "He is alive, or at least he was before we left. He was injured and could not make the journey here. But we will go back for him, I swear it."

Rafe looked to Cedric, but his expression was inscrutable. The orange flames of the fires reflected in his dark eyes. He had always been a strong fighter, and capable. But he was also unpredictable. Rafe had never wasted an opportunity in letting it be known who was the superior sibling. And yet he loved his brother, Cedric knew. When Merek's mouth would get him into trouble with one knight-in-training or another, Rafe's fists would often end the conflict.

Rafe nodded, and a piece of Cedric, the piece tightly wrapped into a ball of guilt over what he'd done to Merek and how he'd left him behind, loosened just a fraction.

"I have no doubt," Rafe said, his voice even.

"He's being taken care of," Liv piped up from her position on the other side of the fire. "LA has some of the best doctors in the world. Or world*s*, I guess I should say."

Liv popped a piece of bread in her mouth and chewed slowly. Seeing her sitting there, across the fire, calmly eating a piece of hardtack, was extremely disconcerting to Cedric. Here he was, finally home in Caelum, surrounded by the trees and the air he'd grown up with, but nothing felt quite the same as when he'd left. His whole world looked different now that *she* was walking around in it.

Liv—clever, fast-talking Liv—was a creature of Los Angeles, with its lights and sounds and oddities. To see her here, resting on the long grass and wrapping a blanket around herself to keep out the night chill as if she were completely at ease could not be more strange.

He knew that allowing her to take up too much space in his thoughts was distracting at best and dangerous at worst, especially when there was so much at stake. But it was incredibly hard to ignore her as she sat there, just five feet away, her hair like burnished gold in the firelight. She looked as natural as could be, although she was in *his* world, under *his* sky. She looked almost as though she could belong here, which was the most terrifying prospect of all.

Cedric could not afford to start thinking Liv had any place in his life.

"Merek in another world," Rafe said, shaking his head. "Hard to imagine."

"It is best if you don't," Cedric cut in. "Merek is safe, but he does not belong in that place."

"None of us do," Kat said.

Cedric frowned at Kat's words, but he knew she was right. The sooner he turned his mind away from Los Angeles and toward his mission here, the better.

"Is it truly that awful?" Rafe asked.

Cedric saw Liv look at him, waiting for his response. "I certainly understand now why our ancestors thought it was hell," he forced himself to say. Liv's eyes filled with hurt, and she looked away. It was better this way, for all of them.

"Well," Rafe said, raising his voice as if to smooth over the tension Cedric had purposely created, "If this world created a creature as lovely as the one who sits across from me now, I do not see how it could be all bad."

Liv quickly rolled her eyes at the compliment. But in the light of the fire, Cedric could see she was flushed. He resisted the urge to throw the rest of his bread at Rafe's head.

Instead, he took a deep breath and told himself to focus, again, on what mattered. "What can you tell me of the situation here?"

Rafe picked up an arrow that was lying by his knee and began to turn it over in his hands. The silver tip caught the glow of the fire as it slowly twirled.

"The initial attack happened quickly, from all accounts," Rafe began. "I was on a hunting trip near Lake Vorail, due back at the castle for the summit. I thought it odd that we found not a single wrath on that trip, but there was no way I could have guessed . . ."

Rafe shook his head slightly. "Our party was halfway back to the castle when we came across the first refugees from Westing. Barely a hundred managed to get out. They were the ones who told us what happened. The wraths amassed with their full numbers in the forestland just outside the city. No one knows how the first of them found their way into the city walls, but once they did, they knew immediately who to kill. They slit the throats of every single lookout guard, seemingly at the same time, since not one alarm was raised."

Cedric's jaw tightened as he remembered the men who manned the lookout posts at the city walls. How many times in his life had he passed those men as he went in and out of the city? How many times had they bowed their heads to him and managed to hide their smiles as he struggled under the weight of a sword half the size of his body?

"After the lookouts were killed, the wraths killed the guards at every gate on the wall," Rafe continued. "Then they opened the gates. The city was overrun almost instantly. Some stayed to terrorize homes, while the others went directly to the palace."

Rafe stabbed the tip of his arrowhead into the ground. "I have never heard of wraths mobilizing in such a way as the refugees described. They have always lived and hunted separately, in small clans. For them to come together in this way and take the city so quickly . . ."

"We were not prepared," Kat murmured, her voice thick.

"The wraths had help," Cedric added. "They had someone to bring them together, someone who knew when the summit would take place, someone who maybe even knew a way into the city. Malquin."

Rafe raised an eyebrow. "I heard that rumor as well. But why would a Guardian—even a crazy, outcast one—help the wraths overthrow our castle? It makes no sense."

"He is not a Guardian," Cedric said, his voice steely. "He is from the other world."

Cedric looked up, briefly, and locked eyes with Liv across the fire. He then explained to Rafe how Malquin had created a portal to Caelum years before and, unable to get home on his own, had struck a bargain with the wraths. He would help them raise an army and organize an attack on the heart of Caelum so that they might have free rein over the realm. In exchange they would send some soldiers to Earth to help Malquin defeat his own enemies there.

Rafe shook his head slightly. "It is difficult to believe. That one man could cause so much destruction."

Cedric did not reply. Malquin was not a formidable figure on his own, but he had enough cunning to somehow rally the wraths to a single cause. How could no one in the palace—no one in the kingdom—have seen that alliance coming?

"How many wraths are in Westing now?" Cedric asked.

"My father said there were hundreds outside the castle that night. It is why we went through the portal instead of trying our luck escaping through the city."

Rafe shrugged. "We have been trying to determine that very thing. At first, we organized major assaults, but the wrath numbers were too large, and they were safe behind the walls *we* built to keep enemies out." Rafe took a breath, his eyes on the ground. "All attempts to take back Westing have failed."

Cedric lowered his own eyes as this information sank in. If Guardian forces hadn't even been able to broach the city walls since the attack, the situation in Caelum was worse than he'd imagined.

"We send mostly small scouting parties now, and raiding groups. We have had more success in picking off small groups of wraths like the one that nearly caught you all tonight. Our whole plan has been to weaken their numbers slowly until we can starve them out, but if it is true the royals—our families—are still alive inside the castle . . . as I said, that changes everything."

Cedric nodded. "Now that I am back, we can amass every remaining Guardian and launch an assault large enough to take back Westing."

Rafe cocked his head and opened his mouth as if to respond, but then paused a moment. Finally, he met Cedric's eyes. "I am not sure that is the wisest plan . . . my prince."

A silence fell around the fire.

"Before we go into talk of plans and wisdom, we should get to a stronghold," Kat said, sitting up with a grimace. She looked to Rafe. "I assume you have one?"

Rafe slowly nodded. "We do, about a ten-hour walk from here. The old village of Duoin."

"And are there any fighters left?"

"About two hundred. Many of the country folk have fled south, believing the royals dead and the city fallen."

"Has anyone come from my family's lands? The northern regions have a thousand fighters, easily," Kat said.

"None yet," Rafe replied. "We've sent groups to ask for help, but none have returned. The wraths around Westing have also blocked the passages to the north."

Kat looked dismayed.

Cedric turned to Rafe. "And at this stronghold, who's in charge?"

Rafe turned to Cedric and tilted his head. "At your service."

Cedric managed a weak smile in return.

"Though, I suppose now you've returned from the dead, you will be looking to take command yourself," Rafe said, almost as an afterthought. His tone was light, but Cedric sensed something else behind his words, a question.

Cedric smiled again, and struggled to think of the right response. Something diplomatic and thankful, yet firm. He was the crowned prince, and leadership should, by rights, fall to him. But Rafe had three months of wartime leadership under his belt already, and likely the loyalty of the fighters. It would be smart to stay on his good side.

My father would know the exact words to say, Cedric thought. But as the seconds passed, his tongue grew thicker in his mouth.

His eyes bounced to—of all people—Liv for help. But it was Kat who responded.

"I am sure that together we can find the best solution to free Caelum once again."

"Of course," Rafe replied. He pushed his arrow against a log in the fire, stoking a flame. The fire reflected in his eyes, and his expression was now blank, impossible to read. "I will take you to Duoin at first light."

Cedric shot Kat a grateful look and breathed an internal sigh of relief. What would he ever do without her?

BRAVE

"I want to go home."

Daisy had barely whispered the words, but her voice carried far in the dead Knight's lonely backyard. Shannon sat next to her on a small patch of dry grass while Merek paced a few feet away. The yard itself was depressing, littered with fast food wrappers and lined with a plastic construction fence that sagged in several places. It looked even worse under the dim orange sky and its thick, brown clouds that seemed to be pushing themselves toward the ground as night grew closer. Then again, the yard was a virtual oasis compared to what was going on inside the house.

"I know," Shannon managed, her throat tight. She put one hand on Daisy's shoulder, but she knew the gesture wasn't enough, could never be enough. She wanted to say something more comforting to Daisy, but at the moment she couldn't even figure out how to comfort herself.

She could still smell him, the dead man. As though the air in that closed-off living room had followed them outside.

"We're gonna get out of here soon," Shannon said, this time more to herself than to Daisy. After she'd barged into the house, Joe had immediately directed her to wait outside so he could call the police. She hadn't needed to be told twice. "We'll leave soon, and you'll go back with Joe."

Daisy shook her head. "No. I want to go *home*."

Of course you do, Shannon thought. But she could only nod and pat Daisy's shoulder again.

"Who would have done this?" Merek asked. He continued to pace, his brow furrowed. "If that man was truly a Knight, why kill him and just . . . leave him there? For what purpose?"

"I don't know," Shannon replied, helplessly.

Joe made his way into the backyard then, stepping around the busted-up remains of an old lawn chair. A bit more color had returned to his face, but his phone hung limply from his hand.

"The police are on their way . . . sometime. I suppose they have more urgent things to take care of," Joe said, gesturing vaguely at the streets, the city, the sky beyond them.

"Do you know what happened in there? Did you find anything?" Shannon asked. Her legs felt shaky, but she stood anyway, just to prove she could.

Joe paused, as if weighing his words, but ultimately just shook his head. Shannon didn't quite believe him, but she wasn't up to pressing him on it. Not right now.

Daisy stood up and crossed her arms. "I can't go back there," she said. Her voice was no longer a whisper, but came out sounding forceful.

Joe looked taken aback. "You don't have to, Daisy. None of us need to go back inside that house."

"No, I mean to Los Angeles. I can't." Daisy's voice broke as she spoke, and Shannon could see tears at the corners of her eyes. She was looking everywhere but at the three of them. "I wanted to help, I wanted to get Liv and Peter back, too, but I can't . . . I can't . . ."

Daisy's head finally fell down, and tears streamed past her nose and cheeks onto the parched ground. Shannon moved forward, at a loss for how to help but knowing she needed to . . . but Joe beat her to the punch, taking two steps toward Daisy and pulling her into a hug.

"Oh, Daisy, you don't have to do anything," he said, his voice both gentle and sure. "I know your brother and sister would want you safe. *I* want you safe."

"It's just too . . . much . . . ," Daisy said through hiccups, her eyes on the back windows of the house. Shannon thought of everything Daisy had been through recently—discovering her biological brother and sister, getting kidnapped, living through a near-apocalypse. Nearly stumbling into a dead body wasn't the worst thing to happen to her by far, but she was right—it was too much.

"I'm sorry," Daisy said, still not making eye contact with any of them.

"There's absolutely no need to be sorry," Joe said, reaching into his back pocket and pulling out a travel-size packet of Kleenex. He handed them to Daisy. "We'll get you back to your parents as soon as we can."

Daisy sniffed. "My old nanny lives in Santa Barbara. I know she'd take me in if I asked, and the news says the sky is still normal there. Do you think . . . I could stay with her? Until my parents come?"

"Of course. We'll find her," Joe said.

Daisy nodded as she wiped her nose with the Kleenex. She already looked a little better than she had moments before.

"What next? For the rest of us?" Merek asked.

Joe sighed. "I think we all need a moment to regroup. It'll take a while for me to get Daisy to Santa Barbara, and in the meantime you need a place to stay." Joe looked off into the distance, thinking.

"He can stay with me," Shannon said. She'd barely formed the thought before the words came out of her mouth. And she had no idea how she'd get this past her parents. But it felt good to be able to do something, to help somehow.

Joe nodded, and Merek just lifted an eyebrow, which Shannon took for agreement.

"And after that?" Merek asked.

"Like I said, I think we all need to take a breath," Joe said. "And what I said to Daisy applies to all of you—you're under no obligation to put yourselves in any danger, do you understand? Your only job is to stay safe."

Shannon thought about contradicting him, but she didn't have the energy. Part of her wished she could be like Daisy right now, asking for a tissue and a one-way ticket out of this place. She knew that leaving wouldn't solve anything, but she couldn't think past the sight of the dead man, killed in the worst way and left to rot in his own living room. It was the best she could do just to nod in Joe's direction and follow him silently away from this place.

⊱⊱⊰⊰

"Can you . . . hurry . . . up?"

Shannon gritted her teeth and turned away from Merek's backside, which was currently located just two inches from her face. Merek shifted awkwardly in place, his feet pressing down on her right thigh.

"I am trying," he said, his voice coming out muffled from the other side of the window they were trying to sneak him into. Shannon suspected he wasn't trying all that hard.

If it had been just another regular day, there would be no need to sneak Merek into her garage. Shannon's parents would be safely at work instead of watching for their daughter through the house windows like hawks. But obviously, it wasn't just a regular day. There might not be any more regular days for some time.

So the only way to get Merek into Shannon's garage unnoticed was through the tiny back window, which he could only reach by using her like a ladder. He lifted one of his feet and planted it on her shoulder, using his elbows to scoot farther into the window hole. Finally, his weight was lifted off her body and he pulled himself through, tumbling down to the other side.

"Oof!"

"Are you okay?" Shannon hissed toward the open window. There was no response. "Merek? Did you pull your stitches?"

Silence.

"Merek?"

"Why in all that is holy is this entire room pink?"

Shannon leaned against the side of the garage in relief. "Don't touch anything. I'll be inside in a sec."

She raced back around the side of the garage and slipped past the hedges lining the driveway. When she hit the sidewalk, she doubled back, making her way up the front walk as if she'd just arrived. Even though she knew it was almost nine p.m., the sky above her wasn't going dark. If anything, the orange was just turning a slightly darker, slightly sicklier shade. Shannon wondered if she could blame her lateness on that, but very much doubted it.

After going inside and talking her parents down—which took much longer than usual—Shannon slipped back out into the garage. She'd fixed up and decorated the space herself when she was twelve, transforming the whole garage into something her parents referred to as the "Glitter Den." It was where she did her homework, watched movies on her iPad, and at times had even tried to stash Liv when a foster home wasn't working out. And yes, it was mostly pink.

Shannon opened the door to find Merek had made himself at home on a neon beanbag chair.

"Sorry, I couldn't sneak out any food or pillows yet without making my parents suspicious. But there's some chairs and a little air conditioner. As long as you're quiet, you'll be good here for now."

Shannon reached for a small purple blanket on the ground and tossed it in Merek's direction, remembering too late that the blanket was also covered in kisses and rainbow-colored unicorns. Merek caught the blanket in one hand and looked down at it for a second. He glanced back at Shannon, and she waited for the sure-to-come sarcastic commentary. But instead, Merek just sank back in the beanbag chair, blanket over his knees.

"Thank you."

"It's just a blanket," Shannon said, with a half shrug. "From when I was a kid," she hastily added.

"I don't mean just for the blanket," Merek continued, averting his eyes. "I know you are putting yourself at risk by allowing me to stay here, but I have . . . nowhere else go. I appreciate your generosity, and I want you to know it."

Shannon stood stock-still, at a loss for words. The last thing she'd expected was sincerity.

"Even if your generosity includes chairs that somehow stick to one's skin." Merek's expression slid back to its usual one of mild disdain as he tried to separate his arm from the beanbag chair beneath him.

"Ah, there's the guy I know and . . . well, tolerate," Shannon said, moving forward and plopping down in the neon-green beanbag chair next to Merek's. "And you're welcome."

"So what shall we do?"

There were a lot of possible answers to that question. They could decide to take Joe's offer that they back out of this whole crazy mission, lying low until their friends returned from another world. Or they could keep helping, keep putting themselves in danger.

But Shannon didn't want to think about that right now.

She didn't want to think about dead bodies or crumbling cities. She didn't want to think at all.

"Wanna watch a movie?"

"A movie?" Merek's eyebrows raised. "Liv talked about those. A lot."

"I'm sure she did. And if it were up to her, the first movie you ever watched would be an old black-and-white one or, like, a movie that won a bunch of Oscars for something boring like sound editing. But I'm going to show you something *good*. Something with zero dead people in it."

Shannon got her tablet from the far side of the room and sat back down, moving her beanbag chair closer to Merek's.

"Are you ready?"

"I suppose?"

"Good. I think you're gonna like this. A modern classic of our time," Shannon said, queueing the movie up and pushing play. "It's called *Mean Girls*."

THE BEST MAN

The village of Duoin had been around for centuries, and looked it. The stone walls surrounding the main portion of town were crumbling and in some places had even fallen to dust. These areas were all manned by gruff, bearded guards in rough-spun tunics. They eyed Cedric warily as he approached the wall with Rafe and the others.

"Back alive, then?" the nearest guard said to Rafe. His front teeth were yellowed, and he picked at them with a grimy finger.

"Do not look so excited, or I will start to think you miss me when I'm gone," Rafe replied with a grin. The guard guffawed, and Rafe held up a large, misshapen pack. After they'd eaten at the fire the night before, Rafe and his men had gone back to the dead wraths to collect their weapons and supplies, which now knocked together as he lifted the bag.

The guard's eyebrows raised. "Good haul, then. And who's this?" He motioned to Cedric, then to Kat and Liv a few feet away. His eyes narrowed in confusion as he took in Cedric's odd clothes—worn denim from the other world, as well as a shirt that read LA DODGERS. Not the most royal of garments.

Cedric opened his mouth to speak, but Rafe beat him to it. "Surprise guests. Come, open the gates and join us inside. All will be revealed."

The guard stared at Rafe through narrowed eyes, as if slowly working through his words. Finally, he climbed down from the wall and produced a large key from his belt, then used it to open a thick set of wooden doors.

Cedric followed Rafe inside to the center of Duoin, the others close behind. The village was made up entirely of stone buildings and grasses of various heights. A group of thin goats bleated weakly from a small enclosure near the main wall.

But if the goats looked pathetic, the people looked worse. Here and there, worn-out men and women walked down dirt paths or sat on sagging porches, watching as Cedric and Rafe and their group filed past. Many of them were injured, sporting bandaged arms or makeshift crutches. One was missing an eye.

"Where are the soldiers?" Cedric asked Rafe.

Rafe moved his arm widely, in a gesture that seemed to take in the entire town. "All around you."

"But these aren't trained fighters. Did none of the king's guard escape? What of the village's own hunters?"

Rafe's mouth was a thin line. "Many of our best fighters were involved in the first full assaults against the wraths, and their numbers were . . . depleted. This is what's left."

Again there was a coldness to Rafe's voice. Cedric turned around to see Kat limping slowly through the village next to Liv, who looked around with wide eyes. Rafe's other bowmen brought up the rear.

"Here we are," Rafe replied, stopping in the middle of a

round patch of dirt that Cedric assumed must be the village's center. A cluster of buildings lined the edges of the patch.

"Duoin!" Rafe shouted, turning in a circle. "We have returned from the hunting party, and with news!"

Cedric watched as men and women emerged from the buildings, slowly gathering around the edge of the circle. Their eyes slid warily over Cedric to land on Rafe, whom they watched eagerly.

Rafe threw his arm out toward Cedric. "I have found, wandering in the wood, none other than the one who we all believed to be dead. People of Duoin, I give you Cedric West, Prince of Caelum. Warrior son of the Oaken King! He lives!"

Stunned silence. Not just from the villagers, but from Cedric as well. His throat felt tight, and he wasn't sure exactly what to do with his hands. He wished suddenly that he was holding a sword, or even an arrow—anything he could grip to keep his fingers still and occupied as the hundred or so villagers around the circle stared him down.

The crowd started murmuring, some looking to Rafe in disbelief, others training suspicious eyes on Cedric.

"Hello," Cedric said, his voice sounding unsatisfactory to his own ears.

No one moved. The silence stretched until finally one toothless old woman stepped forward. Her milky eyes raked over Cedric, and after a few moments her mouth stretched into a smile. "He has the queen's eyes."

Cedric nodded at the old woman, grateful.

"Believe me, Duoin," Rafe said, "this boy who stands before

you is none other than the prince."

Cedric bristled at Rafe's use of the word *boy*, but worried that to correct the person who'd saved his life and led the village for months would seem petty.

"The prince has been wandering in another world, but he is back now, and he has a plan to retake the city and free the king and queen."

Another silence.

"I . . . well . . ." Cedric shot an angry glance at Rafe, but the duke's son was no longer meeting his eye. He knew exactly what he was doing.

Rafe barreled onward. "Of course, now that we know the royals are alive, my trusted men and I have a plan as well. One that will build on the knowledge we've gained over the last months, the knowledge we've earned by fighting and shedding blood to protect our lands. The knowledge that has led to one of our biggest wrath kills yet!"

Before Cedric could interject, Rafe lifted the arm that held his sack and tipped it over onto the ground. And what came tumbling out wasn't just weapons, but bloodied, hacked-off wrath horns. At least ten of them, maybe a dozen.

From behind him, Cedric heard Kat gasp. But he couldn't take his eyes off the gory sight on the village ground, or the triumph in Rafe's expression. For as long as he'd been alive, he'd been taught to fight wraths to keep them from Guardian villages—even to kill them, if necessary. But this, taking trophies . . . it turned something necessary into something . . . ugly.

But the villagers of Duoin didn't seem to agree. When they

saw the carnage on the ground, their coarse voices went up in cheers. Many of them clapped, and the old woman who'd compared Cedric's eyes to the queen's even jumped up and down—with joy. The villagers were no longer watching Cedric at all. Their eyes were trained on Rafe, who thrust his fist up in triumph, basking in their cheers.

"Tonight, we celebrate sending these monsters back to the hell from whence they came! But tomorrow, we determine our next move against those who hold our entire way of life hostage. The prince deserves to have his plan heard out, but I believe I have earned that right as well."

Rafe gestured to the mound of wrath horns at his feet.

"Just as I believe *you* have earned the right to decide for yourselves how and when you want to fight, to win back what was taken from us. What say you, mighty villagers of Duoin?"

The cheers were deafening.

Rafe turned to Cedric and bowed his head slightly, nothing in his expression betraying the shrewdness of his actions. But they *had* been shrewd—and fast. It was clear the villagers loved Rafe, and there was no one here to back up Cedric's authority as prince—no king's guard, no king's army, no king. Just Cedric himself, standing in these ridiculous pants, without even a sword to hold in his hand. Before he'd even had time to catch his bearings in this altered world, he'd been thoroughly outplayed. He had no plan to present to Duoin.

And he had no idea what to do next.

BEFORE SUNRISE

Liv missed sirens.

Not just sirens, but also helicopters. And car honks. And the lady who used to scream show tunes to the fire hydrant at the corner of Liv's street. Because all those noises meant people—tons of people all around. Caelum was too quiet, too empty. It was filled with too many wide-open spaces that seemed as if they could silently swallow her whole.

Plus, it smelled weird. Like manure and pinecones and people who only bathe once a week.

Liv walked under the shadows of trees that lined the path near the village's tiny inn, where she'd been given a room for the night. Everyone else in town was down at the village's largest building, celebrating Cedric's return (though they mostly toasted Rafe). Someone had even brought out a jug of a brownish drink to share, but Liv had taken one look at it and passed it to the next person without taking a sip. She didn't want to appear snobby, but if the thought of cheap keg beer always made her stomach churn, she didn't know if she'd be able to handle whatever ale was cooked up in a medieval inn's single stone bathtub.

Besides, she didn't feel like celebrating. Not until she had at least some idea of how to save Peter and the others from Malquin. After Rafe's big display in front of the villagers, Liv knew they would debate the specific *hows* of their plans the next morning. But she hated the thought of waiting even that long. So she'd left the party to get some air instead. Now she wrapped her arms around herself and headed along the main dirt path in the village, wrinkling her nose at the stench in the air.

There wasn't a single soul outside that she could see. No street lamps, no late-night dog walkers. Certainly no taco trucks just around the corner. She hit the end of the path, looking past the crumbling rock wall and out to the darkness and shadows beyond the village. With a shiver, Liv realized she was afraid. She hadn't been alone like this—truly alone, like out-of-range-of-another-human-being alone, scream-and-maybe-no-one-will-hear-you alone—in . . . maybe ever.

She turned around, heading back the way she'd come. She tried to get her mind off her fear, to imagine something comforting, something from home that was bright and cheerful. She pictured a string of white stars rising over a mountaintop, the word *Paramount* perched on the peak . . . then the beats of pop music . . .

"So okay, you're probably going, is this, like, a Noxzema commercial or what?" Liv whispered, trying to conjure the neon opening scenes of *Clueless* as she stomped around a pile of mud in another dimension. "But seriously, I actually have a way normal life for a teenage girl—"

A crunching sound stopped Liv in her tracks.

She looked around, but saw no one. Ahead of her on the path was a large building, where she knew Kat had gone to get her wounds treated. She started walking faster to reach it.

"Brave to be walking out alone in the dark."

The deep voice came from Liv's right side, but when she whipped her head in that direction, she saw only shadows. After a few moments, she was able to pick out one shadow in particular.

"Rafe?"

She could see him more clearly now, sitting down on what appeared to be a bunch of rocks, or maybe a crumbling stone fence.

"I—is there a reason I should be scared out here?" Liv remembered how Rafe's eyes had gleamed that afternoon, as he'd dumped that bagful of bloody horns onto the ground.

"In a manner of speaking," Rafe replied. In the dark, she saw his teeth and realized his was grinning. "You *are* about two steps away from a particularly ripe pile."

It took a second for Liv to understand his words, and then her shoulders sagged in relief. But when she took a giant step backward to avoid what Rafe was really warning her about, one of her shoes immediately sank into squelchy mud, putting her off balance. She reached out to grab on to something to keep from falling, but her hands found only air. Luckily, Rafe made it to her side in a hurry. He grabbed her hand and helped pull her free.

"Thanks. I'm not really used to dirt roads. Concrete's more my thing."

Rafe's face broke in a confused smile. "I am not sure what you mean, but it is certainly my pleasure to keep you from falling."

Liv pulled her hand from his and stood up straight.

"Are you looking for Cedric?" Rafe asked. "I believe he and Katerina have retired for the evening."

"Oh," she replied, a small voice inside wondering if they had retired *together* for the evening. She pushed it aside. "No, I'm not looking for him."

Rafe tilted his head. "Well, I am still glad you came this way. I've never conversed with someone from another world before."

"Oh, uh . . . it is kind of strange, the first time."

"Would you care to sit? Unless you have someplace to be . . . ?"

Rafe pointed to the pile of stones on the side of the dirt road, which Liv could now clearly see actually did make up a small wall—or once had. She shrugged and sat down on top of it, several inches from Rafe. Now that her eyes had adjusted to the dim light from the stars, she could make out more of his features. He looked a bit like Merek, but there was something else to him—a sureness.

"I actually do have somewhere else to be; I just don't know how to get there. That's the problem."

"What do you mean?"

"My brother, Peter. He's with Malquin. Or I think he is.

Cedric thinks he's in the castle by now, but I can't stop worrying about what might be happening to him."

"I understand what you mean," Rafe said. The smile slipped from his face. "For so long, I thought my parents were dead. But now that I know they are alive . . . all I can think about is how to get them free."

"And you think you can do that better than Cedric?" Liv bit her lip. She hadn't meant to be so blunt; but, then again, Rafe wasn't exactly hiding his intentions.

"I know I can."

Liv shook her head. "I may not have known Cedric as long as you, and he and I might not be on the best of terms right now, but if there's one thing I know he's good at, it's fighting wraths."

"True, Prince Cedric has always been an able enough warrior. Growing up, he would constantly tell tales of how he smashed this wrath or that. Not the worst trait, but . . . we need a cooler, more experienced head at the moment. *Especially* now that we know the royals are alive and at the wraths' mercy. We need a plan that is built on stealth if we want to save our families," Rafe said, his eyes glittering as he leaned closer. "Including your brother," he added quickly.

Liv considered his words. Wasn't this what she wanted to hear? A plan? But she couldn't dismiss Cedric so easily, no matter how intent he seemed on dismissing her.

Rafe sensed her hesitation. "I do not mean to speak against the prince. Like I said, he is a fine fighter, and I even believe he could make a good king someday. But right now, we need

someone else to take charge. Someone more experienced, someone—"

"Like you?"

A surprised laugh escaped from Rafe's lips. "Direct, aren't
you? I can see why Cedric has taken to you."

Liv smiled, but shook her head. "I don't think you're right
on that one. Not anymore, anyway."

"His loss," Rafe said, smiling. "But yes, I believe I am the
man to take on this charge. I have been here, every day, fighting
against these wraths. I know the ways they have organized, and
I know what they are capable of. The men and women of Duoin
will follow me without question, and I believe we should spare
as many of their lives as possible."

Liv sighed, thinking his words over. They did make sense,
and Rafe spoke with a confidence that was easy to get swept up
in. But to say that out loud felt too much like betraying Cedric.
Instead, she changed the subject.

"You know, it's hard to imagine that you and Merek are
related."

"You are not the first to make that assessment," Rafe
said with a laugh. "Merek makes enemies faster than friends.
Whereas I find that friends are more useful." He turned to Liv.
"Are you very much like your brother?"

"I . . . I don't know. We're not exactly close. We didn't grow
up together. We sort of just reconnected, before he came here."

Rafe raised an eyebrow. "You traveled across worlds for a
brother you do not even know?"

"He's family. I don't really have a lot of that to spare." Liv
pictured Peter in her mind, with his skinny frame and glasses,

his Dungeons & Dragons T-shirt. But the image of his eighteen-year-old self faded quickly into the image of him as a child, the one Liv had held on to in her mind all those years she was on her own. How much had Peter changed since then? Would the brother she remembered ever really be returned to her?

"I understand," Rafe said, quiet. "I know more than most that family can be . . . complicated. But they are worth fighting for. I think what you are doing is brave."

Liv gave a rueful laugh. "Maybe in theory. But it turns out, going through the portal was the easy part. Now that I'm here, I don't have any idea how to actually save Peter."

"Maybe not yet, but know this, Liv. When the time comes for you to rescue your brother, I would gladly be at your side."

And even though the words were coming from the wrong person, and Liv was looking into unfamiliar brown eyes instead of blue, she felt comforted.

For a moment, she even forgot about the smell.

⊱┈┈⊰

Cedric paced across the wooden floorboards in the small healing room, balling his hands into fists. Kat lay propped up against the wall, watching him. Under her clean linens, fresh bandages covered her wound.

"I am growing dizzy just watching you," she said, trying to swing her legs over the side of the bed. She winced.

That got Cedric to stop pacing. "You should not move so suddenly until you are healed."

Kat waved her hand and sat up straight. "I have been injured worse."

Cedric resumed his steps. "When?"

"Well . . . I cannot think of when at the moment. It is impossible to think while you attempt to walk a hole through the floor."

"I'm sorry," Cedric said, going to sit by Kat on the bed. Up close, he could see that color was returning to her cheeks. He'd rather not cause her more worry, but if anyone could help him sort out his jumbled thoughts, it was Kat.

"I just cannot understand why Rafe would do this. All of Caelum hangs in the balance, and now he wants to pit himself against me, dividing the loyalties of the village in two?"

"To be fair, I do not think Rafe believes the village will be all that divided."

Kat's words sank in, and it felt like they were pressing Cedric even further down in his seat. "Ouch."

Kat shifted on the soft bed, so she was facing Cedric completely. "We should have anticipated this—that your return after so long could be met with challenge, particularly after the biggest upheaval our land has faced in centuries."

"But there's no time! The important thing is getting Malquin and the wraths out of our lands for good."

"You're right," Kat said. "And what is more, *you* are the prince. You do not have to go along with Rafe's ridiculous scheme to have the villagers choose between you. You could *demand* the people follow you—that is your right."

Kat's words hung in the air, and Cedric considered them. He knew this is what his father would do if his own command were ever challenged. But he thought about the beaten-down, weary people of Duoin, and couldn't stomach the thought of taking another choice from them. Not when they'd lost so much.

"It cannot be like that," Cedric said, shaking his head. "But I also don't think Rafe realizes what kind of threat he is truly facing. He has dealt with the wraths, yes, but not with Malquin. He'll see us coming; I believe that. I just need for the fighters of Duoin to believe it, too."

Kat nodded. "Now you are talking like a true leader." She leaned forward slightly, and her dark hair fell down over her shoulders, its tips tickling the skin of Cedric's arm. He cleared his throat then and shifted a bit away from her. Sometimes, Cedric relied so much on Kat for guidance and advice, he forgot that he was also talking to his future wife. He forgot, in some moments, that she was a girl at all.

This was not one of those moments.

In the dim candlelight of the room, with Kat so near to him, it was all too easy to remember what lay in store for them. Thankfully, Kat didn't seem to be following Cedric's line of thought. She pursed her lips together, mind busy on the actual problem at hand.

Which was so very like Kat to do.

"You think I can do this? Win the people over without forcing them as their prince?"

"I do," Kat said, her eyes brimming with belief. And not just belief—belief in *him*. "I think Rafe miscalculated. He has challenged the Cedric he once knew, the one who led us away from wraths in the palace dungeon without a thought as to what would come next. But you have changed, Cedric. Rafe was not counting on that. Tomorrow morning, you will show him—and everyone else, too."

"You are aware that, in order to succeed, I actually will need to think up a brilliant plan to counter Rafe's?"

Kat grinned. "We have all night."

STAND BY ME

The alehouse was full to bursting the next morning, and Cedric's stomach twisted as he looked over the faces of every man, woman, and child in the village. He suddenly wished he'd taken Kat's suggestion to have some eggs for breakfast.

How could it be he was more nervous to face a roomful of his own people than to face a handful of wraths bent on killing him? If only being a ruler were always as easy as charging into battle. There was no sure outcome for this morning, especially after Rafe had spent an hour whipping the alehouse into a fury of support for himself. His plan (delivered while wearing a wrath horn on a cord around his neck) involved leaving Duoin immediately with a small band of fighters and finding and torturing wrath after wrath until they came across one who would sneak them into the palace. Not a terrible plan, Cedric realized, but one that had too many risks attached. The wraths had more loyalty to Malquin than Rafe anticipated, and they were much more organized. It was far more likely Rafe's team would give themselves away and lose fighter after fighter until there would be none left to take back the city.

Cedric knew all the drawbacks of Rafe's plan, but the words were frozen in his throat. Kat stood steady at his side as he faced the room, many of whom were still talking loudly with each other. Across the room, Liv stood alone near a window. The morning light settled on her features, highlighting the green flecks of her eyes. When Liv caught Cedric looking at her, she smiled. He quickly looked away.

He needed to focus.

"Thank you all for gathering this morning," Cedric said, gripping the handle of a sword. At Kat's suggestion, he'd dressed in scrounged-up battle gear for the announcement of his plan. Which suited him just fine.

"I know you have been fighting long and hard these many months, and you are eager to expel the wraths from our lands once and for all."

Across the room, Rafe joked with some men who sat in a circle of stools around him, eager to refill his mead glass whenever it ran low. When Cedric met Rafe's gaze, the joking stopped, and Rafe made a show of paying attention.

Cedric turned back to the crowd and raised his voice. "As Rafe mentioned yesterday, I have not been here to share the burden of the past few months with you. I *have* been in another world."

The crowd shifted. The muttering died down a bit, and more and more eyes focused on Cedric alone. He took a big breath. This was the hard part, when he would have to say the exact right thing or else everything would fall to shreds. And then Rafe would be right—he wouldn't be the best person to lead these people.

"But I was not resting in this other world. I was fighting wraths. And I faced Malquin there as well. Which is why I know how foolhardy it is to try to outmaneuver him, to rush a plan against a foe who is always two steps ahead—"

"So you will not fight?" a voice called out. Cedric turned to see it belonged to a tall, bulky man who leaned up against the wall. He recognized him as one of the men who had been in the forest with Rafe. As soon as the man spoke, more muttering broke out among the crowd.

Cedric tried to focus. "Not today, no. I have a plan, but it does not involve leaving immediately, or torturing wraths—"

Cries from the crowd. Someone threw a glass to the ground, and it shattered. From the corner of his eye, Cedric saw Liv flinch.

A second man rose, his face a mask of anger. "You have sympathy for those beasts? My brother was a guard at Westing, and they cut his throat without a second thought. A true prince would stop at nothing to avenge his people."

Cedric's heart stuttered at the words *a true prince*. He was losing them.

"I have no sympathy for the wraths," Cedric said, struggling to get his words out before the crowd grew too much against him. "But neither will I provoke a longer war with these creatures."

Cedric straightened and looked out over the crowd. "We

cannot defeat the wraths in Westing with our numbers, and to pick the creatures off one by one is too risky. Which is why I propose we increase our numbers. A great number of our men are in the north, beyond the main city—"

"The wraths have cut off the north," Rafe objected. "I told you, we have sent three parties to try and reach the northern lands. None have returned."

"None have had the secret weapon that we have." Cedric gestured to Kat, who at this point came forward, just as they'd planned. Though Cedric could tell that walking was causing her some pain, she hid it well. Anyone who did not know her would not have guessed that she had recently been stabbed.

"The northern lands are my home," Kat said. "And I have traveled from there to the southern holdings countless times with my own father and his men. I know of a passageway under the Westing Mountains that will take only a few days to traverse."

"How do you know the wraths will not be waiting in this passageway?" the bulky man asked.

"I have not been in them since I was small," Kat continued, "but I remember how tightly we fit into them. I do not believe the wraths could get far inside, even if they were to find the tunnels."

More murmuring broke out among the tables, but this time it held notes of excitement. Rafe sat in one corner, watching his men as they watched Cedric. His eyes narrowed.

"We will send a third of our forces through the tunnel," Cedric said. "Once they reach the other side, they can join with our men in the north. Together, we may have the numbers necessary to overwhelm the wraths in the city. If the men in the north and the south attack the city walls from both sides at the same time, we can overwhelm them and cut off any possible escape routes."

"A solid suggestion, my prince," Rafe said, rising. Cedric was impressed that he was managing to keep his expression neutral. "But assuming the men in the north have survived, and assuming we can find and unite with them, and assuming they can make their way to the city, how will we be able to coordinate our attack? Any messengers caught by wraths would be killed on sight."

"That's true," Cedric said, maintaining eye contact with Rafe. "Which is why we will not be using messengers. We will be using these."

Cedric reached into the bag by his feet—the one he'd taken from Liv's room that morning—and pulled out two dark, boxy devices. Their casings looked impossibly shiny in the dim lighting of the pub. The townspeople fell silent, so still that Cedric could hear only his own breathing.

"Wh-what are those?" Rafe asked, his voice finally faltering.

In answer, Cedric handed one of the devices to Kat, who took it and walked to the other side of the pub. Cedric pushed down on the button on his device, what Liv called "the walkie," and spoke. "Message to Katerina—"

He wasn't able to complete his sentence before the pub broke out in gasps and exclamations. His voice had carried from the device Kat held, ringing out as clearly as if he'd been standing next to her.

"How is this possible?" a woman asked, clutching a hand to her chest.

At this, Cedric looked sheepishly at Liv. She cleared her throat.

"It's, um, radio waves," Liv said. She seemed to notice then that every eye in the pub was on her, and she sat up straighter. "Sound travels on these invisible waves, and . . ." She looked up and to the right, as if she were trying to remember something and thought the answer might be written on the ceiling. "The walkies use those waves to send sound across distances. I'm pretty sure. It's been a while since eighth-grade science. . . ."

The villagers of Duoin looked at Liv as if she were speaking another language. Some looked amazed, others afraid.

"They're not dangerous," Liv said quickly. She turned to Cedric. "But you shouldn't overuse them—I'm not sure how much battery is left, and it's not like we can just run out to a Rite Aid."

Cedric nodded. "We will use them sparingly."

Liv smiled, and caught off guard, Cedric smiled back. For a moment—just a moment—it felt as though they were alone in the room. If Liv was speaking a foreign language, he was the only one in Caelum who could understand it. He gripped the device in his hand, liking that he carried around a part of her world.

Cedric looked back to the crowd, who no longer seemed so critical of their prince. Even the group of men around Rafe looked rapt.

"We will take the next few weeks to work out the details of the plan, sending out small scouting parties to ensure that the land around the tunnel entrance is free of wraths, and to watch their patterns for guarding the city."

Cedric took a breath then, and looked to Liv again. He noticed her eyebrows draw together, her expression stony. Cedric's stomach pinched with guilt; he knew Liv would be upset at the delay in rescuing her brother. But there was nothing to be done about it. He turned away, facing the crowd again.

Finally, Rafe spoke up. The faux friendliness had dropped from his voice. "You want us to wait weeks, though we now know for sure our royals are alive within those walls? And to risk all of our lives on devices that work on . . . *invisible waves*?"

Rafe looked around the room, incredulous. But though every head in the pub swiveled to look from him to Cedric, not one of them backed Rafe up. Cedric felt a surge of hope.

Rafe's eyes flared in anger. "You speak well, Prince. But while you have been dallying in other worlds, we have been fighting for our lives. You have no idea—"

"You are right," Cedric said. "I have been in another world. And I was not dallying; I did fight wraths there. You told everyone in this room as much last night. But I also learned there are *better ways* to fight. I made mistakes, and learned from them, and I will use that knowledge to defeat the wraths and Malquin here. You bring up the royals, but that is not just my king in those walls—it is my father. My mother, my sister. Know that I will not stop until I see them free, until I see our entire world free."

Cedric's voice carried a steadiness he did not entirely feel. Rafe stared at him, and the silence in the room grew thick. Cedric knew that this was the moment that would decide everything.

But it wasn't Rafe who spoke. It was the man next to him who suddenly stepped forward, then kneeled to the ground.

"I will follow you, my prince."

The man standing next to him, who had a beard down to his chest and was carrying a cup of ale though it was just past dawn, kneeled as well. "I will follow you, my prince."

One after the other, men and women kneeled.

Cedric didn't know what to do, how to move. Men had kneeled for his father, but never for him. He looked up and saw Kat beaming at him from across the room.

They'd done it.

As the villagers started to gather around him, and as the drinks started to flow, Cedric began to truly feel, for the first time, like the plan might be successful. He was doing it right, taking precautions and not just reacting on a whim like he had in the past. He was going to act not like a young prince, but like a future king.

⊱⊰⊱⊰

Cedric exhaled slowly as he made his way over to the wooden post fence that ran alongside the small yard behind the pub. He'd finally managed to slip away from the crowd of villagers who'd been clamoring to give him mead, claiming to need some air. The claim wasn't entirely untrue.

On the other side of the fence was a tiny spring, surrounded by white wildflowers. Cedric didn't even hear Kat until she leaned up against the post next to him.

"That was not so bad now, was it?" she asked, her voice light.

Cedric gave a brief, surprised laugh in response.

"Could have gone worse, I suppose."

Kat bumped a shoulder into his. "Come now, modesty has never really been one of your strengths."

Cedric's face broke out into a grin. "You're right. I was fantastic. And what's more, I had complete confidence it would work the entire time."

"Obviously."

Cedric grinned again, and Kat broke out into a laugh. She'd had few opportunities to truly laugh during the past few months, and to hear the sound of it now was like seeing the sun at the end of a long, cloudy day.

"Honestly Kat," Cedric said, "I could not have done any of it without you."

"Of course not," she said, still smiling.

"I mean it," Cedric continued. "Not just today, but the past few months . . . if you had not been there, I don't know what I would have done . . ."

Kat's smile twitched, and her dark eyes locked on to Cedric's.

"You would have done whatever you had to do. As the future king of Caelum."

And there was such confidence, such sureness in her eyes, that Cedric could barely stand to look in them. He glanced to the ground.

But Kat just grabbed his chin and tilted his head up, so he was forced to look at her. "I am not sure when exactly it was you lost your faith in yourself, but what you said in that pub just now was true. Everything that happened in LA, all that we went through, even the mistakes . . . it *did* make you a better leader. And even if you do not believe in yourself at the moment, know that *I* believe in you. Not just because you are the prince. But because you're *you*."

Cedric's heart thudded in his chest at her words. Her fingers against the skin of his face were rough from fighting, her grip gentle but firm.

"I could not be me without you," he said.

Without planning it, without thinking at all, Cedric moved closer to Kat. Her face, the face he'd known so well and for so long, was just inches from his. For a moment, she looked surprised as he moved closer, but then her mouth parted in a smile.

"You admit it, then," she said. Then she was moving closer to him, too. She was so beautiful, this close. It was hard to do anything but stare. "Finally."

Cedric closed his eyes, and pressed his mouth to hers.

Her lips were smooth and soft as they pressed back. He tried to focus on the sensation of it, tried not to think about how he was kissing Kat—*actually kissing Kat*—but it was impossible to turn off his thoughts.

After all, this was the Kat he'd known since they were children, fighting each other with wooden swords. She'd been taller than him then, her hair a mess of braids.

This was also the Kat he trusted more than anyone to fight by his side, with her sure responses and quick movements. Her mouth was quick now, moving surely . . .

Cedric fought to stay in the moment. He moved his hands

up to Kat's shoulders—was that where they went? What was he supposed to do with his hands? It hadn't been this way when he'd kissed Liv. This kiss was different. Not *bad*-different, just . . .

Don't think about Liv.

Cedric kissed Kat harder, and she gave a soft noise of surprise. Her mouth spread into a smile, and she pulled away a fraction, looking up at him. Suddenly Cedric found it difficult to look into her eyes. He'd seen those same eyes a thousand times, but now there was something new there. For the first time in a long time, he couldn't tell what she was thinking.

Cedric looked up, then, and saw a figure standing not ten feet from them, across the yard by the open pub door.

Liv.

She was looking right at him. At *them*.

Cedric's heart thudded as he saw the shock on Liv's face, but before he could react, she quickly turned and disappeared back into the pub. Without thinking, he took a step away from Kat, toward the spot where Liv had been standing.

Kat instantly took a step back as well. Cold rushed into the space between them. Too late, Cedric backtracked to move a bit toward her. She leaned away.

"I-I'm sorry," Cedric started, faltering.

"You're *sorry*?"

"No, I mean, it is only . . . For a moment I thought that I should maybe . . ." He gestured lamely toward the doorway.

"You mean to go after her?" Kat asked, her voice flat. "Is that really what you want to do?"

And there it was again—that unknowable look in her eyes, the one that made a stranger of his oldest friend. Cedric knew he'd done something wrong, that he shouldn't have pulled back so quickly, but he didn't quite know how to fix it. He knew Kat would eventually understand, just as she always did. But Liv?

"We will need her on our side in the coming weeks, is all," Cedric said. "I do not want for there to be any . . . confusion."

"I do not think *her* confusion is the issue."

"Kat . . ." He reached out to her, but she took another step away. Her head bent down for a moment, and when she lifted it again, the strange look in her eyes was gone. They were once again shuttered and fierce, no longer vulnerable in any way.

"No, you are right. We need Liv as an ally," she said. She brushed hair out of her face with one casual sweep of the hand. "Go, now. Before she runs into the woods and gets herself eaten."

"Are . . . you sure?" Cedric asked.

Kat just raised an eyebrow.

"All right," Cedric said, with a quick nod. He moved to follow Liv. Out of the corner of his eye, he thought he saw Kat's face fall. But when he looked back, she was still giving him a cool stare.

As he went, however, he couldn't help but feel he'd done this all wrong.

It was a familiar feeling these days.

‡‡‡‡

Liv hated the air in this place. It was too thin, which made it hard to catch your breath just when you needed it the most. She walked quickly along the dirt-and-stone road, trying to gulp in air as she went.

No way was she going to cry.

It would be so, so dumb to cry.

Cedric had told her from the beginning that he was engaged to another girl. She knew from the start (even if she hadn't believed it at first) that he was a prince with a whole country counting on him. The two of them together—it was impossible. And she *knew* that. But still . . . walking out of the pub and seeing Cedric and Kat together had felt like innocently turning a corner and smashing headfirst into a steel wall.

It hurt.

Liv shook her head gently, trying to clear the image from her mind. She hadn't come to Caelum to try to win over Cedric. She had to focus on finding her brother and bringing him home. Before this world could do any irreversible damage to either of them.

Liv walked without knowing where she was going. Away from the pub, away from Cedric and Kat in that sunlit backyard, her hand on his face, him leaning toward her . . .

Stop.

A few villagers passed by Liv as she walked on, giving her openly curious glances. She kept her head down, avoiding them all. Now that they knew who she was and where she'd come from, they seemed to have so many questions for her. And she didn't want to explain what sound waves were one more time, just like she didn't want to pretend to be excited about Cedric's plan that would leave her brother stranded for weeks.

Just as Liv was rounding on the small inn where she'd spent the night, she heard footsteps behind her. She knew exactly who it was.

She spun around quickly and faced him, savoring the small expression of surprise on his face as he stopped short. For a moment they just stared at each other, a few feet away. They'd stopped underneath a large tree that shaded some of the road, and light dappled down through the leaves to fall over Cedric's face.

Cedric cleared his throat. "I am sorry—"

"Sorry? That's all you have to say for yourself?"

Cedric's jaw twitched. He looked pained.

"I did not want to hurt you. I . . . I only want you to understand, that Kat and I—"

Liv put a hand up to stop him, barely able to look at his face. "This isn't about you and Kat. And it's not about you and me."

Cedric's brows pushed together, confused. And was there a little hurt in his expression, too? Liv felt a spike of irritation. Why should *he* get to be the one who was hurt?

"Not that there is a 'you and me' anymore, obviously. I mean, that's pretty clear, right?"

Cedric blinked. The leaves above him shifted in the breeze, casting shadows over his face. After a beat, he nodded. "Yes. I suppose it is. So . . . why are you upset?"

Liv threw up her hands in exasperation. "*Why am I upset?* Why do you think I was looking for you out there in the first place?"

Cedric's eyes moved over her face, as if searching for the answer. "I . . . I don't know."

"We've been here for a few days now, and we're not any closer to rescuing Peter than we were when we came through the portal. In fact, we've moved farther *away* from him. And then you and Kat come up with this whole walkie-talkie, wait-several-weeks-to-do-anything plan, all on your own, and . . . I mean, did you even think to include me in your planning session at all?"

Cedric's mouth fell open a little, and he looked at Liv the way he did when she said some modern-day word he didn't understand. "I . . . no," he said, simply. "We needed to come up with a viable strategy quickly."

"I get that. But you're not the only one with something at stake here. My brother's counting on me, and I have no idea if he's hurt, or what Malquin is doing to him . . . every day that he spends here could be putting him in more danger. Then you come up with this plan that'll take weeks to put together. *Weeks.* Can you promise me Peter will stay safe that long?"

Cedric squared his shoulders. "I promise I will do everything I can to save your brother. But this is about so much more than him. I have a whole realm to protect. Do you not care about that?"

"Of *course* I care."

"Then why can't you support a plan that is best for my people? To wait is the safest course of action, to defeat the wraths entirely before entering the castle."

"And what if they decide to hurt the prisoners while you're busy storming the walls with your army? What if before you even get in the city, Malquin takes it out on Peter? Or your parents? Or sister? Did you think about *that?*"

"It was a possibility we discussed."

"You and Kat."

"Yes," Cedric said, his voice strained.

Liv shook her head. "You're not the only two people with family in there. I should have had a say."

Cedric finally threw his hands up, exasperated. "Fine. I am sorry we didn't come to you, an untrained, uncooperative Earth girl whose only battle experience involves watching silly imaginary pictures move across a screen, to ask you for strategy help."

Liv took a step back, the words hitting her like a physical blow. Her arms dropped to her sides. "That's what you think of me?"

Cedric gave a short sigh, and looked slightly abashed. But also slightly frustrated. He ran a hand through his hair.

"Okay," Liv said, trying to keep her voice calm, to hide how much Cedric's words had stung. "That's good to know, really. Whatever. But even if you don't take me seriously, what about Rafe?"

Cedric's eyes narrowed. "Rafe?"

"Yeah, you know, the guy who's actually been running this place for months? The guy whose brother you nearly put in a coma back in LA?"

This time, Cedric was the one who looked like he'd been punched. Liv knew she'd gone too far, but it was too late to stop now. Plus, Cedric's words about her still rang in her head.

"Rafe's idea makes a lot of sense," Liv continued. "He told me all about it last night."

"Did he." Cedric's voice was flat. His entire expression had gone still, his eyes dark and steely under the shadows of the tree.

"Yep. Apparently, *some* people don't just think of me as a stupid, untrained Earth girl."

When Cedric spoke, his voice was still as cold as ice. "Rafe has been working against me since the moment we arrived."

Liv rolled her eyes. "Questioning your absolute authority over all things isn't the same as *working against you*. He saved your life, remember? And he wants to free his family, too. *Without* putting them in more danger."

"He may want to free his family, but he doesn't want to do it alongside me. He wants the glory all to himself."

"You've cracked." Liv shook her head. "You so badly want to be the one who's right all the time, the guy with the plan that finally works for once"—a flinch from Cedric, but Liv ignored it—"that you're ignoring good advice from someone who's *on your side*."

"Rafe is on his own side, and no one else's."

Liv put up her hands, palms out. She shook her head. "I don't even know what to say. You've changed since coming here. Or, I don't know. Maybe this is who you've always been, in Caelum." She paused. "And I'm not sure I like this you a whole lot."

She turned and walked away before he could respond, the knot in her stomach pulling tighter and tighter with each step she took.

⊱┊┊⊰

Liv's fists stayed clenched as she wandered around the village roads for the next half hour, replaying the argument again and again in her head. Sometimes she would think about the words she'd said and start to feel a twinge of regret, but then she remembered everything Cedric had said and the anger would flare up just as fierce as before.

She walked quickly, as if she had someplace to be. And she did—though she didn't realize it until the crumbling stone wall came into view.

"Going somewhere?"

Rafe sat on the exact same spot he had the night before, though now he was wearing a hood and half a scowl. His mood seemed to match her own.

"I wish," she replied.

Rafe smiled. "Really? And where is it you wish to go?"

Liv let out a long sigh and looked around her. There was a dirt road leading off in two directions, surrounded by grass and trees and the occasional wooden house on each side. Everything was foreign. Where *could* she go?

"In an ideal world, I'd go save my brother before Cedric's war puts him in any more danger, then get the hell out of this place."

Rafe cocked his head, measuring her up. "But this is not an ideal world?"

"I don't know," she whispered, hearing the defeat in her voice. "I don't know anything about this place, really."

"But I do," Rafe said, his own voice lowering. "Remember what I said last night? About how I would help you?"

Liv swallowed. "Yes, but . . ."

"Of course, I would not want you to do anything that might cause a rift between you and Cedric."

Liv scoffed. "It's a bit late for that."

"Then what is holding you back?" Rafe asked, his eyes now boring into hers. "Did you not just say you want to save your brother?"

"I . . . yes. But how can we do that without ruining Cedric's whole plan?"

Rafe straightened, suddenly all business. "We would have to be careful. Move quickly to get to the palace and find a way inside before the fighters arrive. We would have to be cunning and—"

"Sneaky?"

"Yes. Very sneaky," Rafe said, smiling.

A trickle of static ran down Liv's spine. "I can't believe I'm actually talking about doing this." She shook her head, but she didn't move away.

"There would be risks, of course," Rafe said.

"I already jumped through a hole into another universe to save my brother. It's a little too late to start worrying about risks now."

Rafe responded with a short, barking laugh. "Well, let's be off, then," he said, pushing himself away from the stone wall.

Liv started. "Wait, like, right now? Seriously?"

Rafe's eyes narrowed. "When else?"

Liv looked back in the direction of the village, the direction of the tree where she'd just spoken with Cedric. She remembered the things he'd said, the way he'd dismissed her. This was maybe the best shot to get Peter she'd ever have.

"Okay. Let's go."

STEP UP

Shannon woke to the sound of Sigourney Weaver scream-ing.

Half of her face was plastered against the sticky plastic of a beanbag chair, and half was mushed up against something warm. On the screen, inches from her eyes, Sigourney Weaver was shooting flames at a needle-toothed alien with saliva falling from its mouth in strings.

"That creature looks a bit like you when you're sleeping," rumbled a voice just inches away.

Shannon shot straight up, blinking sleep from her eyes. She looked down and realized the warm surface she'd been sleeping against was Merek's arm. And there was, indeed, a small wet spot of drool on his sleeve.

"I have no idea what you're talking about," she said, wiping the back of her hand quickly against her mouth and combing her hair out of her face.

Shannon had been hiding Merek in the garage for almost a full day now, and they'd spent most of that time burning through Shannon's movie collection and trying to make as little noise as possible. Her parents had barely questioned the amount of time she spent in the garage—not after she told them she needed to get away from their constant arguing (which wasn't even a lie).

The fighting between Shannon's parents was just the latest weird thing to come along in this semi-apocalypse. But it upset Shannon almost as much as the constant sirens and frequent earthquakes. Her parents mostly argued about what to do next—her mom wanted to get out of the city as soon as possible, to load up the car and drive to her sister's place in Salt Lake City. But Shannon's dad didn't think it was safe to leave yet. Most of the highways were still jammed with traffic, accidents, and even abandoned cars. The I-5 going north had been shut down entirely by a fire. Shannon's dad claimed it was safer to stay and wait—at least a few more days—until the roads became clearer. He thought it was possible the worst was over.

Shannon doubted that was true, but knew she couldn't explain that to her parents. Not that she didn't want to. She especially wanted to talk to them about the horrifying discovery she'd made in a small house just outside of town . . . the image of the dead man, bled out on his carpet, was impossible to expel from her mind.

Her stomach rolled over on itself every time she thought of it.

"When did you start watching this?" Shannon asked, squinting at the screen.

"When you were asleep. I clicked around for more movies

on your comp-ter, the way you showed me. This one is quite good. I do not understand a lot of it, but the creature is very effective."

"Of course you'd like *Alien*," Shannon said. "Being that you practically are one."

Merek didn't rise to her bait. "Why didn't you show me this sooner? I found it here. . . ." Merek minimized the movie screen and pointed to a folder labeled "Special Projects." "Why is this one special?"

"No reason." Shannon shrugged, maybe a bit too forcefully. "It's stupid."

Merek just raised one eyebrow.

"Ugh, fine, it's just this project, okay? I took it on over the summer. Liv was doing her whole film school thing, and I just felt, I don't know . . . like I should do something like that, too. My parents won't let me take acting classes, so I'm kind of . . . studying."

Shannon exhaled and looked up at Merek, expecting to see a smirk on his face. But that's not what she found. Instead, he looked curious.

"Studying?"

"Yeah, I made this list of important female performances and started working through them, watching them . . ." Shannon trailed off, wondering why she was explaining any of this. It almost made her skin itch to admit how much she actually cared about this stuff. She hadn't told anyone about her "special project." She'd never admit it out loud, but she kind of guessed that no one really took her acting aspirations that seriously—not her classmates, her friends, her parents, or even Liv. Not that it was their fault; after all, Shannon often joked that she'd just as soon become the next Kardashian as the next Jennifer Lawrence, so long as she was famous. But secretly, she wanted to be *good* at something, the way Liv was good at making movies.

That's how Project Watch Great Actresses Until You Secretly Also Become Great came about. Not that she'd gotten very far. It was too easy to get distracted, first by scrolling through her social media and shopping online, later by otherworldly demon creatures and the actual apocalypse.

"Whatever, maybe it's a dumb way to learn acting. And it's not like I'll ever be as good as Sigourney Weaver is at playing Ripley. I'll probably shoot for a reality show, maybe one of the dating ones. Or I'll just give up entirely and get some boring job that comes with a business card to make my parents happy."

Merek was silent for a moment. Again, Shannon was sure he'd turn the conversation back to more comfortable, sarcastic waters. Again, he surprised her.

"Your parents have expectations of you?"

"Well . . . yeah. Don't everyone's?"

"Not mine," Merek said, his expression darkening. "They save all their expectations for my brother. Rafe is the one who can do everything—fight, hunt, hold court. Me, they just want to stay out of the way."

"Guess you pulled that off pretty well," Shannon said, smiling.

Merek half exhaled, half laughed in response, and the warm air hit the skin of Shannon's arm. "That's true. I am pretty far out of the way at this point."

"Seriously, though, that sucks about your parents," Shannon

said. "I always thought I'd want a sibling to take some of the weight off. But that sounds just as bad."

Merek tilted his head just slightly toward Shannon, as if thinking. "Sometimes. In Caelum, everyone would compare me to Rafe, and I would always fall short. After a while, it became easier to stop trying. At least then I could never fail."

"Yeah," Shannon said, suddenly quiet. Her eyes went back to the movie playing on the screen. "I get that."

Shannon watched on her laptop as Sigourney Weaver pushed the alien out of the shuttle airlock, finally getting herself free. It made her feel very small, sitting on a beanbag chair and watching someone else—even a fictional someone else—be so strong. Her eyes went to the dark orange sky out the tiny garage window.

"But you're not in Caelum anymore."

"No, I am definitely not."

"And maybe . . . maybe it's time we actually do . . . try," she said, thoughtful. "Or at least, stop hiding."

"What do you mean?"

"I mean that we're two of the only people in this world who know what's really going on in this city. And we're just going to, what? Curl up in here and wait for Joe to fix everything on his own? Because we're afraid?"

Merek eyed her skeptically.

"Is that what Ripley would do?" Shannon asked, gesturing to the computer screen.

"I thought you told me those people on the screen were not real."

"Okay, then. Is that what *we* would do? Just . . . nothing?"

"We are waiting to hear from Joe."

Shannon shook her head. "Come on, Merek, he's not going to call. I *know* he's not going to call. He gave us an out, and he assumes we took it."

Shannon picked up her cell phone and hit Joe's number. It rang several times before going to voice mail.

"We'll have to go to him."

She cast a look at the garage door, imagining her parents in another room, two walls away. They'd be beyond pissed if they caught her sneaking out again, especially now. And yet . . .

"*We?*"

Shannon looked over at Merek, still sitting on the beanbag chair. She sighed. "Fine, you can feel free to sit here alone, moping about the friends who left you behind. Or you can help me. You can *do* something. If you ever want to open another portal again and get home, we have to figure out how to fix this."

"Who says I want to go home?"

Shannon took a moment to figure out if he was joking. He didn't seem to be.

"You don't want to go back to Caelum?"

"Maybe not . . . at least not yet," Merek said. "There are many things here I still have not seen."

"Okay. So LA is great and you want to stay here and figure things out, just like a hundred thousand other people who move here every single year. Doesn't change the fact that the city's currently kinda wrecked. If you want to stay here, that should give you even more motivation to help fix it."

This time Merek looked out the window. After a moment, he stood up ungracefully from the beanbag chair. "And if I don't come, I suppose you will leave me alone in this pink nightmare of a room?"

"Yes, and you'll have nothing to eat but the Halloween candy I hid in the toolbox three years ago."

"Then it looks as though I have no choice." Merek shrugged. To anyone who didn't know him, it might have been a sign that he didn't care—didn't care whether he helped, or stayed in that beanbag chair forever, or watched the world fall apart around him. Just a few days before, Shannon would have rolled her eyes and made a sarcastic comment back to him. But now she saw past the shrug and the defensiveness, past what he wanted her to see.

Not that she would ever tell him that.

"Great. Then saving the world it is. We just need a way to the hotel where Joe's staying." After the warehouse fire, Joe had thought it best not to go back to his own house, guessing that the Knights—and even his own brother—might track him down to get to Liv and her siblings. They'd stopped at this hotel briefly after getting Merek out of the hospital so Merek could borrow some of Joe's clothes. "There's no way I can take the minivan without my parents noticing. . . ." Shannon's eyes fell on the glittery purple bike in the corner. "Guess that'll have to do."

"What is it?" Merek asked. He looked at the bike distrustfully. "Certainly not a mode of transportation."

"Yup. Think of it like a horse. And those handlebars?

They're your saddle."

Merek looked at her as though she were insane. Maybe she was.

She grinned. "Let's ride."

⊱⊰

Shannon was certain the bike would give out on her at any second. And if it didn't, her legs definitely would. She huffed in giant breaths as she finally made the turn onto Sunset Boulevard. Her legs wobbled as she stood up, pedaling the old bike forward. Merek sat stiffly on the small seat behind her, having flatly refused to sit on the handlebars. He held his long legs up to keep them from hitting pavement, and his hands gripped her waist at every single turn. As she hit a bump, he moved closer, fingers digging into her skin.

"Ow," Shannon panted.

"Sorry," Merek mumbled, releasing his grip by just a fraction. Riding with Merek felt very, very different from when she and Liv used to double up to ride the bike together.

"Are we nearly there?"

Shannon rolled her eyes, even though Merek couldn't see her face. And even that took almost more energy than she had to spare.

Shannon had been dropping speed every minute, and by the time she'd pedaled onto Sunset, her legs felt like rubber on a hot day. And the view did nothing to perk her up. Sunset Boulevard had always varied from looking glamorous in one blink to seedy in the next, but now it looked like something straight out of *Dawn of the Dead*.

It was dark out, though not the usual dark glow of Hollywood at night. The ruined sky gave everything a sickly brown overtone. The roadway was entirely empty of cars—this particular street didn't provide a quick route out of town—and garbage was blowing freely across the empty pavement. The sidewalks were mostly empty as well, not a tourist in sight. When Shannon pedaled past Arclight Hollywood, with its giant, geodesic dome advertising the last blockbuster of summer, three military jeeps drove by the street on her right. None of them seemed to notice her and Merek.

Most of the stores were locked up, windows barred, though a few had clearly been smashed into. One restaurant's entire front end was blackened char, as if the building had caught fire and been hastily put out. The concrete walkways that bore pink stars with celebrity's names imprinted on them were covered with trash. Hollywood was still technically here, but everything that had ever made it important was gone.

Finally, Merek tightened his grip on Shannon's waist and motioned to a small two-level motel set just off the side of the road. Shannon tucked the purple bike out of sight behind the building and followed Merek up to Joe's door.

She knocked, but no one answered.

"There's no way he's still with Daisy in Santa Barbara, right?" she asked, more to herself than to Merek.

"He might have left," Merek said, peering around the empty motel lot. "Everyone else did."

Shannon felt prickles of fear in her stomach. What if Joe *had* left to try to fix everything on his own? What if he'd gone tracking down more leads without them and had gotten hurt?

"We have to go inside."

"The door is locked," Merek said, as if that settled that.

Shannon raised an eyebrow. "So? You've got superhuman strength, right? Can't you break it down?"

This time Merek was the one to raise his eyebrow. They stayed like that, staring at each other with their equally arched eyebrows, until Merek finally broke away. "I might try the window."

"That works, too."

Merek kicked at the metal railing that lined the concrete walkway outside the motel room until one of its bars loosened, and he pulled it free. Shannon kept a lookout in case the sound attracted any attention, but if there was anyone left in this run-down hotel in apocalypse city, they weren't leaving their rooms to investigate strange noises.

Merek smashed the window open with the bar railing, then kicked aside the jagged, broken pieces near the sill.

"Perfect," Shannon said, smiling. "It's like you were born to be a juvenile offender."

"Was that almost . . . a compliment?" Merek asked, his mouth lifting in a smile.

"Almost." Shannon turned away to hide her own smile and crawled through the window and opened the door for Merek. Together, they looked at the small, dark room with its two twin beds and tiny, scratched-up desk pushed up against one corner.

"God, this is depressing," Shannon said.

She moved to the desk, which was covered with books and

papers. Most were pieces of scrap and notebook paper with messy handwriting scrawled across them. Shannon picked one up and saw a series of names written in untidy pen. Some of the names had question marks by them, others check marks.

"What is this?" Shannon murmured.

Merek moved closer, looking over the papers. But he only shrugged. "My ability to help ended at smashing the window."

"Where did he go?"

They heard a creaking noise from behind, and Shannon and Merek both whirled around. Merek's hand immediately rose up in a protective motion that covered them both, but then fell back down almost as quickly. "I might have some idea," he said.

Joe stood in the doorway, staring down Shannon and Merek with disapproval.

Shannon, no stranger to being caught in the act by a parental figure, immediately opened her mouth to try to come up with an excuse. But before she could say anything, Joe's posture changed abruptly. His shoulders fell, and he wiped one hand across his face, tired.

"Suppose I should have seen this coming."

"Well . . . yeah," Shannon said, caught off guard. "I mean, what?"

"Keeping Liv in the dark never worked out, either."

"Oh. Yeah. I mean, I appreciate you letting us off the hook on this whole search after . . . what we found in Pasadena. And I get why Daisy wanted to leave. But I can't just sit back and do nothing, Joe. I *can't*."

Joe sighed a long sigh. It looked like he'd been up for days, ever since Malibu. "You're just *kids*."

"Liv is just a kid, and she's off storming a castle or something."

"And I am not a *kid*," Merek responded, sounding genuinely insulted. "I have been trained to fight by the best instructors in Caelum."

"Yeah! And I . . . well, I can't fight much, but I can help you with research and stuff." Shannon gestured to the table. "That's what all this is, right? You can at least tell me what you're looking for."

"I'm looking for more Knights of Valere." This time, Joe pointed to the pieces of paper on the table. "I found those papers in Pasadena, in the house of the man who was killed—"

"I knew it! I knew you found something!" Shannon cried. "Sorry, go ahead."

"It's a list of names. I believe they're the contacts for other Knights. I thought I'd start tracking them down, see if any of them are willing to talk."

Shannon looked back over the list of names. "And what? Couldn't find any?"

Joe waited a moment before answering, his eyes on the floor. "No. I found them."

Once again, Joe ran a hand over his beard. Shannon noticed how greasy it was, like Joe hadn't washed his face or showered in a while. And maybe she was imagining things, but it looked like it had much more gray in it than she remembered. Joe looked up, his tired, bloodshot eyes resting on her own.

"They're gone. All four Knights I've managed to track down

from that list . . . all gone. Missing or . . . dead."

Shannon swallowed. "Oh."

"Which explains what I found on the top of the papers," Joe said. He moved over to the desk and shuffled the pieces of paper, bringing one forward. At the top of the page, in block handwriting, were two words: "WARN THEM."

"Warn them?" Shannon asked, her voice shaky.

"The Knight in Pasadena must have known someone was coming for him—coming for them all."

"But the Knights are the bad guys, right? Aren't *they* the ones who go around killing people?"

"Traditionally, yes," Joe said.

"So if someone's taking them out . . . who would do that? Who's bad enough to take on bad guys? Isn't Malquin back in Caelum?"

Joe shrugged. "As far as I know, he is. I don't know. But whoever's doing it, they're working fast, and they're being thorough. And if they finish what they started and wipe out the rest of the Knights . . ."

Joe looked out the dingy hotel window to the angry sky that had already become familiar, and shook his head. "Then there won't be a person left in this world who knows how to fix it."

GONE GIRL

Cedric couldn't remember the last time he'd felt nervous to speak with Kat. Even when they'd sometimes fought as children, he at least always knew what to say to make things right again. Now he had no idea.

Now he'd changed everything.

But he couldn't hide out on the perimeter of the village forever. He took a deep breath and forced himself to push open the door of the pub. Through the dim air inside, he could only make out a few figures. Some men clustered around tables, drinking and eating. Kat was sitting on a stool near the bar, clutching a cup of mead in one hand.

Cedric slowly moved over and took the stool next to Kat without saying a word.

"How did it go, then?" she asked without turning to face him.

"Pretty terrible."

Cedric signaled to the bartender to pour him a cup of mead as well.

"I cannot say I am surprised," Kat responded with a sigh.

"No," Cedric said. "I suppose not." His mind returned again to the conversation—no, the fight—he'd had with Liv. He felt as though every single thing he'd tried to say had come out wrong, and if he could just have a chance to do it over . . . but no. It was better this way. And it was already done, anyhow.

"And . . . how are you?" Cedric asked.

Kat gave a half smile and lifted her cup. "Believe it or not, this actually helps a bit."

Cedric's gut twisted. "I did not mean to—you know I would never have left you there if . . ."

But Kat just snorted. "My God, Cedric, how large *is* that head of yours? I was talking about this—" She tapped gently against her lower hip. "My stab wound? The village healer said a glass of mead might cut some of the pain while it heals."

"Oh! Of course, that's . . . right then."

Kat laughed—her short, brief laugh that was so familiar to Cedric—and he finally smiled. This was his Kat again, the one he knew inside and out. And if there was maybe a sliver of hardness, of caution, in her eyes that hadn't been there before, he was going to pretend he didn't notice.

"So you truly do not want to discuss . . . what happened?" he asked.

Kat tilted her head, as if considering. "Not at the moment, if it is all the same to you. I understand how complicated things are bound to get between us, how everything will change when this"—she lifted the silver betrothal ring from where it hung on a chain around her neck, and spun it on her fingers—"becomes a reality. But there is no need to rush things. There will be time for all of that once Caelum is safe again."

The relief that flooded through Cedric was instantaneous and all-consuming. He felt his whole posture change, and he knew Kat could sense it.

"I very much agree," he said.

Kat nodded, then turned her head back toward the bar. She took another sip from her glass. Again, there was just a hint of standoffishness in her movements . . .

But he wouldn't dwell on it. He chose to listen to her words instead.

"So," Kat said, a bit louder than necessary. "I think we should go through the men and women in the village, particularly the fighters and scouters. We should assess their strengths and weaknesses—"

A hand clamped down on Cedric's shoulder, and he turned around. The broad face of Rafe's right-hand man loomed over him. Cedric remembered his name was Abe.

"Highness, Rafe is missing. He's left the village."

As Abe's words sunk in, Cedric sighed in mild irritation. He wondered how this development would impact his plan. Rafe's help would certainly be valuable, but they would be able to carry out the strategy without him if necessary.

"Well, if he does not return soon—"

"There is more," Abe said, then cleared his throat. "The otherworld girl, she is missing as well."

"What?"

Cedric stood quickly from his stool, regretting sipping on

the cup of mead. It churned in his stomach now, forcing an acidic taste up his throat.

"And there is this." Abe thrust his arm out toward Cedric, who saw a small piece of rough parchment in his slab-like hands. Cedric took it and opened it. Inside was a messy scrawl, smudged in several places.

Cedric,

I'm sorry we fought, but I think it was for the best. We have different missions now. You need to win a war, but I need to make sure Peter survives it. Rafe is going to help me with that. I hope everything works out for you. I also hope you can read this, since I've never used a quill before. I—

But there the words were smudged so badly Cedric could no longer make them out. Though the signature at the bottom was clear.

Liv.

Cedric stared at the parchment, unable to move, unwilling even to blink. He barely noticed when Kat dismissed Abe and stood up, taking him by the shoulders.

"Please, Cedric, do not do this."

For a moment, Cedric was confused by her words. But when he looked into Kat's concerned eyes, he knew she understood everything, even the things he hadn't yet voiced. Because his first thought, his only thought, was to go after Liv and bring her back. Just as Kat knew it would be.

"I have to," he said. "There are wraths out there, and she is alone—"

"She is not alone," Kat said, her voice taking on a fierce edge.

Cedric scoffed. "You think *Rafe* can be trusted?"

Kat released her grip on Cedric's shoulders, and exhaled gently. "Liv obviously trusts him enough to leave with him. And that is her choice to make."

"You cannot be serious," Cedric said. "They will never succeed. If I go after them now, I can catch them—"

"And then what? Throw them both over your shoulders and bring them home? You cannot control what happens to them now. You can only control what we do here."

Cedric shook his head and started pacing in front of the bar. Every part of his body wanted to turn and run out the door of the inn, just run and keep running until he found Liv and apologized and kept her safe, with him.

"Cedric," Kat started again. "We have had this conversation before. I know you care for her, but your people need you right now."

Cedric whirled on her. "What if it were me?"

Kat blinked, taken aback.

"What if it were me who was out there, possibly in mortal danger? If you had to choose, between saving Caelum and saving me, what would you choose?"

For a moment, Kat's mouth parted slightly, and she shook her head as if she couldn't even conceive of the question. But then her eyes focused, and Cedric knew she had an answer.

Suddenly, he didn't want to hear it.

"Forget it," he said brusquely. "It does not matter. But I know I can stop them and still launch the attack successfully—"

"Cedric . . ."

"But I cannot do it alone. Will you help me?"

Kat stared him down angrily for a few more moments, then reached over and picked up her cup of mead. She tipped its remains back into her mouth, then slammed it back on the counter. When she looked back at Cedric, her eyes were clear.

"Of course I will help."

"Good, because I am leaving within the hour."

Kat shook her head, but said nothing. Cedric realized that he had never gone against her advice before, not about something this big. It made him doubt that he was doing the right thing. But then he looked down again at the parchment in his hands, at Liv's messy scrawl. He pictured her writing it, hunched awkwardly over a quill . . . and then he pictured her deep in the darkness of the forest, surrounded by the shadows of horns and claws and teeth. . . .

Right or wrong didn't matter, not now. Nothing would stop him from reaching her—before the monsters did first.

⊁+·+⊰

Liv hummed as she set her pack down in the dirt. She'd been marching through the forest for hours, and now that night was falling, it was getting harder to keep images of ink-black eyes and pointed teeth from her mind. It was even harder to keep the *Jaws* theme song from running through her head every time she heard a twig snap or branches rustle. Humming it out was the only thing that helped.

"Is your plan to *lure* the wraths to us?" Rafe whispered roughly as he sat down on the ground and pulled a piece of bread from his pack.

Liv stopped humming.

"Sorry," she mumbled.

"The point is to be as stealthy as possible," Rafe said, ripping off a piece of bread and tossing it in his mouth. "Hence, no fire, no beaten paths, and absolutely no loud humming."

"Got it. Honest."

Liv opened up her own pack and pulled out her own piece of bread. The bag also had some granola bar wrappers, some refilled bottles of water, and a flashlight. She'd left the walkies behind for Cedric to use in his grand battle plan. She might have been angry with him, but she didn't want him to fail.

It still hurt to think about Cedric. Liv kept turning around, half expecting to see him next to her, and finding a blank space instead. It was like reaching for some valuable, familiar thing—a favorite DVD or T-shirt—and finding it gone. Then remembering *she* was the one who had thrown it away. She'd cooled off since their fight, but the damage was done.

"How long do you think it will take us to get there now?" she asked Rafe.

"Two more days, if we are lucky."

"Hmm," Liv said, thinking it over. "That'd probably be just a few hours if we had a car. Really should have brought one of those through the portal instead of an earthquake kit. Still, Kat said her 'northern people' were just a few days away, too. Caelum must not be that big, huh?"

Rafe shot her a look as though she'd just said something

completely dumb. "You have only seen a portion of Caelum. We have villages on the outskirts of our lands, bordering the mountains and the wrath hunting grounds, that are a two-week journey by foot. Three in bad weather."

"Oh. Um . . ."

"Is your world bigger than *that*?"

Liv wondered how far she'd get from Los Angeles if she walked for three straight weeks. Sacramento?

"Just a bit." She decided to change the subject. "You said it would take two days to reach the castle if we were lucky. What if we run into some wraths?"

He smiled. "Do not worry. I am more familiar with these woods than any man in Caelum. If wraths are approaching, I will hear them."

"And then we'll . . ."

"Fight them, if there are few. Outrun them if there are many."

"Oh, cool. As long as there's a solid plan, then."

Rafe laughed. "Our plan is to make it to the city in good time, without running into wraths on the way. What we should be determining is how to sneak into the castle without alerting anyone and free the royal prisoners."

"Plus my brother."

"Of course."

"Well, my experience with breaking into castles is pretty much limited to Final Fantasy games, and even those I was never very good at."

Liv sighed, leaning back on her pack and stretching out her

legs, which were sore from walking more in the past few days than she usually did in a few weeks in LA. When she looked over at Rafe, his eyes were following the lines of her legs as well. She cleared her throat and raised an eyebrow, but when he looked up at her, he didn't seem embarrassed to be caught at all. Instead, he grinned. Liv could just see the outline of his face and his white teeth in the dark.

"There are also other ways to pass the time," he said.

Liv folded her legs back up. "What happened to focusing on the castle problem?"

Rafe just shrugged. "Sometimes I do my best strategizing when my hands are . . . otherwise engaged."

Liv made a face. "How about you keep those hands where I can see them—"

Rafe suddenly went rigid, his mocking grin sliding from his face.

"What—"

Rafe held a hand out, silencing Liv. He looked toward the tree line on his right. Liv's heart thudded, and she tried to still the shaking in her limbs as she rose. She peered into the shadows all around her, but saw only the dark outlines of trees and leaves. She heard only the sound of her own breath catching in her throat.

Next to her, Rafe slowly slid his sword from its sheath. He did it so quietly that Liv could barely hear it brushing against the leather.

Then she did hear something.

A crunch. And another. Rhythmic, like footsteps.

Rafe's entire body was taut, ready to move. Liv still didn't know if she'd be fighting or running.

Then something pushed through the brush directly in front of them, and Rafe sprung forward, sword out.

A scream broke through the night. It belonged to a man—his voice cut out just as Rafe's sword reached the skin of his throat. But the metal edge stopped just in time, and instead of slicing through skin, it rested firmly against the man's neck. The man looked just a little taller than Liv, and his face was hidden in shadows.

"Who are you?" Rafe barked.

"I—I am unarmed," the man replied. "Harmless."

A tingle ran down Liv's spine. She recognized the voice.

Liv stepped forward, ignoring the hand Rafe thrust out to keep her back. As she came closer, the man's features grew sharper in the moonlight. His round, brown eyes were open wide. His beard, though dirt-streaked and home to a few leaves, was a shocking white, contrasting sharply against his brown skin.

Liv stopped walking forward, suddenly paralyzed. She swallowed hard.

"Professor?"

NO COUNTRY FOR OLD MEN

Professor Leonard Billings stood before Liv, looking worse for wear in the middle of the unfamiliar woods.

"You," he choked out. His voice sounded rough, as though he hadn't used it in a while. Or maybe that was a side effect of having a sword pointed at his throat. "How are you here?"

Rafe shot Liv a confused look. "You know this man?"

Liv stared at the professor. The person in front of her looked tired, dirty, broken. His shoulders slumped, and he seemed years older than the first time she'd seen him, sitting behind his desk in a cozy university office filled with books. But no matter the change in his appearance, this was the same Leonard Billings, the one who'd tried to knife her down in a motel room. The one who'd shot at her in a warehouse full of monsters, just before he'd fallen through a portal to another world. This world.

"He tried to kill me," she finally said. "Twice."

Rafe tightened the grip on his sword, taking one small step forward. The professor lifted his hands in surrender.

"I am unarmed," he said again.

"Who is he?" Rafe still addressed Liv, ignoring the professor's words entirely.

"He's one of the Knights. Of Valere."

"Valere?" Rafe shook his head slightly. "I have never heard of such a knight. No knight of any worth in Caelum would attempt to kill a young woman."

"He's not from Caelum. He's from my world."

"I'm not going to hurt you," the professor said, his voice raspy, but calm. "And again, I'm unarmed. So I couldn't even if I wanted to."

"That's not super reassuring," she said back.

The professor kept his hands up in surrender while Rafe checked him for weapons. Billings's eyes stayed focused on Liv, and she shifted under his gaze. He'd tricked her so completely in San Diego, never letting her see his true self. For someone to lie so easily and so well . . .

"He *is* unarmed," Rafe replied.

Liv shook her head. "He's still dangerous."

"I understand why you'd think that," the professor replied. His voice was still rough, and he cleared his throat. "But I was only trying to do my duty as a Knight. Though I failed, and it is probably too late to undo the destruction you've caused—"

The professor broke into a fit of coughs, and Liv let his words sink in. Destruction? But before she could ask what he meant, he took a deep breath and continued, "Still I was sworn to try, to protect the Earth—"

"By killing me," Liv interrupted, heat rising in her throat.

"And my brother and sister. And Joe's brother, and countless children before that?"

The professor gave a small yelp, and Liv realized that Rafe had pushed the knife blade farther into the skin of his throat.

"You kill children?" Rafe asked, his voice suddenly low and threatening.

The sword blade pushed in deeper and the professor made a gurgling noise.

"Wait!" Liv heard herself yelling.

Rafe stopped. He held the blade carefully still. He spoke without turning around, and his voice was strained. "You claim this man murders the young. If that is true, he is no better than a wrath. He deserves to die."

"Maybe," Liv said, taking a cautious step forward. Part of her couldn't believe she was doing this—defending the man who'd tried to kill her and Daisy. But her mind caught on the professor's words—*too late to undo the destruction you caused.* And an image sprang forward, the last glimpse she'd seen of LA before she'd gone through the portal. Daisy and Joe staring up at the sky, a sky gone orange in the middle of the day . . . She'd convinced herself that it was her own eyesight playing tricks on her, a side effect of going through the portal. But what if . . . ?

Liv put a hand on Rafe's shoulder. "But I have some questions for him first. It's important."

After a few moments Rafe's sword arm pulled back a bit, though he kept the blade up and ready.

The professor put a hand up to the small cut on his neck, then directed his eyes to Liv. "Thank you."

"Don't thank me," she said, crossing her arms. "What did you mean when you said it was too late? What destruction did I cause?"

The professor looked from Liv to the sword in Rafe's hand, as if weighing his odds. He rubbed his neck, then drew his fingers away, looking at the blood on their tips.

"Water," he said. "Please, give me water, and I'll tell you everything. There may be a chance to fix things still." The professor moved slowly, lowering himself with great care and favoring his right leg. His face twisted into a grimace as he sat down.

"You're hurt," Liv said, matter-of-fact, while she retrieved one of the water bottles she'd refilled at a spring earlier in the day and handed it over. He looked at the clearly American-manufactured label before opening the bottle and drinking greedily. Standing three feet away, Rafe watched the professor with a look close to disgust on his face. He still held his sword gripped tight, at the ready.

"It was the portal," the professor said.

"Joe told me the portals aren't meant for us. They chew us up and spit us out—that's what he said. That's what happened to his broth—to Malquin. Humans have to have wrath blood on them to cross safely."

"Well, that would have been nice to know," the professor said with a rueful sigh. "I lost consciousness coming through. When I came to, I was in the middle of a forest. Malquin must have left me for dead. I certainly thought I was dying." The professor paused before speaking again, taking another sip of water from the bottle. "I couldn't move. I was alone, but I saw the portal up above me, still a black hole in the sky."

Liv just barely kept herself from nodding. She knew how jarring it was, to fall out of one world and into another. But she'd had Cedric and Kat there to help her through. To wake up alone . . . She felt a prick of sympathy for the professor. She looked away from his tired, lined face and tried to remember instead how he'd looked as he'd aimed a gun at her chest and fired.

"Why didn't you just go back through it?" she asked, trying to sound as uncaring as possible.

"I could barely sit up," he replied. "My ribs are surely broken, and my left leg . . . it won't move right. I was still trying to stand on my own when I heard someone coming through the woods, and I hid. What I saw . . . those *creatures* . . ."

"Wraths."

"I forced myself to get up and put some distance between them and me. Once I was clear of them, I decided to wait until they left so I could go back to the portal, even if going through again really *would* kill me. But I got turned around in the woods. Couldn't find it again. And . . . here we are."

Before Liv could respond, the professor swiveled his head sharply in her direction. "But you can open another portal for me."

Liv scoffed. "And why the hell would I do that?"

"I have to get back."

"There's literally a million other things I would do before helping you," Liv replied. "You were so against opening portals that you were willing to *kill* me to stop it from happening. But now that it's your skin on the line, suddenly you change your mind? Hypocritical much?"

"It's not for myself alone that I want to return to Earth," the professor replied, his voice rising. "I have to go back. To save the world."

This time it was Rafe who scoffed. But Liv couldn't brush off the professor's words so easily.

"What are you talking about?"

"Why do you think the Knights of Valere exist at all? I tried to tell you, I tried to *explain*—" He smacked one hand against the ground in frustration, which sent him into another coughing fit. He hacked as Liv and Rafe waited. Finally, he wiped his mouth with the back of one hand and took another sip of water.

"You said you wanted to keep portals from opening so wraths wouldn't come to Earth. But it's a little too late for that."

"Yes, that is part of the reason," the professor replied. "Wraths constituted a great threat to humanity a millennium ago, and they are no less dangerous now. But there are other dangers, too. You remember when I told you about the Quelling Theory? In my office?"

"Yes." Magic had existed on Earth until it became too dangerous—around the time Guardians and wraths alike were banished to Caelum—and then the quelling started, like the Earth's defense mechanism against magic. "But magic's not even on Earth anymore," Liv said. "That's the whole point, right? It was quelled?"

"It's not on Earth, no, at least not in any amount that

could cause damage. But it is *here*."

The professor lifted one of his arms and gestured to the woods around him. Liv followed his gaze, peering into the shadows of the forest. The professor talked about magic as if it were a physical thing on Caelum, but she saw nothing but tree trunks and green-gray grass.

"Magic came through to this world when the first portal was opened, along with the wraths and Guardians and anything tainted with that power," the professor continued. "And as long as the wall between the two worlds stayed closed, magic was no longer a threat to Earth."

"And the wall is no longer closed?"

"It's getting torn apart, little by little," the professor responded. "Every time a portal opens between Caelum and Earth, more magic slips back into our world. But after all these years, the Earth is no longer used to handling that much magic, and its quelling defenses will soon go into overdrive. It will start fighting back—hard. If it hasn't already started."

Liv felt like her head was spinning as she tried to follow the professor's words. "Fighting back . . . what does that even mean? How can a whole *world* fight back against something like magic? Something like . . . I mean, what even *is* it?"

"It's a force. It's an invisible thing, but powerful."

"And it's bad for us?"

"Not necessarily, it's . . ." The professor sighed, shaking his head in frustration. "Magic in itself isn't inherently bad, but our world's reaction to it will be. Just . . . imagine what happens to your body when it's infected with a virus. The virus is small, and invisible to the naked eye, yes? But your body still knows it doesn't belong inside of you, and it starts fighting against it. Your immune system kicks in, and that's what causes all of the symptoms that make you sick—not the virus, but your own body fighting it."

Liv tilted her head, thinking. "So the virus is magic. And now that it's back in our world, the Earth is . . . sneezing?"

"Yes," the professor exhaled, closing his eyes. "In an incredibly destructive way. Our world will try to push magic back out of itself by any means necessary. And if it continues to do so, it will tear itself apart. Literally."

"The earthquakes . . . ," Liv breathed.

"Exactly. And it will only get worse from there."

"Worse how?" Images of earthquake destruction popped into Liv's head. Pictures from movies she'd seen and news feeds she'd watched in school. Destroyed houses, floods, great chasms in the ground . . .

The professor shook his head. "I don't know for sure, because we've never seen it happen before. But I do know that the more the Earth fights off the returning magic, the more volatile things will get. That is why it was so necessary to kill the children of the scrolls, before . . . before any of this could happen."

Liv swallowed hard. She looked over at Rafe, who was looking at the professor with a glare. "You believe this man?"

No, Liv wanted to say. And, *maybe*. He was a liar, it was true. He'd twisted facts before to get what he wanted. But if there was even the tiniest possibility he was right . . .

"I don't know." Her voice came out small.

Rafe twirled the sword in his hand and cocked his head at the professor. He gave a half smile. "I will not pretend to understand all you have spoken of. I know nothing of your world, or of 'viruses,' or even the portals, for that matter. But I do know liars. They are often born of desperate men."

Rafe suddenly stopped twirling the sword.

"And you, old man, are desperate."

"Rafe, wait," Liv said, keeping her eyes on the professor. "Is there a way to fix it? If you are telling the truth, I mean?"

The professor took a deep breath. "Possibly."

Liv shook her head. "That's not good enough. If you want me to consider taking you back home with me, I'm going to need more than that."

"There is a man back home," the professor started. He looked down at the ground, eyebrows knitting together as he spoke. "He's a Knight, or he once was. We were assigned to the same team and sent to terminate a group of scrolls who had recently been discovered. Three brothers."

Joe. Liv sucked in a breath.

"But something went wrong that day, as you know. We could only locate two of the brothers, and the eldest escaped. The younger was only five or six. The Knight who was with me, Martin, it was his responsibility to . . . eliminate the target."

"Eric," Liv said, gritting her teeth. She could still picture the pain in Joe's face as he'd told her this same story. "His name was Eric."

The professor just barely lifted his head, his eyes meeting

Liv's briefly before returning to the ground. "Martin was never the same after that. I tried to make him see that by fulfilling his duty, he'd helped keep the world safe, but . . . he no longer heard me. He started taking extended trips for 'research,' talking about crazy theories. He had this idea that there was a way to keep the portals and magic from harming the Earth and ensure that no children of the scrolls would have to die again."

"Did he find it?"

"I don't know," the professor said, sighing. "His behavior got him exiled from the Knights. I never saw him again. But if you take me back to our world, I can find him. I can see if there's a way to fix what's happened."

Liv kept her eyes focused on the professor's. She wished she could tell, just by looking at him, whether or not he was telling the truth.

The professor gave another frustrated sigh. "The longer we wait, the worse it will get. Martin might be our only chance. And we have to go *now*."

"Liv is not going anywhere now," Rafe said. "We are already in the middle of a mission of our own."

"What could possibly be more urgent than this?" The professor threw his hands up in the air. In response, Rafe clutched the grip of his sword hilt—a slight movement, but enough to quiet the professor.

"Something you wouldn't understand." Liv stared the professor down. He stared right back.

"Is this something more important than saving the entire world?"

Liv thought of Peter, and didn't respond.

"Liv, I would advise against listening to this man," Rafe interjected. "You said yourself you did not trust him."

"I don't, but . . ." Liv looked to the professor. "Would you come with us to the castle? Once I've done what we came here for, we can talk about going home. Together."

The professor and Rafe voiced their objections over each other.

"We can't wait that long! It's imperative—" the professor started.

"He could jeopardize our entire plan—"

Liv held up a hand, and both men fell silent. "Wow, I didn't think that would actually work. But listen." She turned to the professor. "I get it, the world is sneezing and the stakes are high—assuming you're not lying to me. Again. And you"—she looked to Rafe—"if there's even the slightest chance the professor *is* telling the truth—and I'm, like, forty percent sure he might be, then we need him. And I won't leave him behind. Agreed?"

"He will slow us down."

Liv just stared at him, and Rafe exhaled through his nose.

"I'll take that as a yes. Now I'm going to get some sleep. Rafe, wake me up in a few hours so you can get some rest, too. We'll keep heading to the castle tomorrow."

Liv turned her back to the men and laid her head down on her pack. She wasn't the least bit tired and doubted she'd get to sleep in this patch of dirt, but this seemed as good a way as any to win the argument.

For now.

⊱┼┼⊰

A hand shook Liv roughly around the shoulders, and for a brief moment, she thought she was back in one of her foster homes, being woken up for school.

"Liv! Liv, you must rise."

But none of her foster parents had ever talked like that.

Liv opened her eyes to the see the bright, whitish Caelum sky. A good portion of it was blocked out by Rafe's face.

"Where is he?" Rafe asked.

Liv stretched her shoulders, which were stiff from sleeping on the ground. "Hmnnh?"

"I woke you a few hours ago to take watch," Rafe continued. "When I closed my eyes, the old man was here. Now he is gone."

"Wait . . . what?"

Liv got quickly to her feet, looking around. She remembered now—Rafe stirring her awake in the middle of the night so he could get some rest. She'd leaned up against her pack, taking small sips of water, willing herself to stay awake. . . .

"I fell asleep," she murmured.

Rafe cursed and ran a hand through his hair.

"The professor was right there." She pointed to the spot on the ground where the professor had been lying in the night. "He was *right there.*"

"Well, now he is gone."

"D-do you think wraths took him?"

Rafe shook his head. "If it was wraths, they would not have left us alive. Or taken the rest of our water supply and the spare knife I kept in my boot."

This time it was Liv who ran her fingers through her hair.

"I'm such an idiot. I can't believe I let myself fall for his crap, even a little bit. I could *kick* myself. Or—"

She kicked out at a nearby log on the ground, then yelped in pain.

Rafe just stared at her, a smile fighting its way across his face. "Did that help?"

"No," she responded, reaching down to rub her toe. "I don't understand—where would he go? Even if the professor was lying about the end-of-the-world stuff, he still wanted to get home. And I was his best shot to get there."

Rafe shrugged. "I can barely understand the motivations of madmen *here*, let alone those from another world entirely."

"Maybe he thought it would be faster to find the portal he fell through instead of coming with us to the castle first?"

Again, Rafe shrugged. "Possibly. You did tell him how to get back through it safely. With—what did you say was needed? Wrath blood? Maybe that's why he took my knife."

"Ugh. I hope I never see that man's face again." Liv felt another surge of irritation, but it was more at herself than at the professor.

"Good. I was worried you might get it in your head to go off after him."

"Definitely not. If he wants to go face a wrath on his own, then fine. He can." Liv didn't voice her secret question—was *any* of what the professor said the night before true? If it was all a lie, it had been a good one—enough to keep her from letting Rafe kill him until he could escape. And if even a small part of it had been true . . . well, she'd worry about that *after* saving Peter.

Liv looked around their small clearing, then back at Rafe. "So what now?"

He scooped up his sword with one hand and held the other arm out to her.

"Now? We go onward. Unless you have more business to settle with that log."

"No," she said, reaching to take his arm. "I think it learned its lesson."

CRUEL INTENTIONS

Kcchscckkt!

The loud, unfamiliar noise filled the air around Cedric and seemed to travel up his spine. He flinched and stopped walking, then reached for the device at his hip. He pushed the small button on its side.

"Kat? Are you attempting to reach me?"

No response.

Cedric had been marching through the woods for more than a day now, trying to track Liv and Rafe's trail, and in that time had communicated with Kat several times via the walkie devices.

And at least half of those times were on purpose.

"Damn. I—" Kat's distorted voice sounded out, improbably, through the device. Then it disappeared. Cedric tried the button again.

"Kat?"

A brief silence.

"Cedric?" Kat finally responded. "Sorry, I keep hitting this blasted button. But it is good I reached you anyway. The men and I are nearly at the tunnel entrance."

"Any sign of wraths?"

"We came across three of them this morning, but dispatched them easily. You?"

"Not yet."

"And Rafe and Liv?"

Cedric sighed, suddenly glad Kat couldn't see his face.

"Not yet."

Kat didn't respond, so Cedric assumed she had all the information she needed from him. She'd been a little chilly toward him ever since he'd made the decision to follow Liv into the forest. They'd had to push up the timing of their plan and rework some things, but Cedric didn't think the changes posed too big a risk. Kat disagreed.

The fighters of Duoin who didn't go with Kat were a half day behind Cedric, marching in small groups so as not to draw attention to themselves. The new plan was for Cedric to find Liv, bring her back to the ranks, and approach the city from the south just as Kat's forces were reaching the other side from the north.

The whole attack plan hinged on perfect timing, aided by the walkies, and on Cedric finding Liv and Rafe—soon. He hadn't thought that would be a problem, but it turned out Rafe was much better at covering his tracks than even Cedric would have guessed. Plus, though he hated to admit it, Cedric had gotten himself lost more than once since starting to track Liv and Rafe. There had been a time when he knew these woods as well as the hilt of his favorite sword, but now he kept having to second-guess each fork in the trail. He'd glimpse a pond and wonder if it was smaller than it had been before. There seemed to be fewer trees than he remembered. And were the ends of some of their branches looking a bit . . . shriveled?

But no, it had to be his memory playing tricks on him. He'd only been away from Caelum for a few months, after all—there was no way it had actually changed in his absence. But as he passed through various parts of the woods, he couldn't help feeling that it was . . . less, somehow. Different from the images stored in his mind, the ones he'd gone over and over when he'd been lost in Los Angeles and aching for home.

Cedric was ruminating on this odd feeling once again, and wondering to himself whether now would be a good time to stop and make himself a quick meal, when he heard a noise up ahead. It sounded like . . . *splashing*. He walked carefully through dirt and fallen leaves, making his way toward what looked like a small stream. The silvery surface of the water peeked through the trees as he moved, and the sound of the stream grew louder.

But over the burble of the water, Cedric heard something else—voices.

He braced himself behind the trunk of a large tree and leaned out slightly. Through a web of branches, he saw two figures sitting side by side along the bank of the stream. Liv was filling a small bottle with water, and just inches away from her, Rafe washed his hands.

Rafe said something in a low voice Cedric couldn't make out, and Liv laughed. She reached out and put one hand lightly on Rafe's shoulder. Cedric bit the inside of his mouth, nearly drawing blood.

Cedric had spent the past few days wrapped up in regret over their argument, but Liv looked almost carefree sitting by that stream.

And Rafe had made her laugh.

The longer Cedric stood watching them, the more he felt like an unwanted intruder. And yet, he couldn't think of a good way to announce his presence.

Then he felt the hairs on the back of his neck rising up, as though he were being watched. Cedric whipped his head around, staring into the dark spaces between the trees. Nothing looked back at him. But just as he turned his head toward the stream again, a huge form came flying out of the woods to his right.

It was a wrath, covered in leathers and holding two broadswords in its clawed hands. And it was headed right for Liv and Rafe.

Rafe jumped up to face the creature, but by the time he got to his feet, the wrath had already reached him. Liv screamed and fell backward, her hands grappling in the dirt for a weapon that wasn't there. The wrath lifted the swords over its head. The blades formed a perfect X shape, and if they swung down, they'd meet again when slicing through Rafe's neck.

Cedric plunged through the tree line with his own sword out. He slashed at the wrath's shoulders, hoping to break his swing. The creature howled, his arms dropping slowly enough to give Rafe enough time to jump backward. Rafe landed in the stream with a splash, his eyes looking to Cedric with surprise.

They nodded at each other briefly before Rafe reached for the sword at his hip. The wrath turned on Cedric, swinging wildly with the sword in his right hand. Cedric blocked easily, but before he could make another move, the wrath swung out with his left arm.

Cedric just barely ducked in time. The wrath let out another tortured yell, and Cedric saw a sword tip protruding from its midsection. Rafe stood behind the wrath, and he pulled his sword, black with blood, out of the creature's back.

But the wrath didn't fall. It looked between Rafe and Cedric, calculating quickly. Then it jumped away from them and turned, running back into the woods.

"If it gets away and tells any others we are here—" Cedric started.

Rafe nodded before sprinting after the creature, whose blood left a dark trail over the dirt.

Cedric turned to Liv. "Are you okay?"

Her face was pale, but she nodded.

Cedric turned and ran after Rafe and the wrath. He caught up with them not two hundred yards away, under the trunk of a tall pine at the bank of the stream. The wrath only held one sword now, and it clashed violently against Rafe's. As soon as Cedric jumped into the fray, he and Rafe quickly forced the wrath backward—its one sword was no match for their two.

It was Rafe who delivered the fatal blow, his silver blade slicing through the creature's heart. It fell heavily to the ground, never to rise again.

Both young men stared down at the wrath, panting.

"We cannot leave it here for others to find," Cedric said.

Rafe nodded. "I know of a place to hide it, not too far from here. I can drag it myself. You should stay with Liv, in case more appear."

With that, he grabbed the creature by the shoulder and started hauling it off to the woods. Cedric wiped his sword off on some nearby leaves and made his way back to Liv. She stood on the bank of the river, her eyes staring wide at the smear of black blood on the ground at her feet.

As soon as he reached her, Cedric opened his mouth to speak, but couldn't find what to say. He wanted to yell at her for running away, but with the same breath he wanted to ask how she was doing.

Instead he said nothing, and they stood, looking at each other over the inches of space between them. Her eyes were impossible to read. Was she glad to see him? Or angry still? The seconds stretched onward, wrapping around them in a thickening silence.

And then she moved, closing the space between them in an instant and throwing her arms up around Cedric's neck. His arms went around her quickly, naturally. He pressed the side of his chin against her hair without giving it a second thought. Her skin was warm in the sunlight, but her arms were shaking slightly—

"I thought we were going to die," Liv finally said, her words coming out broken and raspy just inches from his ear. She gave a nervous laugh that tickled his skin, and Cedric gripped her tighter. "That wrath came out of nowhere, and we didn't have time to . . . if you hadn't jumped out when you did . . ."

"It's all right. You are safe," he murmured.

He felt her slowly relax in his arms, and for a moment he couldn't remember what they'd fought about. He hadn't thought he'd ever get this close to her again. He had been so careful not to really look at her, not to even touch her since . . . well, he couldn't remember that, either. His brain was a blank as her face moved under his, as her head tilted up . . .

"Liv—"

And her body stiffened. She pulled away and cleared her throat. The moment turned to awkwardness so quickly that for a moment Cedric wondered if he'd imagined her being so near him at all.

"Sorry, I didn't mean to . . ." Her face flushed, and she crossed her arms. She looked back up at him. "Not that I'm not grateful for the save, but . . . what are you doing here? Don't you have a whole war to plan?"

Cedric sucked in a breath, stood up straighter. "I came for you."

"For me? Why?"

He stared at her a moment. "I had to."

She looked up at him then, as if surprised by his answer. She didn't say anything, though, and once again the moment dragged on. He hastily added, "It was the right thing to do."

She looked down, pursing her lips. "Right. Of course. I should have known . . . I am really sorry, Cedric, for taking off and just leaving a note behind. I mean, I was angry, but that's no excuse. I didn't mean for you to worry."

Cedric shifted, his feet sinking slightly into the mud on the creek's edge. He felt suddenly at a loss for something to say. How was it he could be more clearheaded when battling a giant wrath than when simply having a conversation with Liv?

"I am sorry, too. For the things I said. I did not mean—"

"I know." Liv gave a small smile. "But now that you know I'm fine, are you going back? Or are you coming with us to the castle?"

"No, I must return to the men who are approaching the city behind me. But I intend to take you with me."

Liv raised one eyebrow. "Oh, is *that* what you intend?"

"It is the reasonable course—"

"So once again, you've made this plan concerning me without thinking to consult me at all."

Cedric shook his head, frustrated. "No, what I meant was— would you please come back with me? It will be safer for you to stay behind battle lines and enter the castle once we've taken the city back—"

"We've had this exact discussion before." Liv shook her head, a look of disgust crossing her face. "Everyone Malquin is holding prisoner could be used as leverage or even killed during the fight, and it's like you don't even care."

"Do not be ridiculous. Of course I care," Cedric said, growing angry again. How did every conversation with Liv go so far off course, and so quickly?

"Really. Then why doesn't it make sense to sneak into the castle and free our families just before the war starts?"

"That . . ." Cedric started to argue back, before letting her words sink in. "*That* is your idea?"

"Yes."

"That . . . is a good idea."

Liv crossed her arms. "Yeah, I know."

Cedric started to pace now, his mind whirring. His hand went to the walkie device at his side, but he didn't want to reach out to Kat until he had a firmer grip on the plan starting to form in his mind.

"If we could coordinate it, and somehow sneak a small group into the castle to free the prisoners just before the battle begins, it might also cause enough of a distraction to lure some wraths away from the city gates before our forces strike. . . ." Cedric bit his lip as he paced. "Combining both of our plans could be the best chance we have to take back the city and keep our families from becoming casualties."

Liv's eyes glittered in the morning light. "We should go find Rafe, and fill him in on this—"

"Right. Rafe." Cedric's stomach tightened at the thought. But he tried to push his negative thoughts aside. Rafe was a strong fighter and strategist, and could be key to the success of this new plan. No matter how much he was able to make Liv laugh.

Liv looked around. "Where is he, anyway?"

"He went to dispose of the wrath's body."

"What if he ran into more of . . . them?" Liv's eyes filled with worry, and she scanned the edge of the forest.

"We can follow his trail and meet up with him," Cedric said, taking his sword from its sheath once again.

He gestured in the direction Rafe had gone, and they took off together, side by side. After walking quickly for a few minutes, Cedric saw the line of flattened grass and broken sticks ahead of him lead into the mouth of a cave.

"He took it in there?" Liv asked.

Cedric motioned for her to stay put, but of course she followed him anyway. They had to duck to get inside the cave, which was small enough that they could have reached out and touched the walls on either side at the same time. It extended backward into the ground past where Cedric could see. The whitish light from outside touched only the first few feet of the cave, and Cedric's eyes were slow to adjust to the dimness.

Which is probably why he didn't see the body until he tripped over it.

Cedric quickly righted himself and looked down at the figure at his feet. At first, all he could see was dark fabric and what looked like whitish hair. He didn't recognize the face until he knelt down to get a closer look. The man's dark eyes were open wide, directed at Cedric just as they had been at a small inn two hours outside of Los Angeles.

"Oh," Liv said, as she recognized the grayed face of the professor. "Oh God."

Cedric gently closed the professor's eyes with two fingers and stood.

"Was . . . was it a wrath?"

Cedric shook his head. "His throat was slit cleanly, with a knife. That is not how wraths . . . do things."

"How is he here? I just saw him *last night*."

"What?"

Before Liv could answer, footsteps sounded out from the back of the cave. Cedric put a hand against Liv's mouth and pressed her back against the dirt wall. But the figure that quickly emerged from the shadows wasn't a wrath—but an out-of-breath Rafe.

Cedric didn't need to see Rafe's face to know what had happened, but it helped to confirm his suspicions. After all, what were the odds that Rafe would attempt to hide a dead wrath in the exact same cave where another body was hidden?

"Why?" Liv choked out.

For a moment, Rafe looked caught, maybe even contrite, but that quickly melted away into defiance. He squared his shoulders. "This man was a murderer. Of *children*. You said so yourself. He would have slowed us down, or worse."

"So you just . . ." Liv trailed off, her eyes wide and staring at the professor.

"I did what was right," Rafe replied, his voice tight and defiant.

"If that was true, you wouldn't have waited until I fell asleep." Liv said, looking up at Rafe with eyes that seemed to blaze even in the darkness. "You wouldn't have lied."

"You do not understand how things work here—"

"You're right, I don't. And I don't want to."

Liv whirled and ran out of the cave. Rafe sighed and ran one hand over his forehead.

"Well, this is rather unfortunate. Why did you follow me here, anyway?"

"Liv was worried," Cedric said, unable to keep the acid from his voice.

Rafe narrowed his eyes. "Do not tell me you are upset at this as well. You know what we do to murderers in Caelum, Cedric. He admitted his guilt to me, and he showed no remorse. This is what he deserved."

Cedric said nothing, but turned to follow Liv from the cave, leaving Rafe behind with the professor's body. He knew that, technically, Rafe was right. He had not broken any of Caelum's laws, which decreed that anyone who killed another human be put to death. But that knowledge did not lessen the sick feeling in his stomach.

He found Liv not too far away, leaning back against a massive tree trunk with her head hanging down between her legs. She was taking big, shaking breaths.

"What are you doing?" Cedric asked, trying to make his voice as gentle as possible.

"Trying not to throw up."

"Liv—"

"How could he do that?" Liv whipped her head up, her face red and blotchy. "Just slit a man's throat and be so . . . so . . . *cavalier*? Just la-di-da, he deserved it."

Cedric took a step closer to her. "Rafe . . . he is many things, but cavalier is not one of them. He does not act without forethought."

Liv closed her eyes for a moment and shook her head. "I just feel so . . . lost here. Every decision I make, who to trust and who to save, it always turns out wrong."

"Believe me, I know how you feel." Cedric wanted to reach out and touch her shoulder, or her hand. He looked down instead.

"The professor is dead," Liv said. "I know he tried to kill me. Like, more than once. But still . . ."

Cedric closed his eyes and saw again the ashen body of the professor lying on the ground, the empty, unseeing eyes. "Still."

Liv looked toward the cave and inhaled sharply. Rafe had emerged and was making his way to them.

"We have to keep him with us, don't we?" Liv asked, her voice low.

Cedric sighed. The last thing he wanted to do was keep Rafe with them. Rafe had challenged his authority, tried to turn the villagers against him, taken off with Liv into a forest filled with monsters. But he was a skilled fighter, and he knew the most about what awaited them in Westing.

"Yes," he finally said. "We need him."

"Can you trust him?"

"I trust that he wants to free his parents. And right now, we need his help to do that."

"I am touched at your confidence in me," Rafe said, getting closer.

Liv glared at Rafe, but Cedric stepped toward him.

"We have the same goal, just as we always did. Are you willing to put everything else aside to work together? To save our families, and then the kingdom?"

Cedric stuck out his hand. Rafe eyed it for a moment before grabbing it in his own.

"To save our families, and the kingdom."

"Well, let's do it soon," Liv said, pushing herself up and off the tree trunk. "Because I am *beyond* ready to get out of this place. And never come back."

Liv started walking back to the creek ahead of Cedric and Rafe without turning around to look at either of them. Cedric didn't know if she'd been referring to the woods or to Caelum as a whole when she'd said "this place" in such a tone of disgust, but he suspected it was the latter.

It cut him deeper than he wanted to admit.

RISKY BUSINESS

"Well, at least all those zombie apocalypse movies got *something* right."

Shannon peered through Joe's windshield at the Ralphs grocery store across the parking lot. The area between the Jeep and the store's front door was packed with cars, some parked haphazardly in spots, others left in aisles with their hazard lights on. The honking was endless. A line of people extended out of the doorway of the store, where a single police officer was desperately trying to keep order. Two women were fighting over a shopping cart on the sidewalk, and as one yanked on the handle, another dropped a canvas bagful of fruit. A single melon rolled away down the asphalt and disappeared beneath the front tires of a pickup truck.

"Shannon, this isn't the apocalypse." Joe said, keeping his eyes trained on the apartment building that butted up against the grocery store parking lot. "And there are no zombies."

"Yet," Shannon added. But despite Joe's assurances, what was happening in Los Angeles sure felt like the end of the world. It seemed like half the city had already fled from the earthquakes and skyrocketing heat. Schools and government buildings were closed (so much for senior year). The National Guard were on the scene with the LAPD, but they couldn't be everywhere at once.

Shannon, Joe, and Merek were supposed to be staking out the apartment building in front of them. But she couldn't tear her eyes away from the action in front of Ralphs.

"Whoa, did you see that woman get clocked in the face with a bag of frozen peas?"

"Shannon, if you really want to help, keep your eyes forward, not on the store."

Shannon sighed and directed her attention to the grim, boxy apartment building they'd been watching for forty minutes, hoping to spot the member of an ancient cult who might have information on how to fix the (zombie-less) apocalypse.

"Still no movement," Joe said, his eyes on a second-floor window of the building. "I'm going to check inside."

"We'll go with you," Merek said from the backseat.

"I'd prefer if you stayed in here for now—"

Shannon started to protest, but Joe cut her off. "I'll let you know if I need backup. But if I get up there and find more of what I've been finding at these Knights' homes . . . there's no need for you to see that."

Shannon thought again of the dead man in his living room, the brown blood on the walls. She nodded, staying put as Joe got out of the car.

Merek sat back in his seat, wiping sweat from his forehead

onto his shirt. "I never knew it was possible to be this hot."

"Yeah," Shannon said, lifting the ends of her hair off of her shoulders. Even with the air conditioner running, the inside of the Jeep was stifling. "Who knew saving the world would involve so much sitting around in our own sweat?"

The heat outside made Shannon feel tired and slow. Her thoughts were slow, her movements were slow . . . it was amazing she'd been able to sneak out of the garage fast enough to not get caught. Not that she had any idea of whether she'd be able to sneak back *in*—but that was a problem for later.

"What is that?" Merek asked, his voice suddenly sharp.

Shannon followed his gaze to one of the second-story windows of the apartment building. It had been shut and dark before, but now it was thrust open. A tall man in high-waisted jeans and tortoiseshell glasses began shimmying out of it, onto the balcony.

"That's the apartment, right? What do you wanna bet that's our Knight?" Shannon asked.

As she spoke, the tall man lifted one leg over the balcony ledge, gripping the railing with his hands.

"Holy crap, is he gonna—"

The man swung his other leg over the ledge, until he was hanging, his legs dangling in the air. He released his grip, dropping to the ground.

"—jump?"

Shannon and Merek exchanged a quick look before flinging their car doors open at the same time. Several feet away from them, the tall man had already started running away from the apartment building, toward the Ralphs.

"Follow him!" Shannon yelled as she pulled out her cell phone.

Merek took off after the man, Shannon running behind him. The man turned his head, saw he was being chased, and raced ahead. With one hand, Shannon called Joe.

"Shannon?" he asked, his voice echoing through the phone.

"He's out here, Joe! He's running!"

Ahead of her, the Knight dashed down the length of the Ralphs, dodging a tipped-over vending machine. As Merek neared him, the man jumped toward a loading dock door and flung it open, running inside and slamming the door behind him.

"Hurry!" Shannon yelled into the phone before hanging up.

Merek jumped toward the loading dock door, opening it again with a bang and racing inside. Shannon started to follow him, but then stopped in her tracks, her feet skidding against the concrete. If Merek was about ten seconds behind the Knight, the fleeing man might make it out the front door of the store before Merek could reach him. Shannon quickly doubled back toward the Ralphs's entrance.

When she got closer to the main door, Shannon started pushing through the line of people waiting to get inside. Some hands reached out, grabbing at her clothes, pulling at her arm, but she slipped away before they could stop her.

"Hey, she's cutting!" someone yelled to the cop. But he was busy pulling apart two men who were fighting over an open handicapped-parking space.

Shannon finally slipped inside, but if anything, the chaos was worse here. People raced past her, some with carts and baskets, others just filling bags as they went. They grabbed everything they could find—cans, packages, boxes of food—often without even looking at what they were taking. One woman reached out an arm and swept an entire shelf full of graham crackers into her cart before heading toward the checkout line that extended to the back of the store.

Shannon stopped, looking around for the Knight in the tortoiseshell glasses. But it was hard to spot any one person in this madhouse of panicked activity—like the most messed-up game of Where's Waldo in the world. But then, Shannon heard a loud crashing noise and looked up to see the Knight barreling toward the glass door behind her. Merek skidded around a corner and ran after him. Shannon was dismayed to see, even from this far away, that the bandage over Merek's collarbone was turning red. He must have reopened his cut in the chase.

"Hey!" Shannon yelled at the man. "We just want to talk to you!"

She positioned herself in front of the door, planting her feet on the ground.

The Knight raced toward her, past an overturned bin of browning daisies, past a man stacking his basket with batteries. People looked up as the running Knight passed, but none moved to stop him.

And then the running man was so close that Shannon could see the brown of his wide, panicked eyes behind those tortoiseshell glasses. Only one person stood between him and the exit.

And he wasn't slowing down.

"Stop!" Shannon yelled, her heart racing. She put out both hands, as if they could stop this man before he collided into her, before he ran right through her.

But the Knight didn't stop. He dropped one shoulder down low, and it took Shannon a moment to recognize the movement—one football players made before they bowled down an opponent—

The man smashed right into Shannon's outstretched hands, hard, knocking her back and sideways into the metal edge of the store's front door. She felt different points of her body connect with the metal—her head, her elbow, her hip. For a moment, her vision went red, then black. When full color returned, the man was gone, and Shannon was on the ground. Merek kneeled over her, his eyes wide.

"Are you hurt?"

Yes. Shannon didn't even need to look herself over to know something was wrong. Not just where she'd hit the door, but where the Knight had hit her. He'd collided into her hands, snapping back her wrists, and now—

The pain in her right hand was sharp. When she tried to move it, she let out a cry.

Merek winced as he looked over Shannon's hands. He didn't even seem to notice that he was injured, too. He gently moved one of Shannon's arms over his shoulders and heaved her up. There was no sign of the Knight at the door, and the police officer allowed a new group of people to enter the store, as if nothing had happened. One running man hadn't been enough to catch his attention in this chaos.

"Did he get away?" Shannon squeaked.

Merek just grimaced, his eyes going dark as he glanced, quickly, over the heads of the crowd and out the door.

"Not for long." His voice was steely, no trace of its usual sarcasm.

Shannon pulled her damaged wrist close to her body, whimpering every time it jostled. "Well, this'll teach me to try to be an action hero."

Merek's eyebrow twitched. "You were brave to stand in his way like that. Stupid, possibly, but brave."

The half compliment took Shannon off guard, and she barely knew how to respond. No one had ever called her brave before. She'd never thought of *herself* as brave before. And really, all she'd done was try to stand in someone's way, and fail. "Um, thanks."

"Just like Ripley," Merek added. He looked back toward the parking lot before he could see the smile spreading across Shannon's face.

Outside, it was impossible to see one man amid all the confusion. By the time Joe reached them, the Knight was completely gone, like he'd disappeared into thin air.

THE RESCUERS

The castle was a surprise, to say the least.

Of course, Liv had seen plenty of castles in her time. They were all in movies, sure, but at least she thought she knew what to expect. Stone walls, check. Turrets, check. Moat, check. But what she hadn't been prepared for, at all, was the sheer size of the building before her. It turned out those movies and television shows couldn't really capture the *scope* of such a thing.

Which was why she'd been staring at the castle for the better part of the afternoon, even though she was supposed to be helping Rafe and Cedric keep track of wrath scouts. The castle was made of a dark gray stone, much of its lower half covered with dense green ivy and moss. It was so large that it cast a shadow covering nearly half the city. Silhouetted against the bright white sky, it was impossible to take in all at once. And Liv couldn't keep her eyes off it.

"There are two more," Cedric whispered from her right.

The three of them were hiding behind a rock outcropping

just outside the city walls, and for the last few hours had been keeping track of when wrath guards passed in front of a small side entrance.

"It still does not make sense," Rafe said, shaking his head. Liv bristled at the sound of his voice, just as she had every time he'd spoken on the rest of their journey here. "Why would there be only two at a time, every half an hour or so? In every previous attempt our forces made this close to the city walls, we encountered wraths in groups of no fewer than ten, sometimes even fifteen. Why would they thin their numbers?"

"Maybe they suspect something," Cedric said.

"Maybe it is a trap."

"Or maybe we just got lucky for once?" Liv chimed in.

Neither boy responded. They kept their eyes on the monstrous creatures that passed underneath the city wall a quarter mile away. Looking at Cedric and Rafe, Liv couldn't help but notice their similarities. Both fighters, both strategists. Both possessing the kind of jawlines so strong that some might describe them as "unfair."

But that's where the similarities ended. After the encounter with the professor, Liv could see more clearly now the differences between them. And she could never unsee those differences, just like she could never unsee the specks of blood that had dried on the professor's white beard, just above his slit throat.

"I say we go after these ones now," Cedric said in a low voice. "Use Liv's strategy to get through the gate before any other wraths join their number."

After a beat, Liv nodded, trying to ignore the knot growing

in her stomach. She looked up at the immense, imposing castle again. Her brother was in there somewhere. Waiting.

"Just to be clear," Rafe said, "we are all agreed this strategy is a bit . . . insane?"

Rafe's tone was light, but Liv still bristled. "I've seen it work," she said, defensive. "Many times."

She neglected to mention that those "many times" had always taken place in movies, but there was no need to explain that to Rafe. He looked to Cedric. "You are sure about this?"

Cedric didn't hesitate as he met Liv's eyes. "Definitely."

Rafe shrugged, outvoted. They made their way toward the castle as quickly and as quietly as possible, staying low to the ground and hiding behind trees and rocks. If they were spotted now—either by other passing guards or by any wrath who happened to be watching from the battlements—it was all over.

Cedric and Rafe sneaked up behind the pair of wrath guards who were stationed in front of the wall. The creatures were speaking to each other in low voices and didn't seem to hear Cedric and Rafe as they moved low through the tall grass. They had to be quick in this attack—if the guards had time to signal for any kind of help, they'd be outnumbered in an instant.

Cedric suddenly jumped up from the grass, sword high. He brought it crashing it down over one wrath's head, while Rafe simultaneously plunged his sword into the other's back. The second wrath let out a snarling yell before falling, and both boys tensed up. They looked around the small clearing in front of the side gate, but no one approached.

Liv hid underneath the gray city wall, which cast an enormous shadow over the surrounding grass. Cedric dragged the body of one of the wraths toward a small, wooden door that was set into the bottom of the wall. His muscles strained under the bulk of the creature until Rafe came up alongside to help.

The boys thrust the wrath forward between them, and Rafe pounded a series of four knocks into the wooden door—the same knock they'd seen wrath guards use to gain entrance a few hours earlier.

A small wooden plank lifted away from the center of the door, its edges held by a set of thick, black claws. One black eye filled the hole. Rafe and Cedric both propped the dead wrath up so its chest was at the eye level of the wrath on the other side of the door.

"What is it?" The creature's voice was somehow both guttural and screeching, like someone randomly plucking the strings of an out-of-tune bass guitar.

Rafe and Cedric looked at each other briefly. From her hiding place next to the door, Liv could see beads of sweat coursing down their faces as they held the dead wrath up. Carefully, Rafe removed one of his hands from the body and knocked on the door again, four times.

The black eye blinked, and then backed away from the hole. Liv heard the sound of something heavy sliding around on the other side of the door. Then it opened a crack.

Just as the wrath guard on the other side of the door stepped back to let the new wrath through, Cedric and Rafe pushed forward, shoving the body roughly through the door. It landed on top of the wrath guard, knocking him to the ground.

Rafe used his sword to quickly dispatch the wrath guard struggling on the ground before he could call for help, then pulled both bodies behind a nearby trough. Cedric closed the door in the wall so as not to alert any passing guards that something was wrong.

"I can't believe we actually pulled off a *Weekend at Bernie's* move," Liv said, peeling herself away from the stone wall and going through the door before Cedric closed it. He gave her a questioning look. "And by that I mean I had total confidence it would work the whole time."

The city inside was entirely different from the wild lands just outside the stone walls. Wooden houses, shops, stands, and stalls surrounded streets of densely packed dirt. Some of the buildings had colorful signs attached to their doors, advertising candles or linen or pastries. But every door was shut. Not a single person walked down the streets or into or out of any building. It was like a ghost town.

They took cover in a small alley between the city wall and what seemed to be a butcher shop. A crude wooden cutout of a pig hung over the door. Cedric took the walkie out of his belt and held it up, pushing the button.

"Kat?"

After a few moments, the walkie buzzed in response. "Cedric? Are you inside?"

"Just."

"We are in position, just out of sight of the northern gates. My father's men are here, almost all of them able to fight.

But . . . the Duoin villagers warned us there would be several wraths, and we have only seen a few."

"Us too. But we have no time to worry about that now. Liv and I are headed to the castle. Rafe is on his way to the southern gate to open it from the inside for the Duoin fighters."

"Then we will strike in a half hour to lure the wraths north."

"Be careful, Kat."

"You as well."

Cedric lowered the walkie, and Rafe put one hand on his shoulder. "You will have little time to retrieve our families before the wraths realize we are surrounding them on all sides."

Cedric nodded.

Rafe started to turn away, but then faced Cedric again. "I know you think I wanted to undermine you for my own glory, but truthfully, I simply did not believe you were capable of doing what needed to be done."

Cedric raised an eyebrow. "Is that . . . your version of an apology?"

"It is the truth," Rafe responded. "But nothing that came before matters at this moment. That is my family in there, Prince. Get them out."

Without waiting for a response, Rafe turned and took off, running quickly through the back alleys. Cedric watched him for a moment, then started heading in the opposite direction, indicating that Liv should follow. They stuck close to the alleys behind buildings, always checking before crossing the dirt roads. Every now and again Liv thought she would see someone—a shadow crossing the street just out of the corner of her eye, or a figure ducking behind a window just as she turned toward it.

"Where are all the people?" she whispered as they drew nearer to the hulking castle.

"I wish I knew," Cedric responded, his voice strained.

Eventually, the castle walls grew closer. Cedric led her to a small opening in the stone where the turret met the wall.

"Excellent," Cedric said. "I was hoping the wraths would overlook this."

"What is it?"

Cedric ducked inside the opening, and Liv followed. Immediately, she felt like retching. The smell of spoiled food—and something worse—was overwhelming in the small space.

Cedric put his hands up over his nose, his eyes watering.

"It is a refuse passage out of the kitchens. Our staff always kept it clean, but it appears the wraths did not have the same scruples."

Cedric sucked in a breath and began picking his way around foul-smelling piles. Liv tried not to look too closely at them, but when she spotted a suspiciously human-sized bone lying on top of one of the mounds, she started to gag.

They moved quickly until they came out of the passageway and reached a large, circular room with walls of stone. It was surrounded by wooden tables, cabinets, and four fireplaces. A handful of women and men moved among the tables in the room. They were thin and pale, from the old woman who stood hunched over a giant pot to the young girl—she looked to be no older than twelve—sweeping in the corner. Their clothes were ragged, falling to pieces, and their hands were bound with chains.

A thin man standing closest to the passageway noticed Liv and Cedric come through first. His mouth fell open in surprise, and Liv saw he was missing several teeth.

"Aldis? It is Aldis, yes?"

At the sound of Cedric's voice, the others in the room turned around, some of them gasping in surprise.

The man continued to stare. Finally, he nodded. "Pr-prince?"

"Yes. An army has come to turn the wraths from the castle. They will begin at any moment. I need to know—is my father still alive?"

"I—I do not know, Highness," Aldis responded, then lifted his chained arms by means of an explanation. "The wraths keep us locked in here to cook."

Liv looked around the kitchen-like space and the small piles of rags that lined the walls. At first glance they might be mistaken for garbage, but now Liv saw an older woman lying on one and realized what they were. Beds.

"You have been here all this time?" Cedric asked.

"Since the castle fell," Aldis said, his voice shaking. "We are not permitted to leave the kitchens."

Cedric's jaw tightened, his eyes turned dark. Liv knew that look.

"This ends today." He stared hard at the chains on Aldis's wrists. "I do not have the keys to free you yet, but I will return. I swear it."

Without waiting for a response, Cedric strode quickly toward the door at the far end of the kitchen.

"Sir!" Aldis called out after him, his voice barely louder than a hiss. "There are wrath guards on the other side!"

Cedric paused just long enough to pull out his sword, then quickened his step toward the door. He yanked it open so hard the wooden door went flying back into the stone walls. Liv jumped at the noise, but the two hulking guards on the other side of the door looked even more surprised. Cedric stabbed one of them in the side before he could fully turn around. The other wrath reached for what looked like a giant club with metal spikes coming out of its end. It swung the club at Cedric's head, but he ducked just in time. While the wrath was still following through on its swing, Cedric pushed his sword up into its belly. He pulled it out again quickly as the creature fell forward onto the floor.

Black blood dripped from the tip of Cedric's sword as he turned toward Liv, his face as still and hard as stone. "Coming?"

Liv scurried after him as he made his way through another hall outside the kitchen. The hall itself was dark, with very few windows cut high into the gray walls, leaving little light. Liv could see what looked like torches stuck into the walls, but they were unlit.

"So that was a little scary," she finally said, jogging to keep up with Cedric's pace.

"You have seen more wraths than that in one place."

"Not them. You. I've seen you fight before, but I haven't seen *that* . . . You took them out so . . . brutally."

Cedric kept his eyes forward, his hand tightened on his sword. "Aldis and the others have worked in the kitchens for years. I've known most of them since . . . always. And they were in *chains*. Did you not see? The wraths had them in chains."

"I saw," Liv whispered.

They turned a corner, and then Cedric stopped abruptly. Liv didn't stop in time and crashed straight into his back. He quickly turned and pulled Liv with him, pushing her up against the wall in the first hallway and flattening his body against hers.

"Uh . . . ," Liv started.

"Wraths. Four of them." Cedric whispered low, his breath tickling her ear. "Coming this way."

Liv could feel Cedric's heart pounding in his chest. Her own pulse sped up long before she heard the clattering, heavy footsteps moving down the hall adjacent to them.

"Stay very still," Cedric whispered. "And very quiet."

Liv gave a small nod in response, her ear brushing against his cheek. His breath was hot against the hollow of her neck. This close to him, it was hard not to think of how tightly he'd held her by the stream after saving her from the wrath in the woods. Here she was again, skin humming and buzzing, pulse racing, her body reacting even when she didn't want it to, even when she hated it.

How would the wraths not hear her when her heart was pounding this loud?

The footsteps moved closer to where they hid in the shadows of the darkened hall. Liv held her breath and willed herself to freeze, like an actor having to play dead. She saw a light approaching the hall opening and realized one of the wraths must be carrying a torch. If it happened to look right, no amount of shadows or stillness would hide them . . .

"Hey!" a gruff voice yelled out, and Liv twitched. Cedric pushed against her more firmly. But the voice wasn't from the wrath with the torch. It seemed to come from farther away. Another wrath approaching the group.

"Something's happening. At the north gates."

"What?" one of the closer wraths responded.

"I don't know, do I? We're supposed to go see."

The wrath with the torch sighed in response. "What the hell is it now?" His voice was already moving away, and the light was retreating, too. Soon, all the wrath footsteps faded away down the hall.

For just a moment, Liv and Cedric remained frozen together against the wall. Liv lifted her eyes and saw he was looking down at her, his face only a couple inches away, his eyes shadowed in the darkness. His lips parted—

"We have to hurry," he said.

He pulled away quickly, and a rush of cold air filled the space where he'd been. He turned and started to run, and Liv followed, willing her nerves to get a grip. Through every bend and twist in the hallways, down every flight of stairs, past every heavy door they passed, she ran. If the wraths already knew the city was under attack, she had to get to Peter *now*.

Eventually, the air grew colder and seemed to press down more on Liv's body. She shivered even as she ran, her California skin not used to this level of damp and cold. Cedric reached back and grabbed her hand, guiding her forward so she wouldn't trip in the darkness. Up ahead of them, Liv could see a faint light. As she grew closer, she realized it was a flame from a single torch in the wall. It lit up a long, narrow space with bars on either side. It smelled dank and awful, and every one of Liv's instincts told her not to go in that room. But Cedric's hand pulled her even faster than before, and his eagerness was contagious.

They were practically sprinting by the time they entered the narrow space, which Liv realized was the dungeon. Cedric stopped abruptly and dropped her hand.

"This cannot be right," he said, turning around in one full circle at the cells on either side of them. "It cannot be."

Liv stepped past him, looking left and right. The small torch sent just enough light for her to make absolutely sure—the barred doors on the cells stood open, and every single one was empty.

VERTIGO

"They have to be here somewhere," Cedric said as he led Liv up the twisting back stairs of the servants' quarters.

"You're right. We'll find them," Liv said. But her words had a false, placating sound.

He tried not to think of the dungeons, of the wide-open, empty cells. Of the faces he had last seen behind those bars months ago. He'd been so sure his family would be in the dungeon still, so sure he'd rescue them—

But what if there was no one left to rescue?

His heart twisted. He tried to shove the thought aside, but it wouldn't budge. Instead, he gripped his sword hilt so tightly his fingers ached. He noticed the back of his hand was splattered with blackish blood.

"So where . . . are we going?" Liv panted as they rounded a landing and stepped into a corridor.

The sentence was barely out of her mouth before Cedric stopped in front of a large, familiar wooden door. He'd passed this door hundreds of times in his life, and had had more than one occasion to go through it, when he'd fallen ill as a child or when he'd twisted an ankle on a hunt.

He tried to push the door open, but it was locked. He slammed his fist into the wood near the doorjamb, and the resulting noise was so loud, Liv jumped back.

"Cedric?"

"These are the healing quarters. If anyone was injured, they might have been taken here . . ."

He kicked at the wood, this time sending parts of it splintering away from the door. Liv didn't say anything, but edged slowly away from him.

"This is a good sign, Liv. It would not be locked unless the wraths were trying to keep someone out . . . or in."

On the fifth kick, the door busted inward. Light from the windows of the healing quarters spilled out into the hallway, and for a moment Cedric couldn't see anything in the room at all. But then his eyes adjusted to the light, and he took in the familiar settings—the large, arched windows, the rows of clean beds. Lying on the bed at the far side of the room was a figure propped up against a pillow.

"Peter!"

Liv flew into the room, running over to her brother so quickly she nearly crashed into the bed. Cedric followed, scanning the room once again to make sure he hadn't missed anything.

He hadn't. No one else was there.

"Liv?" Peter asked, his voice full of disbelief. He pushed himself up even more on the bed, though Cedric noticed he didn't get out of it.

"Wh-what are you doing here?" Peter continued. "Emme

said you'd follow, but I didn't think you'd actually come after me—"

"Of *course* I'd come after you!" Liv replied, sounding both relieved and angry. "You idiot!"

Cedric noticed her eyes filling with tears, though she didn't cry.

"I'm so sorry, Liv. I'm so, so sorry. Emme said she needed help, and I thought I could save her, I thought . . ."

"It's okay."

"No. I should never have left you and Daisy behind. And now . . ." He looked down at the bed, where he was covered by a blanket from the waist down.

"What happened?" Liv asked, gently.

Rather than respond, Peter slowly pulled the white blanket aside. His right leg was completely wrapped in strips of linen, from his thigh all the way down to his ankle.

"It was the portal," he whispered. "Malquin said I didn't go through it right—"

"Malquin is here?" Cedric interrupted.

Peter looked up at him for the first time. He nodded, heavy. "He asked me to tell him where you were staying in Los Angeles, but I wouldn't say, Liv. I wouldn't. I made Emme promise not to, either. She felt bad after . . . what happened." Peter looked down at his leg.

"Oh, Peter," Liv breathed, following his look. "Is it . . . ?"

"Broken. Feels more like shattered. But the healer said I'll be able to walk again. Probably."

"We have to get you home, back to a real doctor."

Before Peter could respond, Cedric stepped forward. He wanted Liv to have her moment, but seeing her with her brother only reminded him more of the family he needed to find.

"Liv, I need to search for the others."

Liv nodded, but her eyes were panicked as she gestured to Peter. "He can't walk. How can we get him out . . . ?"

Cedric's mind raced. Every second that ticked by was another wasted opportunity to get to his family before the attack began. He looked around the thick, stone walls of the room.

"Stay in here. It is secure, and less dangerous than sneaking Peter out if he is injured. Bar yourself from the inside when I leave, and do not open the door for anyone but me."

Liv looked terrified, but she nodded again. "Good luck."

The light from the windows fell on Liv and Peter, making the top strands of their brown hair shine in identical shades of red-gold. In that moment, they were undeniably siblings. Cedric blinked at the image before leaving the room and shutting the wooden door behind him.

He barely realized where his feet were taking him until he arrived at another pair of wooden doors, these ones much larger and carved with various delicate depictions of hunting and feasting. His father's quarters.

He pushed his shoulder against the door, surprised when it opened easily. He was even more surprised by what he saw inside.

King James was sitting in the same large wooden chair where he used to sit to scold Cedric when he'd done something wrong as a child, or to clean his smaller weapons during peaceful evenings once the day's work was done. The king who sat on the chair now looked very much the same, and yet . . .

The set of his shoulders was unchanged, as was the fierce look in his eyes. But he also looked grayer and thinner—smaller—than Cedric remembered. The whole room, in fact, felt smaller than Cedric remembered.

Two wrath guards stood on either side of the king. They immediately jumped forward when Cedric entered the room, but stopped at a single motion of the king's hand.

"Father, I . . . ," Cedric faltered, suddenly confused. Why were the wraths guarding his father also obeying his commands? "I am here to rescue you."

"Yes, I can see that," his father responded.

Cedric, thrown, just shifted in place. He suddenly felt incredibly young. It was almost as though the past few months had never happened, and instead of traveling to another world and fighting dozens of monsters, he'd simply been out hunting and drinking too late and was now waiting for a punishment. King James stared at him, his blue-gray eyes unreadable.

"I . . . ," Cedric said. "Are Mother and Emme nearby? Are they all right?"

"Perfectly fine, both."

His father's voice was maddeningly calm. He nodded to the wrath on his right, who moved forward and seized Cedric's arm. Cedric was too surprised to react. He waited for his father to give some explanation, but the king was whispering to the other wrath guard. After a moment, the creature gave a grunt and walked to a curtain in the back of the room. He pushed it aside and walked into some sort of passageway that Cedric had never known existed.

"Father, what . . . ? We have to get out of here."

"No, son," the king responded, his voice even. "We have to wait here for Malquin. He is very eager to see you again."

The world seemed to stutter and stop. The king's words echoed in Cedric's ears, but he couldn't make sense of them.

Nothing made sense.

And then Malquin emerged from the secret passageway behind the curtain and nodded—actually nodded—at the king. Cedric wondered for a moment if he were going insane. But when Malquin turned his dark eyes to Cedric, all of his doubt hardened into anger. He ripped his arm free from the wrath guard who held him and stood straight to face Malquin head-on.

The man looked much like he had when Cedric had seen him last, from his twisted arm to his long, whitish hair. Only his expression was different. Instead of the snarl Cedric had seen on Malquin's face while trying to wrest a gun away from him in the warehouse, there was now a thin-lipped smile. He looked calm, completely in control.

Malquin moved to stand next to the king, putting one hand on his shoulder. Cedric felt bile rise in his throat.

"Cedric," the king started, "I was worried for you when you went through that portal—"

"You were the one who *told* me to go!"

The king put up one hand, signaling that it was his turn to speak. Cedric's mouth clamped shut out of habit.

"When Malquin returned to our world, he put my mind at ease. He assured me you were safe."

Malquin inclined his head forward slightly, all patronizing benevolence.

"He also offered me a deal," the king continued. "One so strong, and with so many benefits for Caelum, that I did not think but to accept it."

"You cannot trust him!" Cedric burst out.

"Hush, young prince. The adults are talking now," Malquin said, his thin smile pulling wider. The king's face tightened at Malquin's words, but Cedric's whole body sprang forward in response. The wrath next to him grabbed him by the shoulders and pulled him back.

"As I was saying," the king continued, "I accepted Malquin's bargain. He has offered our family's freedom, and the autonomy to once again rule over our lands, so long as we double the territory of the wraths who choose to stay in Caelum and agree to stop hunting them within our borders."

"The wraths who choose to stay . . . ," Cedric parroted, confused.

"I promised the wraths a victory over the Guardians," Malquin said with a slick chuckle. "But it turns out, many of them want something even better—a world where they can hide in plain sight and follow no rules but their own. A world in which they're four times stronger than the men who live there. Plus, hot water running straight from the tap. Of course, some wraths will want to stay behind. There are always those who fear change. But they will have territory and the knowledge that they defeated the Guardians through their own power. A fine reward for taking part in the invasion. But most of them—"

"Are going to Earth," Cedric said, the words thick in his mouth. "You're sending them to Los Angeles." Then he remembered how few wraths had been on watch at the city gates, and in the castle. "Or you already have."

"I did not *send* them anywhere. The wraths made up their own minds."

Cedric cast a wild look to his father. "You cannot do this. You think these creatures will obey the laws of the other world, will refrain from taking anything and killing anyone they choose? There will be no way for the people of Earth to protect themselves—"

"That is not our concern," the king said, his voice stern. "Caelum is our only concern. If so many wraths choose to leave, our land will be all the better for it."

"No . . . ," Cedric said, shaking his head. Memories flashed before him—children gazing at giant bones in the museum, hundreds of people walking freely down busy roads, the way the wraths had torn through the police officers in their path one dark night in a brick alley . . . "We were made Guardians for a reason, because we are the only ones who can keep the wraths in check. To let them loose on an unsuspecting world—it is wrong, Father. This is the wrong way."

"It is the only way," the king responded. "Think of it, Cedric. Put aside your emotions and just *think*."

And despite the condescension behind the king's words, Cedric did think. He thought of a land with fewer wrath forces.

Fewer invasions on outlying villages, fewer cattle robberies, abductions, skirmishes. Deaths. He thought of a relative peace returning to Caelum, stronger than ever before. Of his father ruling over that peace. Of Emme safe.

"The deal is a strong one," the king continued. "And it only requires that we turn over to Malquin one thing."

Malquin looked straight at Cedric, his eyes hard. "Another scroll."

Cedric's head shook automatically. *No, no, no.*

"Oh, come on, it's not like I'd hurt them," Malquin said, as though it were *Cedric* who was being unreasonable. "I already have Peter. Daisy and Joe have proven a bit hard to track down, but fortunately I won't have to bother with them . . . since another scroll is already here, isn't she?"

Cedric's head had stopped shaking. He was perfectly still. "What do you want with her?"

"That is my concern," Malquin said. "Tell me where Liv is, Cedric, and all this can be over."

Cedric didn't move.

"This is not a game," the king's voice boomed, his voice rising higher. "Tell us where she is, Cedric. I command it."

But despite his words, the king's voice grew less and less commanding to Cedric's ears. The more his father spoke, the less he sounded like a king. Cedric had always counted on his father to do the absolute best, right thing in every situation. That's why he always claimed to be so hard on Cedric—because he knew what the right course was.

But what if he actually didn't?

What if he was just scared, and doing the best he could in the moment, just like Cedric always did? What if his father—what if the *king*—could be wrong?

Cedric felt movement at his back and turned to see another wrath enter the room, his horns nearly clipping the top of the door frame.

"There is . . . a situation . . . ," the wrath said, his black eyes focused only on Malquin.

Malquin's jaw twitched in annoyance. He quickly followed the wrath into the hallway. Cedric didn't really need to wonder what situation the wrath was referring to. By this point, Kat and whatever army she had gathered were attempting to break through the north wall. While the wraths were distracted there, Rafe was letting the entire village of Duoin in at the south gate. Cedric wondered how far they'd come into the city. All he had to do was keep his family safe until they got here. If he could placate Malquin long enough, make sure he didn't get the chance to harm anyone else before the castle was taken back . . . then his father would see they no longer had to make any sort of deal with this madman . . . he would see . . .

Cedric strained to hear the whispered conversation taking place out in the hall, but only caught snippets here and there. The king was also straining to listen, his head tipped forward. Cedric found his eyes caught on his father's face. It was the same face he'd looked up to his whole life, but now he felt as though he were seeing it in sharper focus, like a thin veil had fallen from it. In the set of those strong features Cedric now recognized so many of his own familiar, conflicting emotions—worry, fear, anxiety, anger—and to see them so clearly painted across a face that had been only one thing for so long was extremely disconcerting. It felt like the world was slowly tipping under his feet, morphing into something new. And Cedric wasn't sure he was ready to face it.

He turned toward the hall instead, where Malquin's voice rose in a sharp whisper. Moments later Cedric heard the wrath's heavy footsteps clomping away. Malquin came back into the room.

"I have thought about your deal," Cedric said. He kept his chin up, his face level with Malquin's own. "And if it means you will leave Caelum and take hundreds of wraths with you, I will concede to your terms."

The king closed his eyes for a moment, relieved. Malquin smiled.

"Liv is in the castle now," Cedric continued. "And I can bring her to you."

Malquin's smile slipped. "Or you could just tell me where to find her."

Cedric shook his head. "If she sees you coming, she will run. Possibly back to the portal she came through. But if it's me . . . she trusts me."

Malquin stared him down for a moment, and Cedric was careful not to flinch or betray himself with the slightest movement.

Finally, Malquin nodded to the wrath behind Cedric. "Stay behind the prince. Give him enough space so you don't spook the girl, but don't let him out of your sight."

The wrath grunted and took one step closer to Cedric, the stench of his breath impossible to escape.

"This won't spook her at all," Cedric muttered.

But even his sarcastic anger was (mostly) for show. He didn't have any intention of leading this creature near Liv. He just needed to buy Rafe and Kat more time, even get outside to help them if he could.

They started through the castle halls, the wrath guard close on his heels. Cedric moved quickly. He made it down the main stairs into the giant front entrance hall, his ungainly guard still keeping pace behind him. The last time Cedric had been here was the night wraths had invaded the castle. His stomach clenched as he remembered how the creatures had dragged Emme by the arm across the stone floor.

Up ahead of him, several wraths ran out the giant front doors. Just before the door slammed closed behind them, Cedric heard shouts and the unmistakable sound of metal clanging against metal.

"Where are we going?" the wrath guard growled.

"To retrieve what I promised," Cedric replied without turning around.

Halfway across the front hall, Cedric planted his feet on the stone floor and braced himself. The wrath following him crashed into his back, nearly toppling him over. But instead, it bounced backward, and Cedric jumped on the creature's moment of confusion. He whirled around, sword at the ready.

The wrath wasn't thrown quite enough, however. He just managed to block Cedric's swing with one thick arm. His mouth curled back in a sneer as he reached for the blade at his side.

The wrath's sword was shorter than Cedric's, but it was plenty sharp. It sliced through the air and hit Cedric's own sword with a clang that reverberated up Cedric's arm and set his teeth clattering.

This wrath was strong.

When the creature prepared its next swing, Cedric dropped to the ground and quickly rolled beneath the wrath's sword, then thrust his own blade upward. Its tip pushed into the wrath's side, right where the two ends of its leather armor met.

The wrath fell to the ground with a final grunt.

Even still, Cedric knew he didn't have much time before more wraths appeared, on their way out to join the battle. What would he see when he pulled the door open? If there were several wraths out there, he would have an even harder fight in front of him. But many wraths were likely already in LA. He just hoped Kat and Rafe had taken out enough of the remaining wraths to destroy Malquin's plans.

Cedric took a deep breath, then flung open the doors.

Rafe stood on the threshold of the castle entrance, bloodied and grinning. Behind him, two dozen fighters from the village of Duoin were flanked in battle formation. Several bodies of wraths lay in front of the castle gates, and in the distance, Cedric could see more fleeing.

"Well?" Rafe rasped, leaning heavily against the door frame.

"What are you standing there for?" Cedric responded. "Come in."

⊁⊱⊰⊀

Energy coursed through Cedric's body. He could only imagine Malquin's face when he pushed back into the king's quarters and told him that he'd failed. He'd never get his hands on Liv, and he'd lost Caelum, too.

Cedric burst through the doors to his father's room, but one glance at Malquin's face told him the madman already knew his plan was ruined. His eyes were narrowed into slits, his lips pressed tightly together in anger. The skin of his face looked even whiter than his hair.

Two wrath guards still stood at the king's side, but they no longer looked like fearsome, confident soldiers. Their large black eyes bounced warily between Malquin and Cedric, their fingers twitching at the weapons in their hands.

"It's over, Malquin. We have the castle," Cedric said.

But it wasn't Malquin who responded.

"Oh, son," the king said, his voice breaking. "What have you done?"

Cedric blinked, took half a step back. Maybe his father didn't realize what was happening?

"It's all right, Father," Cedric said. "You do not need to do what Malquin says any longer. We've won."

Cedric's words seemed to hang in the air, their triumph slowly wilting.

The king shook his head back and forth, slowly.

"They were going to leave us be," the king said. "Forever."

"You . . . you don't understand," Cedric continued. "Our whole army is here, driving the wraths back. *We've won.*"

Malquin's eyes hardened, boring into Cedric. "Is that what you think?" His voice was low, dangerous.

For a moment, Cedric's heart thudded in fear. But then he heard the sound of footsteps racing up the stairs, and he straightened. His army was here, and Malquin's threats were meaningless.

Malquin shook his head. "You've made a mistake, young prince. You didn't just forfeit our deal, you took something that is rightfully mine."

"Liv isn't yours."

But Malquin continued as if Cedric hadn't spoken at all. "Just ask the Knights who hurt my brother. Take something from me, and I'll make you pay tenfold."

Just as Cedric heard men pour into the room behind him, Malquin nodded once at the wrath guards standing behind the king.

They moved quickly—so impossibly quickly—in the space of a breath. One ran a knife across the king's throat, while the other plunged its blade into his chest.

Cedric felt a cry tearing from his throat, but he couldn't really hear it. His body stumbled forward, arms stretched out toward his father, but he was too far away, too late. As the room erupted into chaos, Cedric struggled to make sense of any of the sounds and sights in front of him. His mind kept playing that moment over and over, the slide and the plunge. The way his father's shoulders slumped. He hardly noticed when Malquin slipped through the curtains and into the secret passageway, or when the two wrath guards moved to block any soldiers from following him.

Cedric barely heard the soldiers cry out, in pain, in rage, in disbelief. Some froze in horror while others ran toward the two wraths, weapons ready.

Cedric stared at his father's body on his wooden chair, seeing it again and again.

The slide, the plunge.

And then the blood.

He fell to his knees before the king's chair. His father's blue-gray eyes stared out at the wall over Cedric's shoulder, but they didn't see it. They didn't see anything.

Could he have stopped it? Could he have moved quicker? Could he close his eyes and turn back time somehow? Only a few seconds had passed since it happened, just a few seconds in all the long history of time. Surely those few seconds could reverse, could turn back around, could make this moment *not* have happened?

He closed his eyes tight, but around him time continued to move *forward*, like it always had.

Slide and plunge.

But this wasn't the fault of time.

Cedric was on his feet in a second. He gripped his sword in his right hand, no longer feeling pain in his shoulder, in his muscles. No longer feeling anything. He turned toward the passageway behind the curtain. The wraths blocking Malquin's escape were now busy fighting against the king's own men. Cedric pushed past them all.

And he ran.

The passage was pitch-black, and Cedric had no torch to guide his way. Still, he ran fast and straight, never pausing to get his bearings.

Somehow, he knew where this tunnel would lead him.

He wasn't surprised to turn a corner and tumble almost

directly into a dark wall made of stone. In the middle of it was a small wooden door. He thrust out a hand, pushing against one of the stones in the wall. The door swung open for him, just as it had months before.

Cedric tumbled out into the small courtyard. The last time he was here, it had been covered only by the night sky, but now the setting sun had colored everything in a pinkish glow.

The only thing in the courtyard except for Cedric was the portal that hung a few feet away, a hole made of darkness. It was still and empty and mocking, giving no sign of having swallowed up Malquin only moments before.

For the second time in ten minutes, Cedric fell helplessly to his knees. He didn't get up again for a long, long time.

GOOD NIGHT, AND GOOD LUCK.

The world was looking much grayer than usual.

Shannon knew that was partially due to the painkillers the doctors had given her, and partially because the lights in the hospital room she was in were dimmed. She wondered if maybe it was in an effort to conserve electricity, or because the hospital was probably running on generators after all the earthquakes. It didn't seem worth asking—not that there was anyone around to ask.

The room was filled with four other patients in cots all pushed up next to one another. The doctors and nurses moved from one to the next quickly, their fingers shaking from fatigue, or maybe too much caffeine.

The whole hospital was running on its last legs.

It had been less than a week since the sky turned orange, and already LA had reached its breaking point. Shannon saw it in the faces around her—the other patients, the doctors, the newscasters on TV, her own parents—the heavy grayness of the room wasn't just an issue of lighting, it was a feeling. The time for panic was passing.

Now was the time to cut losses and get the hell out.

A thin figure slipped through the doorway and made its way over to Shannon's bed.

"Merek?"

He smiled, pulling up a chair near Shannon's side.

"How did you get here? My parents . . ."

Her parents hadn't left her side since Merek and Joe had brought her home, slightly bruised and just a bit broken. They'd yelled at Joe until he left, stammering apologies and dragging Merek behind him, and then they'd immediately rushed her to the hospital.

"Joe dropped me here," Merek said. "Don't worry—I did not let your parents see me. They finally left your room to talk with the healers, so I took the opportunity to sneak inside."

"If they find you here, heads will roll. I'm serious."

"I will take my chances." Merek was still smiling, still making jokes. But his eyes were heavy—they had been ever since the Ralphs's parking lot. Shannon gestured around the room again.

"Feels like we were just here, doesn't it?" Next to her, a patient coughed in his sleep. Another moaned across the room. "Guess it's a bit different this time."

Merek's eyes were still focused only on her. "Yes. It is."

"Did you get your stitches fixed?" Shannon reached one hand up to the bandage on Merek's collarbone, pulling it gently to see. He didn't flinch as the light fabric pulled away, revealing the cut underneath. He still stared at her in that strange, intense way.

"I will be fine," he said. "And you?"

His eyes fell down to Shannon's right wrist, which was wrapped up in a cast.

"Broken. But I'll only need the cast for a month. Then the doctors will be able to take it off." She sighed, knowing it would be easier to pull the Band-Aid off fast. "In Utah. Which is . . . far from here."

But Merek didn't look even a little surprised.

"You were eavesdropping, weren't you?"

"Your parents were not exactly being quiet about their decision."

Shannon gave a small laugh. "And they say *I'm* the loud one." She was trying to make light of it, but the truth was that her parents' terror had terrified *her*. They'd been acting strange ever since the sky turned orange, sure, but when they saw Shannon come home with a broken wrist and a bruise on the side of her face, the fear in her mom's eyes had stopped Shannon cold. She couldn't even argue with them when they told her they'd decided to leave Los Angeles immediately. At that point, to ask them to stay seemed cruel.

"It's not that I want to go," Shannon said, looking down at her busted wrist. She couldn't even feel it through all the wrappings—or, no, it was probably the drugs blunting the pain. She wondered if they were affecting her decision making, too. At that moment, she didn't care. All she wanted now was to make sure she never saw that look on her mom's face ever again—that she never *caused* her mom to look that way ever again.

"But they're my parents," she whispered.

Merek was silent for a moment. "I understand."

Shannon couldn't guess what he might be thinking. He'd called her brave at the grocery store. Did he think she was a coward now? Or maybe he was thinking of his own parents, in another world and surely worrying about him also?

"Are you going to go home, too?" she asked. "Joe could open you a portal."

But Merek shook his head. "No. There is nothing I could do at home that Cedric and Kat are not already doing. But this world . . ." Merek sighed, lifting his head toward the room's single window. "In this world, I might do some good. I might be of real use for once, more than just some second son or sidekick."

"Merek . . . you're not a sidekick."

Merek gave a small smile, but it didn't reach his eyes. "We shall see."

He looked down, his eyes hardening when they met Shannon's cast. "Besides, Joe will still need help. And someone needs to find the Knight who did this to you—"

"And get some answers?" Shannon raised an eyebrow. "There's no need to get all revenge-y when there's so much left to do."

Merek shrugged, and Shannon felt nervous for a moment. But then he smiled. "You are probably right."

"Probably? Try always."

Merek laughed. After a moment, the sound faded away, and he finally met her eyes. "Shannon, I . . . this time here, on Earth, it has not been totally unbearable, and I think that is because—"

Merek's head suddenly whipped toward the door, as if he'd

heard something. A second later, Shannon heard it, too—footsteps, and voices. Her parents.

Shannon wanted, more than anything else, to hear how Merek was going to finish that sentence. But there was no time. Her parents had been livid with the stranger who'd brought her home with a broken wrist, and if they caught him in her room now, they might call hospital security.

"You have to go," Shannon said, forcing the words out. "Before they get here."

Merek looked at her once and nodded before turning to slip out the door, taking his unsaid words with him.

BOYS DON'T CRY

Liv stayed by Peter's side for three days.

The castle healer, a pretty traumatized-looking man who couldn't seem to believe the wraths were gone from the city no matter how many times it was explained to him, had done all he could do. He'd told Liv that Peter's leg was "bent, not broken." She translated that to possible Caelum-speak for *fractured*, but honestly would have no idea until she got her brother home and to a modern-day doctor. He'd probably need a physical therapist, too, with how much he was struggling to walk.

But at least he *was* walking. He wouldn't be running up any concrete stairs Rocky-style anytime soon, but he was making full laps around the healing room.

Which meant it was almost time to go home.

Liv was more than ready. For one thing, now that Cedric had won the castle and Liv had her brother back, she couldn't shake the professor's voice from her mind. His dire warnings about how the portals had hurt LA echoed through her thoughts. Of course, there was a chance he had been lying.

But there was also a chance he hadn't been.

And that wasn't the only reason Liv wanted to leave. She missed Shannon, and Joe, and her city. She'd had her fill of living in an honest-to-God castle, even with all the positive changes that had happened in the past three days. Through the healing room windows, she had seen the city bustle itself back to life. The whole city was filled with a mix of celebration and solemnity. The wraths had been defeated. Malquin was gone. The king was dead.

Liv had never met the king of Caelum, but her heart ached for Cedric when she heard what had happened. She hadn't seen Cedric on the few trips she'd made into the castle interior, looking for food or clothes. But she figured he was where he needed to be now, with his family and his people, at last.

She had seen Emme, though. On her second day in the castle, she'd looked up from the bed where she'd been chatting with Peter to see a silent figure standing in the doorway. Emme was dressed all in black, her long, brown hair combed straight and hanging limply past her shoulders. Her face was chalk white, her eyes red and swollen.

Surprised, Liv had stood up immediately, but was unsure of what to say. She'd been so angry at Cedric's sister for stealing Peter and putting him in danger, but all that anger seemed to have burned itself out. Peter was safe, and would go home with Liv soon. Emme had acted to protect her family, and now her father was dead.

"I am sorry," Emme said, her voice low, her eyes not meeting

Liv's. "I never meant for him to get hurt."

Liv nodded, but she wasn't sure what to say. No matter Emme's intentions, Peter *had* gotten hurt. But it felt wrong to yell at the grieving girl in the doorway, her miserable eyes fixed on the floor.

Peter spoke first, pulling himself up into a sitting position behind Liv.

"Emme?" he asked. "Do you want to come in?"

But Emme simply shook her head, retreating so quickly from the doorway it was like she'd never been there at all.

"Man, she looked wrecked," Peter said, his eyes on the space where Emme had been.

Liv sat down next to him again. "Don't forget you wouldn't be in this mess at all if it weren't for her."

"That's not totally true," Peter replied. "I mean, yeah, I wish she'd let me know that going through the portal might squeeze my leg bones till they split, but it's not like she pushed me through. I jumped, pretty willingly. More than willingly."

Liv sighed, looking down at Peter's bandaged leg. He'd given her some version of that speech at least ten times since she'd found him in the healing room. If he'd come through the portal looking for adventure and some storybook idea of destiny, it hadn't taken him very long to get over that idea. Reality had hit him hard, in more ways than one.

Peter absently reached to adjust his glasses on his face, seemingly remembering too late that the glasses had been lost in the portal, too. Liv's heart ached again. Of course, she'd been mad at Peter along with Emme. Mad at him for acting so rashly, for being selfish, for basically forcing her through a portal to another world to come rescue him. But he looked so diminished lying in that cot. It wasn't just his body that had been hurt. A piece of him was missing, and it was a piece Liv had barely gotten a chance to know before it was gone forever.

"Anyway, I'll be okay," Peter said, then gave a small laugh. "I mean, probably. Bones heal, right? But losing a parent . . . Liv, we both know what that is."

"I know," she whispered. She thought of how dazed Emme had looked, as though she couldn't tell if the world around her was real, and her mind went immediately to Cedric. For the hundredth time, she wondered how he was doing.

On the third day in the castle, another black-clad girl stepped into the door frame of the healing room. This time, it was Kat.

She gave Peter one crisp nod and set her eyes on Liv.

"Liv, I require you for a moment. If you please." She added the last part hastily.

"Of course," Liv murmured, rising.

She followed Kat out into the cool hallway of the castle. The walls and portraits were covered in thick black banners, giving the corridor a solemn look. But the halls were also full of people—people carrying platters of food, throwing open doors, cleaning windows. The whole place was simultaneously mourning a death and coming back to life.

Kat walked slowly, seemingly not in any particular direction. Her shoulders were stiff, but her hands fidgeted at her sides.

"I am sorry I did not come sooner—" Kat started.

"Oh, that's okay," Liv interrupted. "You had bigger things to worry about."

"Yes," Kat said simply.

"I'm glad to hear your parents were safe. How are they doing?"

Kat's mouth stretched into a small smile. "Well, thank you. They are resting after their ordeal."

An awkward silence fell over them. Kat cleared her throat.

"I see you have found some new clothes."

Liv looked down at the loose-fitting tunic and trousers she'd begged off the castle healer.

"Oh yeah, my jeans were getting pretty disgusting. At first all I could find in the castle were dresses, but I couldn't figure out how to tie them on, let alone walk around in them."

Kat gave another small smile. "It does take some finesse."

They walked past a large arched doorway in the hall, and Kat stopped suddenly, facing Liv. She reached into the pockets of her skirts and held out a pair of small black devices—the walkie talkies.

"These belong to you."

"Oh," Liv said, surprised. "No, you should keep them. Who knows, might come in handy again, right?"

Kat nodded, looking pleased as she tucked the walkies back into her skirt. "I am sure they will. Now that you are free to return to your home and retrieve Merek, you might send some—what are they, batteries?—back with him."

"Yeah, I can do that."

Kat nodded again, her expression growing more serious.

"I have never really liked you very much, Liv Phillips."

Liv let out a small, abrupt laugh, which seemed to confuse Kat.

"Uh, yeah, I know," Liv said.

"And I assume you feel the same toward me."

"I guess there were times you weren't necessarily my favorite person." Liv had a flash, briefly, of Cedric's fingers in Kat's long hair, when he was kissing her behind the pub in Duoin. She pushed it aside and shrugged. "But you've saved my life a ton of times, which makes you kind of too awesome to *totally* dislike."

Kat looked a bit startled at Liv's words, her mouth opening and closing before she got herself back under control. Even though Liv had meant what she said, she *did* take a little bit of satisfaction in getting a flustered reaction from the unflappable Kat.

"Yes, well . . . ," Kat sputtered, trying to get back on track. "I do not bring this up to spite you, but so that you understand the import of my next request."

"Um . . . okay."

Kat looked around the hallway, exhaling. Whatever she had to ask of Liv, it was taking a lot out of her.

"Speak with Cedric. Please. Before you leave."

Liv swallowed, not sure what to say.

"We both know he has feelings for you, but this is not about that. What he is going through is something I . . . I cannot help him with. Though I have tried. We all have tried."

Kat looked at the ground then, her eyes holding something like defeat. It was at that moment that Liv realized how much this was costing Kat, to ask for her help. How much she must truly care for Cedric to come to Liv at all.

"King James is gone," Kat continued. "And the kingdom needs Cedric more than ever before. They need to mourn their fallen king and place faith in their new one. And Cedric needs to do the same. But instead of honoring his father or looking to the future, he is . . . fixated on Malquin. I fear he plans to track him down and end him once and for all."

Liv thought about Malquin in LA, and what he might be up to there. She felt a pang of sudden fear.

"Isn't that a good thing? Malquin should be stopped. He should pay for what he did."

"I agree," Kat said. "But revenge is not what Caelum needs right now. It is not what Cedric needs right now, either. He cannot run from his responsibilities here, just as he cannot run from his father's death." Kat's voice lowered a bit. "I believe, Liv, that you know this to be true."

Liv didn't say anything. She had no idea what it was like to be suddenly made a king. But she did know what it was like to lose a parent. Putting off your grief to fixate on other things might feel good at the time, but you couldn't outrun grief, or fight it. It would always come back to you in the end and force you to deal with it.

"He refuses to talk about his father with anyone, not even with his mother and Emme."

Kat kept her eyes fixed on the floor.

"Not even with me."

Kat looked up then, her dark eyes meeting Liv's. Her face was pale and taut, beautiful and determined. She looked like more than a warrior princess—she looked like a queen.

"And you think I can . . . h-help him somehow?" Liv stammered.

"Liv, I think you are the only one who can."

⊱┼┼⊰

Liv finally found Cedric on top of a castle turret, his back to her as he leaned forward against a waist-high balustrade. He looked out over the city below, the wind ruffling his dark hair.

Liv hadn't seen him in days, and just taking in the set of his shoulders, his posture, the familiar hard line of his jaw—it stopped her short.

"I will come down in a few moments, Kat," he said, not turning around.

"Um . . . it's not Kat."

Cedric's head turned sharply to the right, though he didn't move from his spot against the stone railing. Liv slowly made her way over to him. She took a spot a respectful few feet away, then peered over the edge of the turret wall. Being this high was sort of like looking out over Los Angeles from the top of the Griffith Observatory. Except with horses in the place of bumper-to-bumper traffic, and tall city walls in the place of the Hollywood sign.

Cedric was still next to her, and silent. She didn't know what to say. Sorry? Of course she was sorry. Everyone was sorry. Whenever people heard that her own parents were dead, the first thing they said was, "Sorry." They meant well, but pity never made it better, and she vowed not to say sorry if she could help it.

What *did* make it better? What possibly could, short of bringing the dead back where they belonged? Talking about her parents' deaths never made her feel any better—in fact, it always seemed to take them one step farther away from her. But talking about their *lives* . . . that sometimes brought them back, at least for a few minutes.

"What was he like?" she finally whispered. "Your father?"

Cedric looked up at her briefly, surprised. He swallowed before turning his eyes back to the city.

"He was . . . ," he started, his voice rough and scratchy. It sounded like he had either worn it out, or not used it in days. "He . . ." His Adam's apple worked its way up and down in his throat, and his hands shook where they gripped the stone balustrade.

Liv's heart squeezed inside her chest. She reached a tentative hand up, and put it on his back. He let out a shaky breath.

"He was larger than most men, in every single way," Cedric said. He gave a small, watery laugh. "Or at least he seemed that way to me. He used to eat roasted meat three times a day. When he issued commands to men, they would drop what they were doing and immediately obey."

"It sounds like he was a strong person," Liv whispered.

"He always wanted me to be better than I was. I used to resent that, but now I think . . . I think he believed I *could* be better, even before I believed it." Cedric's head hung down.

"Maybe he just knew more about me than I did, because he was a king."

"Or because he was your dad."

Cedric turned to Liv, and the pain in his face was so raw, so sharp, that it propelled her forward before she could think. All she knew was she wanted him closer, she wanted to take that pain away. She pulled him against her, wrapped both arms around him and held him tight.

"Will it ever stop feeling like this?" Cedric asked, his lips in her hair.

"Yes," she said. "And no."

"I miss him, Liv."

She nodded against him. "I wish I'd gotten to meet him."

"He would have liked you," Cedric said. "Though he would not have admitted it."

She smiled, and he held her tighter. Wrapped up into him, she could barely feel the wind.

"I cannot believe I will never see him again," Cedric murmured. "I *know* it, but I cannot *believe* it."

For a few moments they stood there together, not moving or speaking. His body seemed to get warmer by the second. He pulled back suddenly, situating his two hands on Liv's shoulders. He looked straight at her, his eyes heavy with a pain all too familiar to Liv.

"And soon I will have to say the same about you," Cedric said.

Liv didn't quite know how to respond.

"I have known, Liv, since the moment you stepped through

that portal to my world, that it would have to end this way. But now that the time is approaching, I cannot seem to face it." His eyes dropped to the ground. "I cannot lose you, too."

Liv was still speechless.

"I would not ask you to stay out of pity for me—"

"Stay?" The surprise finally forced Liv's mouth to work, but just barely. "But Kat said . . . she said you wanted to go after Malquin."

If Cedric was surprised that Kat and Liv had been discussing him, he didn't show it. Instead, his eyes darkened at Malquin's name.

"Malquin deserves to pay for what he did. And I want nothing more than to find him and—" He stopped himself, closing his jaw together so tightly the edges pulsed a bit. The naked pain was slipping from his expression, hardening into something else.

"I hate him," he said suddenly. "I hate him so much that I can *feel* it. It's like a rock that's growing inside me, squeezing out from the inside. I feel it more than . . . anything else."

He closed his eyes then, and took a deep breath. "But what I feel . . . it doesn't matter. I know that now. As much as I want to go find him, to end him once and for all . . . I know I need to be here. I will be—I *am*—a king."

Liv swallowed, barely sure how to react. "Oh," she said, her voice small.

"But Malquin is still dangerous," Cedric said, words tumbling quickly out of his mouth. He put his hands on her shoulders, looking urgently into her eyes. "And I couldn't stand the thought of you going back there, of him hurting you, too—"

"Cedric," Liv interrupted him, shaking her head. So *this* was why he wanted her to stay.

But he barreled on before she could continue. "I know you need to get your brother home to the healers there, and to see that your world is okay. And someone needs to make sure Merek has not got into too much trouble and send him home. But it is not safe for you there, Liv. I don't think Malquin will ever leave you alone."

Liv shook her head. "I can't live my life in fear of Malquin. Besides, he already lost Caelum. What could he possibly need me for now?"

Cedric shook his head. "He did not tell me why he wanted another scroll, but I do not think it had anything to do with Caelum."

"Well, if he wanted to, he could find me here as easily as there. Easier, probably."

"I could protect you here. You and your brother and sister. If you stayed, we could—"

"Cedric," Liv said, trying to make her voice gentle. "Being afraid of Malquin . . . that's not a good enough reason for me to stay."

Cedric swallowed. His hands were still on her shoulders, and his fingers curled against her gently. "Then what about me? What if I were the reason?"

"But . . ." Liv shook her head, still trying to convince herself this was actually happening. "When I told you, on the pier, that I wanted to be with you, you said it was impossible. There were too many reasons why it would never work—"

"There are still reasons. More, now that I am a king."

Cedric looked out over the balustrade's edge, over the city and the land beyond its walls. Liv still didn't even know how much of it was his. She didn't even know what his life would be like now, as an actual king. Cedric looked back at her again, his eyes blue and aching and fierce. He looked so vulnerable but also so sure at the same time.

"What is the point of being a king if you cannot be with the one person who matters most?"

There was a bravery in Cedric's expression, one that Liv recognized. The only time she'd ever really opened herself up like that was on that pier with Cedric, in a conversation much like this one. She remembered how much it had hurt to put it all out on the line and be shut down.

"Do you feel the same?" he asked. His eyebrows rose a fraction, and his voice did as well. He was nervous, Liv realized. Afraid of what she was going to say.

So was she.

"Of course I do," she said. She reached up to take his hands from her shoulders, clasping them instead in her own hands. "That hasn't changed."

Cedric's eyes lit up then, with so much hope that Liv had to look away.

"But other things have."

Cedric shook his head slightly, not deterred. "I know that, but if we want to be together, then what else matters?"

Liv sighed. "Everything else. Everything else matters." She

bit her lip, trying to pick her words. Cedric's hands were hot in hers. "I know how much you're hurting, and that right now, it feels like you're just losing everything, that your whole world is upside down . . . but, Cedric, things will right themselves again. Your life will eventually go on, the way it was supposed to."

"But what if my life was supposed to have you in it?"

"Cedric," Liv said, her voice lowered, "I don't belong here."

His grip on her hands slipped, just a bit. But he shook his head, his eyes still bright.

"I've never been away from Los Angeles before," Liv continued. "Going to a new place was exciting, and you know, terrifying, with the monsters and battles and everything, but this place isn't *for* me."

Cedric shook his head again. "I thought that about Los Angeles at first. My only desire was to go home. But the longer I stayed there, the more I came to appreciate it, the more I wanted to stay—"

"You did? You never said that before."

"That is because it did not matter how I felt. My responsibilities were here. But, Liv, you do not have those same responsibilities. You can do whatever you want, live wherever you want."

"Wherever I want," Liv murmured. She looked down at the stone floor she was standing on. The floor that was attached to an actual *castle*. So many people would give everything for the chance to be here, to see this other world.

But Liv already had the world she wanted—she'd been lucky enough to be born into the exact place she belonged.

"That's the thing, Cedric. I never wanted to *live* in a fantasy story. I wanted to *make* them. I still do. And LA is the only place I can do that. It's my home, Cedric. Being away has only made that more clear."

She took a deep breath.

"I can't stay here. I have to go home."

The light went out of his eyes—she saw it happen. He stepped back from her slowly, his hands slipping out of hers until only their fingertips were touching, and then they weren't.

"I'm so sorry," she said, finally uttering the words she'd vowed not to say.

"Me too," he said back. His body was rigid, and he looked past Liv at the sky and mountains beyond.

"I'll miss you," she whispered, not trusting herself to speak louder without releasing the tears stuck in her throat. "So much."

"Me too," he said again.

She believed him, but she knew it wouldn't change anything.

It was time to go.

⊁⊦⋅⊣⊰

Liv was nervous to go through the portal, even more so now that she knew what it felt like. A handful of people gathered around her in the walled-in courtyard deep in the back of the palace. Peter, of course, was at her side, his arms shaking a bit as he supported his own weight on a pair of rough-hewn crutches. Emme stood off to one side of the courtyard, her eyes on the ground. Kat was next to her, watching Liv, her expression unreadable in the weak sunlight.

Rafe stood across from them, his arms crossed over his chest. He'd given Liv a note for Merek, and made her promise to send him home safe. She'd agreed, of course, though she also wished Rafe hadn't come to see her off. Every time she saw his face, she couldn't help but think of the professor. Of his empty eyes in the cave, and of the warning he'd given her before that.

Had anything he'd said been true? What awaited her at home?

And then there was Cedric. Standing right before her, looking at the dark tear in the sky just behind her back.

Without saying anything, Cedric took a knife and drew it across his palm. The blood that rose up looked ordinary—human—but Liv knew it was tainted with some mixture of whatever ran through the wraths. She tried not to think about it as Cedric reached out to touch her hand, then Peter's.

"This is really all it will take to keep us safe?" Peter asked. He looked back at the portal and swallowed hard.

"It'll work," Liv said, taking his hand. "Cedric's blood is what got me through okay the first time."

Peter nodded, but his face was white as paper.

Cedric cleared his throat, then looked up at Liv.

There had to be some important words to say, didn't there? Something profound for him to remember her by, since that was all they could hope for now. They belonged in different worlds, literally. She would never see him again.

She had to say *something*.

But they'd already said everything.

"Good-bye," she murmured, her voice sounding weak and thin to her own ears.

"Good-bye," he said.

And she knew she had to turn away then. The second she did, he would be just a memory. Not someone she could see or talk to or laugh with or fight with in real time. A pit of sadness opened in her stomach, but it didn't change what she had to do.

She turned away. And she jumped.

SKYFALL

Two Months Later

On any regular Saturday in Los Angeles, the Grove would have been teeming with people. Now the whole place was eerily empty. The plate glass windows of the shops were darkened, or in some cases, broken. The doors were locked and chained. The fountain in the middle of the shopping center was still, its water a flat pool collecting leaves and bits of dirt and trash. Red biohazard tape cordoned off a section of the pavement that stretched from the movie theater to the Banana Republic.

And inside the taped-off section, things were floating.

Liv looked down from her perch on top of the Grove's parking structure, watching as a Sunglass Hut kiosk floated three feet above the ground and gently brushed up against the wilting leaves of a palm tree.

The sight should have been shocking, even terrifying. But over the past two months, it had become the new normal. For reasons no one seemed to be able to explain, there were places in Los Angeles where gravity had ceased to work the way it should.

At the intersection of Santa Monica and Highland, tires, plastic bags, coffee cups, and even an abandoned car looked to be strewn haphazardly on the ground. But the items were actually fixed to the pavement, completely unmovable. No tractor could budge them, and nothing could pick them up.

On a side street in front of a donut shop in Calabasas, a manhole cover went shooting up from the pavement and into the sky. Then gas pumps, mailboxes, an entire bus stop bench. They floated through the air like pieces of paper caught on a gentle breeze, only to fall again and land some dozen or more feet from where they started.

Many people in the country were skeptical about the "Gravity Incidents," as they'd come to be called. Only people who stayed behind in LA (of which there were very few) or brave scientists willing to enter the city had seen the incidents with their own eyes.

Liv was looking down at some of those scientists now as they wandered around the floating kiosk in yellow hazmat suits, waving devices in their hands and seemingly unbothered by the 110-degree heat. Despite their best efforts, no scientists had been able to figure out what was happening in the city. The orange sky was spreading, south over Torrance and north over Thousand Oaks. Earthquakes were a daily occurrence. More Gravity Incidents were popping up every day.

And then there was the lightning storm. It had burned down half of Venice and knocked out electricity for the western half of the city. Shocks of brilliant light shot down from the red-orange sky, forked to the ground one after the other, seemingly without end. Liv had watched the whole thing from Daisy's abandoned Malibu beach house, her stomach a hollow pit of dread.

Turned out the professor hadn't lied after all.

Now she sat with a similar feeling in her stomach, watching some more portal damage unfold. She knew there wasn't anything she could do to help out here. The only way she could be of any use was to keep tracking down Joe's leads on the remaining Knights of Valere, and hopefully find the mysterious "Martin" that Professor Billings had mentioned.

Not that she'd had any luck with his information so far— all of their leads had turned up either empty houses or, in a couple of terrible cases, dead bodies—and she didn't even know if "Martin" was a first or last name.

Still, she would do more good continuing to look for Martin than she would scouting out some scientists. They were out here looking for some reason, some clue as to why all this was happening, and she already knew what had caused it—*her*. Well, her, Malquin, Cedric . . . anyone who'd opened or used a portal between LA and Caelum.

That's the real reason she came to check out this latest Gravity Incident. Even if being here wouldn't solve anything, she wanted to see the damage she'd caused with her own eyes.

After another half hour, the scientists finally wandered away from the taped-off area, taking their instruments with them to a kind of makeshift base camp set up in the parking lot next to the Coffee Bean. Liv used this as her chance to take a closer look. She ran down the stairs in the parking structure, passing the moped she'd hidden near the back wall. Her own car had been towed or stolen from Daisy's street shortly before LA fell to pieces, so she had no idea where it was or how to get it back. But she'd found a set of mopeds in the garage of Daisy's beach house, where she'd been staying for the past couple of months. The find had been fortunate, since the rest of the garage held only useless old toys, beach chairs, and a box of illegal fireworks. Thankfully, the mopeds still worked, ran on little gas, and were easy to maneuver on the closed-off streets of LA.

Liv slipped out of the parking structure and made her way toward the red biohazard tape, careful to keep her back against the wall. From this vantage point, she had a better view of the items floating beside the kiosk. It was a lot of scraps of paper, mostly, plus dirt gently floating in the air alongside some errant palm leaves, a chair, some paper shopping bags, and, weirdly, a bunch of individual pieces of popcorn.

But there were no clues as to how the portals were causing this to happen. And that was the problem, really—how little she knew about this, and how little *anyone* on Earth knew about magic. How could anyone be expected to stop what they didn't understand, or even believe in?

Liv sighed and backed away. She had an afternoon of tracking leads ahead of her, and staying here punishing herself wasn't going to help any. Just as she turned around to go back to her moped, she saw a figure blocking her path, his back to her.

He was tall, nearly a head taller than Liv. He wore an all-black outfit, like some kind of guard or soldier, though the shirt seemed a little tight on his frame. His dark brown hair was cut just above his ears. From his body language, he looked uncomfortable, either from the intense midday heat, or from his too-tight uniform. And then he turned his head, just a little, and Liv saw his profile—the hard line of the jaw, the ready posture of the shoulders, so familiar . . .

Liv froze in place, one foot still up in the air. She could barely tell if she was breathing. The soldier's features were blurred through a slight shimmer, like a heat mirage. But he could almost be . . . he kind of looked like—

The soldier turned again, and disappointment crashed into Liv. It wasn't him. It wasn't even *close* to being him. But before she could berate herself for being so stupid, for getting her hopes up for even a second, she realized she had another problem.

The soldier was staring right at her.

"Hey!" he called out, starting to run toward her.

Liv turned and sprinted into the parking garage. Her feet hit the pavement and echoed across the empty, cavernous space. She heard footsteps behind her. If this guy caught her, he'd turn her over to the evacuation teams, and with phone lines down, she'd never be able to tell Joe what happened to her or where she went . . .

She reached her moped and jumped on, hitting the gas just as the soldier reached out for her. She turned and saw how close she was to him—just inches away. He looked barely older than she was.

She gunned the moped, and the soldier's fingers slipped from her arm. When she turned around, she saw him sprinting—in the opposite direction. She turned her way through the winding parking structure and finally got to the opening, where she had to slow the bike down a bit to direct it around the wooden barrier meant to keep non-paying cars out. Then she was out again under the orange sky, zipping toward the main road, free . . .

The black car came out of nowhere, pulling in front of her and slamming on its brakes. Liv barely had time to twist the handle of the moped and skid it sideways so she didn't run into the car. It wasn't marked—not LAPD or any official government agency that she could see. The same young officer was behind the wheel.

Liv saw two more black cars moving toward her—he must have radioed for backup. They were coming at her quickly, blocking her in from all sides. Her only option was to go back the way she'd come.

She turned around quickly, the moped squealing against pavement. It tipped toward the ground, and she put one leg out to stop it from falling. Then she made her way back inside the parking structure. She heard the black car squeal as well as it turned to follow her. She once again went around the wooden barrier, and a few moments later, she heard a splintering crash as the officer just drove his car straight through it.

His car was faster, she knew. And she was outnumbered.

She drove out the other side of the parking garage, riding her moped through the pedestrian walkway into the shopping center. Amazingly, the black car followed. She heard the sound of metal scraping concrete as it rounded a corner, but it kept on coming. The officer followed her past a boarded-up steak restaurant, alongside empty storefronts, over the unused trolley tracks, until they both neared the red biohazard tape.

But Liv didn't stop as the tape grew closer and closer. She sped up. And behind her, the officer in his black car sped up as well.

The red tape was just a few feet away, and then a few inches, when Liv jerked hard on the handlebar, turning the moped right. It almost skidded out from underneath her, but she managed to get it back under control. She pulled out of the ninety-degree turn and drove around the outer edge of the biohazard tape, sticking to the sidewalk nearby.

The black car wasn't so lucky.

The officer tried to turn at the last minute, too, but his car was just too big, going too fast. He turned a hard right, but the car kept skidding right through the tape, into the heart of the Gravity Incident. For just a moment, nothing happened. The car's momentum kept it skidding across the pavement. But then it started to lift. It was as though the car had hit an invisible ramp, and its momentum sent it soaring up into the sky. But instead of coming back down, it stayed up there, ten feet above the ground.

Liv stopped her moped for just a moment to look. She could see the officer's face through the front windshield, his eyes and mouth opened wide in shock. But he wasn't hurt, and the car stopped rising. It floated gently, its tires brushing against the awning of a nearby candy store.

Before the officer or the panicked-looking scientists could catch their bearings, Liv revved the moped again, this time driving it into the narrow walkways of the farmer's market. If they wanted to catch her in there, they'd have to follow her on foot, and her moped would outpace them easily.

Maybe she'd even have time to pick up some organic trade coffee before heading back home. Or at least, what was passing for home these days. Not that there'd be much time to sit around and rest once she got there.

Los Angeles wasn't the same place she'd left behind, the place she'd been homesick for in Caelum. And if she wanted that place back, she was going to have to keep working day and night to fix it. She was the only one who could.

SUPERBAD

Malibu was pretty far away from the Grove, but Liv didn't mind the trip down the empty Los Angeles freeways. The wind whipping past her face helped cut through the oppressive heat blanketing the city. She weaved through the few abandoned cars on the freeway, only slowing her moped to turn onto the Pacific Coast Highway that hugged up against the ocean. She was almost enjoying the ride, but when she saw white lightning flash through the rust-colored sky off in the distance, she leaned forward and urged her moped to move faster.

The mansions dotting the coast on the way to Daisy's Malibu beach house had all been abandoned. Liv hadn't seen another moving vehicle on this two-lane stretch of highway for days. So she was a little surprised to see a black speck off in the distance growing larger and larger as it made its way toward her. She saw it was a moped as she drew closer, and when the other driver turned into the Ratner family driveway at the same time she did, she knew exactly who it was.

Liv slowed her moped and hopped off, turning around to see Merek do the same.

"Where have you been?" She didn't mean to accuse him, but her words came out sounding that way.

Merek's eyes narrowed. "Out for a ride. Same as you, I suspect."

Liv bit back a response and walked with Merek toward the house. She was still surprised, every day, with his decision to stay in Los Angeles and help her fix what the portals had broken. When she and Peter had come back to find the world a mess, Joe and Merek had helped fill in all the blanks. Liv had given Merek his brother's letter, expecting him to ask her to open a portal so he could go back home right away. But instead, Merek had said he had a "mission" to tend to first.

"They'll be worried about you," Liv had said, confused. "Everything's safe in Caelum now. If you don't go back, Rafe will think something's happened. Cedric—"

Merek had scoffed. "Cedric? He is the one who left me here—*after* giving me a thrashing for no reason, as you surely remember. As for Rafe, I have never been top on his list of worries. I am sure he can wait a while to see his wayward baby brother once again."

At that, Merek had tucked the note from Rafe into his pants and turned abruptly away. Liv hadn't pressed the issue. Truthfully, she was glad Merek was here and willing to help out. Tracking down an impossible-to-find Knight was more than a one-woman job. Actually, it was a job for a whole squad, one with plenty of cars, time, and working Wi-Fi—none of which

Liv had. She'd use any help Merek was willing to give.

Still, as shorthanded and overwhelmed as they'd all felt these two months, Liv was at least happy to know that Daisy and Shannon were both out of Los Angeles. She'd been freaked out to learn that Shannon had been put in the hospital by a Knight. And as much as she missed her best friend, she knew Shannon was where she needed to be—safe and with her family.

Daisy, too, was safe at boarding school, even though Liv hadn't been able to email her since the lightning fire in Venice took out the power on the west half of the city. But Liv's gut told her that her sister was fine—after all, the only upside to someone taking out the Knights of Valere one by one was that the Knights would probably be too busy running and/or getting murdered to try to track down Liv and her siblings.

And as for Malquin—there hadn't been a single sighting of him since he fled the castle after killing Cedric's father. There was no way of knowing where he was or what he was getting up to—or even if he was still in LA—but Liv still wasted many hours wondering about it.

"Are you hungry?" Liv asked Merek as she opened the front door of the mansion. She kept her voice upbeat to make up for her earlier sharpness.

"Always," Merek answered.

"Great, let's grab a quick lunch and then spend the afternoon tracking down another lead?"

Merek nodded, following her inside. But when Liv stepped into the dim front room, a figure bounced forward, blocking her way to the kitchen.

"Finally!" Peter said, moving quickly toward her on his crutch. His leg was still in the process of healing, but he'd gotten much better at navigating around the house. "I've been waiting for you for *hours*."

"What for?"

"Joe said when you got back we could go on a supply run. We're short on water."

Liv frowned. "Again?"

Peter shrugged. "You're the one who insists on washing your hair so much. Can we go now?"

"Twice a week isn't *that* much," Liv muttered, self-consciously touching one hand to her hair. It wasn't like she had anyone to impress, but some habits were hard to break, even in a semi-apocalypse.

"Whatever," Peter said, shrugging. "I've been stuck in this house for two days. I'd drink the rest of the water myself just to have an excuse to leave the house."

Liv sighed, thinking about her plans to spend another afternoon trying to track down Martin. The search should take priority, but Peter was right—it had been two days since he'd been able to leave the house. Because of his leg, he couldn't ride a moped, and they'd decided as a group to use Joe's Jeep only when they had to. Which left Peter stuck, alone, most of the time.

"All right," she said. "Let's go."

Changing her plans was almost worth it to see the smile that stretched across Peter's face. He pushed his pair of replacement glasses up his nose with one hand as he moved past Liv and out into the orange-y daylight.

"Up for a trip?" Liv asked Merek.

He hesitated briefly before responding. "I think we should return to the location on Beverly for supplies."

Liv peered at him. This was the second time Merek had suggested they go to the Ralphs on Beverly for their supply run. "Why? There's, like, three stores that are closer."

"But most of them have been emptied already. That location had the most untouched water containers left."

"Are you sure? I don't think—"

"I remember very clearly." The determination in Merek's voice surprised Liv. She got the sense, again, that there was something going on that he wasn't telling her.

"Who cares which store we go to?" Peter said, his crutch hitting the ground as he hurried back to them. "Can we just *go*?"

Liv pulled her gaze away from Merek, deciding to leave it alone for now. "Yeah, let's go."

Liv drove the Jeep quickly but carefully. The large vehicle was much more conspicuous than the mopeds, but they needed it to haul water jugs and supplies back to the mansion. Liv just had to be careful not to draw the attention of the evacuation crews or anyone who'd stayed behind in the city for less-than-honorable reasons.

When she pulled into Ralphs's parking lot, she maneuvered the Jeep along the side of the building, where it couldn't be easily seen from the street. The parking lot in front of the store was a wreck, littered with shopping carts and abandoned produce. One car with four flat tires was parked across three spaces. But, like most of LA, it was completely empty of people.

"All right, let's do this quick," Liv said. "I'm starving."

"I will scout the perimeter," Merek said, jumping out of the Jeep.

"I don't think that's necessary—" Liv called out after him, but he was already gone.

"Come on, you know how much he loves scouting the perimeter. Why take that away from him?" Peter said, grinning.

Liv gave a half shrug. "Good point."

She got out of the Jeep and followed Peter inside the abandoned Ralphs. The iron gate that usually slid across the doors to keep people out at night was busted up on one side, as if something heavy had been thrown against it—or driven into it. Beyond that, the glass doors themselves had been completely disassembled. The store inside was dark, except for what little light filtered in through the front windows.

Liv grabbed the handle of a lone shopping cart and pushed it toward the soda and water aisle. The shelves were mostly empty, some even pulled away from their metal backs and tossed to the floor. Still, there were some bottles of sparkling water and cans of ginger ale pushed to the back of some shelves, and they might even spot some bottles of still water if they were lucky.

They started hauling bottles into the cart. For the first few weeks after she'd come back to LA, Joe had been the one to go on most of the supply runs, always leaving bills near the cash register to pay for what they'd taken. But then he'd run out of bills, and it wasn't like there was anyone left to claim them, anyway. Liv had convinced Joe that they'd settle up with the grocery chain *after* fixing the city.

Peter hummed as they worked, his voice growing louder and louder until his humming transformed into words.

"It's the end of the world as we know it, and I feel fiiiiine."

"Really?" Liv rolled her eyes as she tossed a six-pack of orange-flavored mini water bottles into the cart.

"Come on, Liv, there's no one in here. There's no one for miles. If you're going to have an apocalypse, you might as well revel in the upsides. Like singing at the top of your lungs in a grocery store without people looking at you weird."

Liv sighed, looking up the darkened aisle. "I don't really think this situation has any *upsides.*"

"You're right," Peter said. "We should definitely be depressed all the time instead. Spend another few hours sitting in the dark, bitching about the heat and talking about the dead bodies you guys keep finding."

"Peter—"

"I know I'm not out there with you, seeing what you're seeing every day. But I'm living this, too. I'm worried, too. About Malquin being here and maybe still looking for us, and about who's killing all those Knights. About if things will ever be normal again. But right now, in this very second, we're in the middle of an abandoned grocery store, Liv. We're filling up a cart with whatever we want, and no one's yelling at us. It's every foster kid's dream. Hell, it's every *kid's* dream."

Liv couldn't help laughing. "I think you and I have very different dreams."

Peter smiled. Behind the lenses of his glasses, Liv spotted a familiar glint in his eyes, one she hadn't seen in months. It was the same sort of spark she'd seen in him when he first came to

LA and learned about the portals. He'd been more excited at the prospect of an adventure than scared of the dangers they were facing. It was that same spark that had made him run off to another world with Emme. But it was also that spark that made Peter . . . Peter. And it had been gone for a long time.

"Maybe you're right." Peter sighed, leaning on his crutch.

Liv looked over the boring items in their cart, thinking. They only ever took exactly what they needed on these supply runs. It had never occurred to her to turn it into something fun.

She looked up at a Peter with a grin.

"Maybe . . . or maybe I just want to keep all the Doritos to myself."

Peter grinned. "You'd have to get to them before me."

"Is that a challenge?"

"It's a promise." Peter repositioned himself on his crutch and threw his free hand into the air. "Then let the Great Doritos Hunt begin!"

Liv couldn't help laughing as Peter hobbled off from her quickly, making his way to the snack food aisle. She turned on one heel and ran toward the front registers instead. She knew that she was wasting time, and that there was so much she needed to do. Get supplies. Keep tracking down Knights. Try not to think about Cedric. Fix the world. But for now—for just this second—she didn't want to think about earthquakes or Gravity Incidents or portals. She wanted, for once, to focus on an upside.

Even if it was just one small, Cool Ranch–flavored upside.

Liv searched through the smaller shelves that lined the registers. Most of the candy, mints, and batteries were gone, the tabloids and magazines left behind. Liv kept her eyes peeled for the shiny corner of a Doritos bag, a smile still on her face. That is, until movement outside the store's large front window caught her eye.

Someone was slipping out a window of the apartment building next to the Ralphs. Merek.

"What's he doing?" Liv murmured. She moved closer to the window, watching as Merek gripped the edge of a railing and dropped down to the concrete.

"Give up already?" Peter called from behind her.

But Liv didn't turn to face him. Instead, she ran outside.

"Merek?" Liv called, her feet slapping against pavement. Across the parking lot, Merek's head shot up. His cheeks colored, as though he'd been caught doing something.

"What were you doing up there?" Liv asked, slowing as she neared the apartment building. "Why—"

But Merek's head jerked—not to look at Liv, but at something behind her. His eyes narrowed, his entire body tensed. Liv's heart raced as she turned, but all she saw was a tall man slowly ambling down the sidewalk in front of the parking lot, heading toward the apartment building. The man appeared to be limping, dragging one foot behind him and wincing in pain with each step.

Before Liv could ask Merek what was wrong, he went shooting off like a snapped rubber band—one aimed directly at the tall stranger.

"Merek!" Liv yelled. She ran after him, but he was a Guardian—too fast for her to catch. The tall man looked up as Merek approached, and Liv got a better view of his face. His skin was paper white, and he wore a pair of tortoiseshell glasses. He tried to run, but he was moving too slowly.

Merek reached the man and threw him, face-first, to the ground.

"Hey!" Liv yelled, panting as she drew closer.

"It's him," Merek growled. He was heaving, his eyes still full of fury. "The Knight who hurt Shannon."

Liv could barely process Merek's words. The Knight who hurt Shannon? *But how?* And then it clicked—the reason Merek always wanted to come to this particular Ralphs, and why he'd been coming out of the apartment building window.

"You've been looking for him, haven't you? All this time?"

Merek didn't bother responding. He put one toe under the man's stomach and rolled him over onto his back.

Liv gasped. Up close, the man's skin was ghostly white and cracking in places, fine dark lines trailing out from the corners of his mouth and eyes. He smelled terrible, like a combination of sewage and rotting meat. But that wasn't what made Liv draw back in shock. It was his eyes—his all-black eyes, big and wide as marbles.

The man wasn't a man at all. He was a wrath.

Merek and Liv both took a step back at the same time, just as the pale man gnashed his sharpened teeth together and then spasmed in a cough.

"That's not . . . possible," Merek said.

"What's wrong with him?" Liv whispered at the same time.

Because even aside from looking like a monster in human form, there was clearly something very, very wrong with this man. He tried to roll back into sitting position, but didn't seem to have the energy to get up off the concrete. He opened his mouth to speak, but a black bubble formed over his lips instead. It popped, dribbling a bit of blackish fluid down the side of his chin.

"What's going on?" Liv heard Peter ask. She turned to see her brother moving across the parking lot as fast as he could on one crutch.

"Stay back!" Liv yelled. "It's . . . a wrath. I think."

"No, he's a Knight," Merek said. "I remember his face. I remember what he did—"

"We should try to get him to Joe," Liv said, cutting Merek off quickly. If she could just think of a plan for what to do next, it might quiet the panic in her mind. "See if he knows anything—"

"*Liv,*" Merek snapped. "This man is a Knight—was a Knight—I saw him just two months ago, and he was a *man*, not a wrath. The same one who hurt Shannon. I am positive."

Liv shook her head. "But that can't be. How can he be a Knight *and* a wrath?"

On the ground, the man gurgled again. More black fluid came from his mouth. His thin hands curled into fists.

"Hey," Merek said to the man—the wrath—whatever. "What are you?"

On the ground, the man didn't respond. His black eyes flitted back and forth, back and forth.

"He is dying."

The man's mouth opened, but no sound came out. Without

thinking, Liv dropped down to her knees next to him. She'd seen eyes like his before—in Los Angeles and in Caelum both. This creature didn't have horns or thick graying skin, but she knew what he was. There was no denying it.

"What happened to you?" she asked, trying to keep the man's attention.

His jet-black eyes settled on hers, but she couldn't read anything in them but fear. His face grew paler by the second, the lines around his mouth getting darker. He stopped trying to talk, and then fell still. Though his eyes were still open and staring, Liv knew they were no longer seeing her.

"He's gone," she whispered.

Merek still looked down at the man, his face twisted in disgust. "Good."

"Merek," Liv said, "no matter what this—person—did, I don't think he deserved this."

"What *is* this?" Peter asked. "What the hell is going on?"

"I have no idea," Liv whispered, her eyes still transfixed on the dead man with the wrath's eyes. If Merek was right, if the creature before her *had* been a man, then somehow he'd been transformed into a monster. She had no clue how that was even possible, or what it meant. No clue if this, too, was somehow her fault. And no clue what strange and terrible thing might happen next.

How could she get used to this new reality—let alone fix it—when the rules kept changing?

THE MAN WHO WOULD BE KING

King Cedric III had an itch he just could not scratch.

Literally—he had an itch above his knee that would be near impossible to reach through his layers of pants and robes. And even if he could reach it, it would be considered rude to interrupt his audience session to do so.

So he bit his lip, trying to take his attention away from his knee and focus on what the man in front of him was saying. It was difficult to do, especially as the air in the audience chamber was so stifling hot that more than a few guards around the edges of the room were on the verge of nodding off. Plus, the man speaking to Cedric had his head down and directed his words at the ground rather than looking his king in the eye.

His *king*.

It still felt unreal to Cedric, though his coronation ceremony had taken place almost immediately after they'd put his father in the ground, nearly two months past. But it was a lot to get used to all at once—the sheer number of men and women, from the guards to the cooks, who looked to him for direction every single day; the way servants no longer joked with him playfully, but instead averted their eyes when he spoke; the way the crown on his head pulled tight at the skin and gave him a constant headache—

Stop complaining, Cedric. Pay attention.

"—almost gone, Majesty. Not all of it, but almost all, and we don't know what to do . . ."

The man standing before the high-backed throne looked just a few years older than Cedric. He had wheat-colored hair covering the top of his head, though it was hard to make out his features as he stared intently at the stone floor. Cedric's mind wandered as he imagined *what* the man was staring at down there, until he eventually realized the man had stopped talking.

And he hadn't heard the last part of what he'd said. Or the first part. Or most of the middle, really.

Cedric looked up for help, and the first face he saw was Kat's. She stood about ten feet away from him in a long green gown. She looked regal and calm, the picture of a soon-to-be queen—that is, a soon-to-be queen with two swords tucked into her belted sash and a look of pure annoyance on her face. She widened her eyes at Cedric.

The room was silent. Everyone expected him to speak now.

"Um," Cedric said, borrowing an expression from Liv without even realizing it.

The wispy-haired man continued to stare at the ground, while Kat continued to shoot disapproval across the room using just the power of her eyes. Cedric shifted in his seat.

"It's almost all gone, you say?" Cedric finally asked, grasping onto the one part of the appeal he remembered hearing.

"Yes, sir," the man said, his eyes still on the ground. "Not cut off or anything like that, just dying away, like's been poisoned almost. But who would poison trees?"

Cedric opened his mouth, but was at a loss to find words. Dead trees? That's what this man had come to him about? He supposed it was better than the last two appeals, which had both been about land disputes, but still. What was he supposed to do about dying trees?

"The wraths, maybe?" the man asked.

Cedric sat up straighter in his chair. "Wraths? Did you see any?"

The man clutched at the hat in his hand before braving a glance up at Cedric. "Not myself, sir. But some o' the children at the edge of the village say they saw two wraths just last week, at the border of the trees. Or, what used to be the trees."

Cedric gripped the edge of his chair. Ever since the Guardians had taken back the city, driving out or killing all the wraths inside, the creatures had all but disappeared. Their organization had fallen apart after losing the castle, their deal to get more territory, and their leader. They were less threat than they'd ever been before Malquin.

Malquin.

Just thinking the man's name made every muscle in Cedric's body clench. White-hot anger coursed through him, and from there, he couldn't stop picturing a knife sliding across the skin of his father's neck, images of Malquin slipping into the corridor, images of the portal hanging empty in the pink light of the dying day, and of Cedric falling beneath it, knowing already that he'd failed.

He couldn't think about Malquin, not now, not ever. Not without falling apart.

But he could think about the wraths.

Those who hadn't already gone to the other world had scattered, retreating back even farther into the lands at the outskirts of Caelum. In the two months since, most of Cedric's time had been taken up with repairing the damage done to the city and the surrounding villages, restoring the army, and catching himself up on all of his father's edicts and rulings. He'd rather have spent that time personally chasing away as many wraths as he could from his people's land, but sightings of them had been few and far between.

So now, Cedric was all attention. His hand went unconsciously to the sword hilt at his side, fingers tapping lightly against the silver handle that had once belonged to his father.

"I will look into this wrath threat personally," Cedric said, his voice echoing out through the room. "Oh, and . . . the trees as well."

A murmur rose up throughout the audience chamber. Cedric looked over at Kat and saw her lips were pursed, as if she were biting back words. She'd have a lot to say to him about this, he knew. After all, kings weren't supposed to go off alone into the woods to investigate threats. They were supposed to send soldiers to do that work for them, while they sat safe on their thrones and worried about matters of state.

Kat and Cedric had been having the same argument for

weeks. After Merek had failed to return to Caelum, Cedric had been sure of the worst. That Merek's injures—the ones Cedric had helped to cause—had been too severe and he hadn't recovered. Or that Malquin had found Merek, Liv, and the others in LA. Every part of Cedric had wanted to travel through the portal to check on them, but he knew he was needed here, in his own world. Being king was supposed to come before everything else. That's what his father had taught him, what Kat kept reminding him every day.

If only being king didn't involve so much sitting around, listening to people complain.

The itch on Cedric's knee returned with a vengeance. "That is all for today," he said to the audience chamber at large.

The nervous man bowed once before retreating from the room with the other townspeople and villagers. Once they'd all left, Cedric leaped from his chair. Kat was by his side in a moment.

"Do you really think that was wise?"

"I have no idea, Kat," Cedric said, running a hand through his hair. "But I finally have the opportunity to go out into our land and do some good. Or at least do *something*."

"You are doing good. Right here. You are helping to heal a country that has been torn apart by war for the first time in centuries."

"*You* are doing more on that front, I think."

Kat sighed, but she didn't deny it. She and Emme had together made sure that the villagers, townsfolk, and even castle servants had been fed and clothed and able to start putting their lives back together after the wrath invasion. Though Cedric's mother was still the queen regent, she had been unable to get out of bed since the king's death. While Cedric had caught up with his father's advisors and planned how to strengthen the remaining army and rule the country, Kat and Emme had been doing all the real work of putting things back together again.

"You are the king, Cedric. Just you sitting up in that chair and listening to your people talk does more to restore this country than almost anything else."

"Yes, I know." Cedric sighed. He didn't want to get into this argument again. But still, he felt useless and weak sitting up in that chair, and if he owed his life to the people of Caelum, he still longed for something he could do, something he could fix with his hands, something he could track or fight.

"But if there are wraths out there on the borders, is that not something worth investigating? What if they are planning another uprising? Or a retaliation?"

Kat just looked at him steadily. He knew his reasoning was thin. The wraths had been pretty effectively crushed, what small number of them remained in this realm. They likely would not try any type of retaliation for some time.

Finally, Kat sighed. "At least let me put together a guard—"

"No," Cedric said, cutting her off. "I have not had a moment away from guards and advisors in months. I will be careful, stick to the main roads."

"What if Rafe went with you?"

Cedric thought about it for a moment. Rafe had been just as busy as Emme and Kat in these past few months, mostly adjusting to his new position as captain of the guard. He'd been rebuilding the broken regiment and training new soldiers, working night and day although it was a time of peace. Cedric secretly suspected that Rafe was expending his energy to keep from thinking about his missing brother. Guilt over how his own actions might have forced Merek to stay in LA indefinitely clawed at Cedric every single time he saw Rafe's face.

"No," he said quietly. "Rafe is busy. I will go alone."

"And if something should happen?"

"Then I will fight. Or run. Just as I did before I became king. Of course . . . you could always join me."

For a moment, Kat looked on the verge of saying yes, and Cedric grinned. Just imagining it—being out in the woods with Kat, hunting stray monsters together like they used to do before the weight of the whole realm was on their shoulders . . .

After a beat, she shook her head. "There is too much to do here."

Cedric tried not to let his disappointment show. Instead, he kept his grin firmly in place, trying to inject lightness into his voice as he sauntered backward away from her with a confidence he didn't really feel.

"Your loss, Katerina."

Kat narrowed her eyes.

"Do not call me that if you know what is good for you, Cedric James Bartholomew the Third."

He tipped an imaginary hat to her before turning to leave the audience chamber, happy to know that a few things, at least, would never change.

It was three days' ride to the outer village where the nervous man said wraths had been spotted. As Cedric rode, he took stock of the land around him. Some of the villages still looked mostly abandoned, while others looked like nothing had happened in the past six months at all. Villagers rode horses and mended fences and hung laundry out to dry. Cedric kept clear of all of them; he wasn't in the mood to stop and chat.

He slowed his pace when he reached the outlying village of Quincy, located about halfway between the base of the Westing Mountains and the start of the Southern Hills. It wasn't far, Cedric noted, from the portal Liv had opened from a beachside in Los Angeles, the one he had come through with her and Kat a few months earlier. Cedric felt a pull to go and see the portal once more. To know that such a doorway existed, and that Los Angeles was on the other side, that Liv was on the other side . . .

But such temptations were for regular men, maybe even princes. Not for kings. He kept his horse moving.

Quincy itself looked relatively intact. A group of men worked to rebuild a pen, and Cedric asked them about the rumors of wraths nearby. They pointed to the children who'd spotted the wraths, who were less helpful than Cedric was hoping. They seemed so equally excited and terrified to be talking to a king that some of them could barely stand still. Eventually, Cedric got one child to point him in the right direction and headed off into the forest.

Immediately, he noticed something was wrong with the trees at the edge of the woods. The changes weren't so big that someone would see them unless they were looking for them, but there was something . . . off. At first, it was just a tree here or there that seemed different from the others. One would be bent at an odd angle, its branches all reaching toward the ground like arms trying to pick up something that had fallen. Another would be a strange, light gray shade, as if all color had been bleached from it. The trees just seemed . . . weaker somehow, *less* than they used to be. Cedric remembered how he'd had the same feeling riding through a different part of the forest on his way to find Liv and Rafe months earlier. At the time, he'd brushed it off, but here . . .

The odd trees grew in number, until Cedric looked around and found himself surrounded by gray and white, bent and broken, stunted and shorn trees. He knew that trees weren't living things in the same way that men and animals were, but still, he couldn't help but think these trees looked to be in pain somehow.

Cedric gripped the reins of his horse as he rode onward, more slowly now. The wispy-haired man had not exaggerated about what had happened to this forest. If anything, he'd been too light on details. Something had gone very wrong here, and Cedric had never seen anything like it before. Was the forest sick?

At one particularly distressed-looking tree, Cedric stopped to get a closer look. It looked less like a tree than like the ghost of one. Cedric reached one finger out to the bark and touched it. When he pulled his finger away, it was covered in a crumbly powder, like clumped ash.

As Cedric examined the dark ground around the tree's roots, some movement in the distance caught his eye. He whipped his head up to see a few branches in the distance snap in the air, as if something—or someone—had run past them in a hurry.

Cedric weaved between the trees and was soon only moments behind whoever was in front of him. Branches slapped backward through the air as the person moved quickly through the woods. Cedric caught a glimpse first of a gray elbow, then a horn. Not a person, then.

The wrath was big, but not as fast as Cedric. He drew closer and closer, reaching one hand out to try to grab on to the wrath's shoulder—when the creature bounded through a final layer of white-gray leaves and into a small clearing.

Cedric crashed through after it. He jumped from his horse and reached for his sword just as the wrath turned around to face him. It was a foot taller than Cedric, and it had not one, but two maces tucked into its belt. But instead of the customary wrath expressions of contempt and rage, Cedric saw only panic in the monster's craggy face.

For a moment, Cedric hesitated. He wondered if it would be possible to ask this wrath if it knew anything about what had happened to the forest. But before he could try, the wrath composed itself. It snarled, jumping out at Cedric claws first.

Cedric's sword was fully unsheathed in an instant, and he lunged at the creature. Instantly, his arms and legs—his entire being—was filled with a purposeful energy. He dodged left, then right. He swung out with his sword, blocking a blow from the wrath's mace and managing to get a swipe in himself. He moved on instinct, almost without thinking, and it took him a moment to realize the expression on his own face was a smile.

It had been months since he'd been able to do this, to get up off his throne and go do something. He felt good. Better than good, he felt like himself.

The wrath barely knew what hit it.

Only after its body fell to the ground did Cedric look around at the clearing. Like the trees surrounding it, the grass here was a gray-white, leached of color. It stretched out around Cedric, looking almost like fallen snow. And in the middle of all that grass was a small cabin, nearly perfectly square, with a thatched roof and a red door.

The door opened, and another wrath emerged. It ducked its head to keep the horns from catching on the door frame. It looked once from Cedric, sword out, still in fighting stance, to the dead wrath on the ground.

Its eyes narrowed. Cedric smiled again.

It took even less time to dispatch this one. Three minutes later, Cedric stood heaving over the second wrath. He wiped the black blood from his sword onto the dull grass.

"Well, you've killed them, then."

Cedric whipped around at the sound of the voice. Standing in the open cabin doorway was a thin old woman with graying hair. She wore a fraying shift and looked at Cedric with calm bemusement.

"Which means either you're here to free me, or to kill me at last."

The old woman looked from the dead body of one wrath

to the other, then shook her head. "Violent, angry things. And absolutely no sense of humor. But still, they were all that kept me company these many years. Old Smelly and the Nut."

Cedric couldn't hide his surprise. "Those were . . . their names?"

"It's what I liked to call them when they were bothering me, which was every day. Ah well, they're gone now, aren't they? Locked me in here for years, and then one quick jab of some pointy metal and"—the old woman clapped her hands together—"that's that."

Cedric's head was spinning, and he wondered if the battle had worn him out more than he realized. Or maybe it was just the disorientation of finding this old, strange woman out in the middle of the dying woods.

"Who are you?" Cedric repeated.

"Mathilde. And who are you?"

"I'm Ced— I'm the king. King Cedric."

"A king? My, this is a big day. Well, come on in, King Cedric, and have a bit of tea. All this unexpected violence has rather tired me out."

Cedric stayed rooted to the spot. The old woman turned around and rolled her eyes. "If you aren't here to kill me or to free me, I'm guessing you're here about that?" She pointed off into the woods and then disappeared through the red door into the cabin. Cedric cast one more glance at the dead wraths at his feet and followed.

The cabin was small inside, and clean. If Cedric hadn't known the old woman had been kept prisoner there, he wouldn't have guessed it. In one corner of the room was a bed, neat and tidy with a quilt pulled tight around its edges. A worn thatch rug was on the floor, and a wooden table under a window had a vaseful of flowers in its center.

Mathilde directed Cedric to take a seat at the table, then started fussing around with a pot near a small fireplace.

"Why were those wraths keeping you prisoner here?" Cedric asked. "Does it have something to do with what's happened to the forest?"

"In a way, yes," Mathilde answered, setting a pot to boil. "And in a way, no. A bit, I suppose."

"So what did cause it?" Cedric asked

"Hold your horses," Mathilde said. She opened up a small cupboard in the corner. Inside were two cups; she took out both.

Hold your horses? The expression was a strange one, Cedric thought. It almost sounded like . . .

"And use your brain," Mathilde added, interrupting Cedric's thought. "You're the king, after all. What do you think is causing the forest to die?"

Cedric sighed. When he'd seen the damage to the trees, only one thing had popped into his mind, one thing that had changed in Caelum, one thing that could have led to such destruction.

"Is it the portal?" he asked.

"Portal singular? Isn't there more than just one out there these days?"

Mathilde finally came and sat down at the table with Cedric, leaving the pot to boil on its own. She looked at him steadily, her brown eyes clear and sharp.

"Yes," Cedric said, on guard. How did this old woman

know about the other portals?

"You're not one for idle chitchat, are you?" Mathilde sighed. "Which is a pity, because I've had scarce opportunity to carry on a real conversation for a while now, let alone exchange anything like banter with a handsome young man. Pardon me—a handsome young king." Her eyes glittered as she smiled at Cedric. "If I were just fifty years younger, you know—"

"Mathilde," Cedric interrupted the old woman before she could finish that sentence. She gave him a sneaky grin, and suddenly it clicked in Cedric's mind, what was so strange about the woman . . .

"The way you talk," he started, leaning back in his chair. "The words you use, the things you say . . . you remind me of someone. Someone who's . . . not from around here."

Mathilde said nothing, but only cocked her head, as if seeing Cedric in a new light.

"Are you from the other world? Did you come through a portal?"

Mathilde laughed then, a loud, barking noise.

"From the Old World? No, goodness, no. Though I can imagine why you'd think so." She got up suddenly to get the pot from the fire. As she spoke, she poured the boiling water into tea cups and mixed it with herbs Cedric couldn't identify. "Like I said, those wraths kept me prisoner here for years. And they weren't exactly much to talk to. But they didn't act on their own—not smart enough by far—and their leader used to visit me often. With only one person to talk to for so long, I suppose I picked up a few of his conversational tics. Even when he wasn't around, I took to talking to him in my head . . . do you think that's crazy?"

Cedric wasn't sure how to respond.

"Ah, well," Mathilde continued. "If I am crazy, at least I came about it honestly. And as much as I hate the man who kept me here, I came to rely on our little chats together, the real ones and the imaginary."

Mathilde set a cup in front of Cedric, and he reached for it.

"It was Malquin, wasn't it?" he asked. He heard the steel in his own voice as he said Malquin's name. His hand closed tightly around the handle of the teacup, making it rattle against the table.

"Malquin," Mathilde scoffed, then made a face is if the word tasted bad on her tongue. "He gave himself that name. I always thought it was a bit of a mouthful."

Suddenly, Cedric set his cup down against the table so quickly that some hot water splashed over the edge and burned his hand. He barely noticed.

"Hold on," he said, sitting up straight, some of his anger fading as another memory came forward. "Malquin told Liv all about you, the old crone he found out in the woods who explained to him why he couldn't get back to his home world—"

"Crone?" Mathilde said, sputtering. "Well, that does sting a bit."

"Sorry, I only meant . . . that is who you are! I hadn't really thought about that piece of Malquin's story before now—I just . . ."

"Forgot?" Mathilde waved a hand. "That's all right.

Everyone forgot about me. That's how John was able to keep me secreted away here for so long."

"But why keep you prisoner?" Cedric asked, leaning forward now. "What exactly did you tell him?"

"Much more than I should have," Mathilde said with a sigh, leaning back in her chair. "I don't know how he found me. Over the years, people like me have grown fewer and fewer in Caelum. I might even be the only one left."

"People like you?"

"People who remember how this world really came to be, and why. Hundreds of years ago, everyone knew the truth. But over the centuries, the information faded out, first becoming a story, and then a legend, and then mostly forgotten altogether. Either those in power wanted to deny the truth for some political purpose, or the people of Caelum forgot it on their own. Or some combination of both."

Cedric shook his head slightly. "The truth?"

"What do you know of our realm's origin? Our history?"

"I know what my tutors taught me," Cedric started. "They said that the Old World had turned into a hell dimension, and we came here to escape it. Of course, I heard a different version on Earth. That we were banished here along with the wraths."

"A lie and a partial truth," Mathilde said, taking a sip of her tea. "In reality, the men in the Old World who banished us here didn't just send us through a portal to another world. They *created* that world."

Cedric didn't fully understand at first. "You mean . . ."

"All this—" Mathilde waved her hand toward the window and the trees beyond, "didn't even exist yet. But the Old World wanted us gone, or at least a sect of people in it did."

"The Knights of Valere," Cedric interrupted.

Mathilde rolled her eyes. "Knights of Valere. Malquin. Who allows these men to pick such ludicrous names? Knights of Pompousness, more like. Knights of Need a Good Butt Kicking."

"But you said they created Caelum?" Cedric said, getting impatient. "How could they *create* a whole world?"

"By accident, obviously," Mathilde said with a dismissive gesture. "Even back then, with all the magic that existed in the Old World, those men couldn't have intentionally lit a fart on fire. They knew magic could be manipulated by those who believed in it, but it still took *hundreds* of them to figure out how to do something so small as open a portal. And of course they did it wrong."

"Wrong how?"

"They meant to send the wraths out of their world, and they didn't care where to. They stumbled on the means to open a portal, not knowing where it went—or if it went anywhere at all. But when they went through the motions of actually opening that portal, for the very first time, they had no idea what changes were taking place in their own world. How it was shedding itself of magic, bit by bit."

"I know that part; one of the Knights, a professor, told me that. The Quelling Theory"—Cedric waved his hand—"never mind. What happened next?"

"Those Knights and their scholars and mages opened the portal, expecting it to suck the wraths through, but it went ahead and took a good chunk of the Old World's magic right along with it instead. Which—ha! They didn't see that coming.

But all that magic had to go somewhere. And there was nowhere for it to go, so it created a new home for itself."

"Caelum," Cedric whispered.

"Built brand-new out of magic and thin air. And just in time for our arrival, too."

Cedric sat back in his chair, stunned by this revelation. He wished there was something a little stronger in the mug in front of him.

"But that doesn't explain what is happening now," he finally said. "Or why Malquin kept you here."

Mathilde looked out the window, her expression suddenly solemn. "This world was created by magic, and it lived on magic. Even if you couldn't see it or feel it every day, it was here. The portals stayed closed for hundreds of years, and there was balance. Until John.

"He came through, ripping a hole between worlds. A hole that stayed open on this side, where magic still existed. And then, a few years later, you and your royal crew went through that same hole, ripping it bigger. Then another portal opened, and another. What did you think would happen when you tore open the wall between the worlds?"

Mathilde's voice became accusatory, but Cedric had no answer for her.

"Magic is seeping back through," she continued. "From our world to the Old One. But magic doesn't exist in an infinite amount. There's only so much of it. And when it leaves here, it takes a piece of our world with it."

"What do you mean by that? How could it take a piece of Caelum?"

"The trees, you idiot," Mathilde replied, exasperated. "Look at the trees. They're losing the force that created them. They're losing life. And if magic continues to seep out of here . . ."

"Oh," Cedric said, slowly realizing. His eyes went large.

"'Oh' is right," Mathilde said. "I know I'm partially to blame. When John found me and began asking questions about the relationship between the two worlds, I admit he flattered my pride a bit. So few people knew or believed the truth anymore, and just to be able to talk about it, to explain about the Old World and the new . . . I know now I shouldn't have told him why he was having such a hard time opening a portal back to Earth. I shouldn't have told him anything . . . but I did. And here we are. If I'd known what he planned to do with that information, or that he would lock me up here to keep me stopping him in any way, I'd have killed him the moment he walked in my house." Mathilde looked away for a moment, her eyes thoughtful. "Not that hard to poison tea."

Cedric warily eyed the cup of liquid cooling on the table before him.

"A joke!" Mathilde said. "Mostly."

Cedric forced a thin smile, but still left the tea where it was. "So he knew?" he asked. "He knew what would happen by opening a giant portal between Earth and Caelum, but he sought to do it anyway?"

"He did," Mathilde said. "Though he handily kept that information from the wraths he promised victory to. They thought if they helped John, he would hand them Caelum on a silver platter. I tried to warn them that by then the platter would be tarnished and bent if not completely ruined, but they never believed me. And now here we are."

"So what can we do?" Cedric asked.

In response, Mathilde shook her head sadly, and shrugged.

"That's it?" Cedric jumped up from his chair then, looking down at Mathilde as she sat at the table. "Our world is about to be destroyed, and you have no idea how to stop it?"

Mathilde made a *tch*-ing noise. "Destroyed? You're just as dramatic as John, you know that? I never said the worlds would be destroyed. Damaged? Yes. Possibly even beyond repair. But even I don't know what will happen if all magic leaves Caelum and goes back to the Old World. This hasn't exactly happened before."

"But it cannot be good," Cedric said. "We have to do something."

"I agree very much," Mathilde replied. "But I've told you all I know, and my fighting days are long behind me. I'm afraid the work of fixing this damage will fall to you, *King*."

Coming from Mathilde's lips, the word felt like a slap. She was right. He *should* know what to do next. His father would. But his father wasn't here. He stood up straighter and kept his eyes locked on Mathilde's.

"There must be something else you know, some idea of how we can stop this . . ."

"I know about the past, not the future. We're all in new territory here." But then she cocked her head, her eyebrows knitting together for a moment. "Though, if I had to hazard a guess, I'd say that in order to stop magic from leaking out of Caelum like a sieve, you'd want to stop up the holes."

"You mean close the portals. Really close them, for good."

Mathilde shrugged. "Just a guess."

"But how do we do that?"

"Well, how did they open in the first place?"

Liv.

And finally Cedric knew, with a blinding clarity, what his next step would be. Fortunately, it was the step he'd secretly been wanting to make for months.

"I have to go back to the other world. To LA."

Mathilde was silent for a beat, and then she nodded. "That sounds sensible to me."

And then Cedric felt something he hadn't experienced in months—a lightness. Some of the tension left his shoulders, and he realized that for the first time in a long time, he had something to look *forward* to.

The only tricky part would be explaining it to Kat. He'd need Mathilde's help for that.

"Will you come with me? Back to the castle?"

Mathilde smiled, and Cedric thought she looked lighter, too. "I thought you'd never ask."

DESPICABLE ME

Liv wrapped her fingers around the handle of the knife. She clenched her teeth and squeezed the handle hard before plunging it down toward Merek's chest.

He batted her hand away in one easy swipe of his arm, then shook his head.

"Are you doing this poorly on purpose?"

"Obviously not," Liv said, her voice tight.

"So are you naturally terrible at coordinating your movements? Or just at following directions?"

Instead of sniping out a reply, Liv closed her eyes and breathed in deep through her nose. In, out. In, out. There was the smell of the ocean, of salt and seaweed and fish. She and Merek were standing across from each other on the back porch of the Malibu house, and sand was blowing across her bare toes. She tried to focus on the feel of it.

"Liv? What are you doing?"

"I'm *trying* to go to a Zen place," Liv replied through still-gritted teeth. "Because every time you talk I want to stab you."

"*Good*," Merek replied. "That is sort of the point of this whole exercise, after all."

Liv's eyes popped open. "You want me to actually try to stab you?"

Merek looked at her, incredulous. "Is that not what we have been doing for two hours? Did Cedric teach you *nothing* in Caelum?"

Liv tried to ignore how her heart pulsed a little harder at even the mention of Cedric's name. Instead, she took another deep breath.

"We were a little preoccupied at the time."

"Yes, I bet."

Liv threw her hands up in frustration. It had been her idea to spend the evening practicing her poor knife-fighting skills with Merek. It had seemed better than obsessing, again, over the discovery they'd made in the Ralphs's parking lot that afternoon and wondering about what it could mean for a Knight to turn into a sort of wrath and then die—right in front of her.

Liv quickly adjusted her hold on the knife, accidentally whizzing it past Merek's ear. He had to lean away quickly to avoid the blade.

"Sorry," she muttered.

"Do not apologize—that is the closest you have come to actually striking me all morning."

"Well, I don't want to *really* hurt you—most of the time—I just want to practice the basics of all this knife stuff. I need to know how to protect myself from the wraths and—well, whatever else might be out there."

"Then maybe we should start with the most basic rule of all, one so obvious, I did not think it needed to be stated. Liv, when you are fighting with a weapon, you cannot just go through the motions. You have to *mean* to strike your opponent."

"But what if I really hurt you?"

Merek gave her an irritating smile. "Trust me, you will not."

Liv gritted her teeth again and lunged. Merek jumped backward quickly, narrowly missing the knifepoint. Liv hadn't hit him, but at least she'd wiped the smile off his face.

"Well," Merek said, swallowing hard. "That was a bit better."

Liv heard a door slam in the distance. Her head automatically perked up at the sound. "He's back."

She left the silver-bladed knife—one they'd "borrowed" from an antique store—on the porch railing and walked along the side of the house, Merek tailing her. She saw Joe coming up the driveway, carrying a shovel in his hand.

Joe's somber eyes lifted to meet hers. "It's done."

Liv didn't know how to respond. She and Merek had both offered to go with Joe to bury the Knight-turned-wrath, but he'd insisted on doing it alone. "I can't spare you much these days," Joe had said with a heavy sigh, "but let me spare you this."

And she'd let him, feeling a little guilty at how relieved she was that she wouldn't have to look at the dead man's face for another second. But now that Joe was back, there was one thing they couldn't put off any longer.

"Joe, we have to talk about this."

Joe leaned the shovel up against the side of the house and nodded. "You're right. Dinner?"

But back inside the house around the Ratners' giant dining table, he went quiet. The cavernous rooms were lit only by the orange glow coming in through the windows and the kerosene lamps they'd arranged around the house. In the dining room, they ate cans of creamed corn under the framed black-and-white photos of Daisy's smiling movie-star parents.

"You guys didn't leave the house while I was gone, did you?" Joe asked, washing a bite of creamed corn down with the orange-flavored sparkling water Liv had taken from the store the day before.

"No," Peter responded. "These two have been in the back, fake-fighting with each other since you left."

Joe raised an eyebrow. "Being careful, I hope?"

"Yes," Liv responded. "Not that I'm getting better, though. Self-defense classes are one thing, but knife fights?"

"If you feel uncomfortable holding a weapon, then maybe it's a sign you shouldn't be holding one," Joe responded in his most levelheaded social-worker voice.

"It's not like I have much of a choice," Liv muttered.

"She should be able to defend herself. If Shannon had had the same training . . ." Merek trailed off and looked away, as he often did whenever Shannon came up. "She might still be here."

"I'm glad she's not," Liv replied.

Merek's eyes flashed. "I disagree."

"I just mean, I'm glad she's safe. Shannon's with her parents, far away, which is exactly where she should be. Meanwhile, we should be focusing on the person—the wrath—the whatever-it-was—that hurt her." She turned to Joe. "You saw his face, Joe."

Joe nodded, pushing his creamed corn away. "He was

definitely a wrath. But what killed him . . . I have no idea. His whole body looked to be falling apart somehow."

"I care less about what killed him and more about how he became a wrath in the first place," Liv said.

"The two might be connected," Joe replied.

No one at the table spoke as they let that cheerful thought sink in.

"But what does this mean?" Peter finally asked. "People can become wraths now? Does this prove what we've thought all along—that the wraths are behind all those Knights being murdered?"

"Which means Malquin's behind it," Liv said.

"We don't know anything for sure," Joe put in.

"That's the same thing we've been saying for two months," Liv said, throwing her fork down on the table a little too forcefully. The clattering noise bounced around the dimly lit dining room.

"I was thinking," Joe said, keeping his gentle eyes on Liv, "maybe we should take a break for a few days."

Liv blinked, not sure if she'd heard correctly. "A break?"

"Give us all a chance to relax for a bit, catch our breath."

"But . . . but this is exactly the time when we *shouldn't* take a break. Not only are we still looking for this Martin guy—who may or may not already be killed or driven off by wraths—but now we know something even worse is going on. The wraths are *up* to something, Joe! This is when we try harder, not catch a breath."

Liv looked to Merek and Peter for support, but they both

stared steadfastly into their cans of food. Joe's eyes filled with concern—with pity—but that somehow made Liv even more angry.

"Come on, guys . . . you can't be serious," she said, her voice rising.

"She is right," Merek said, "if a bit overheated."

"I'm not overheated!"

"Liv," Peter said, his voice maddeningly calm, "we hear what you're saying, and what happened to that Knight is incredibly messed up. But we're not going to solve that problem and fix everything *else* all at once. You've been going out on the moped every day, and now you're practicing knife fighting, too? I mean, I know things are terrible, but we're not exactly action stars here. Maybe you should just chill for a bit," Peter said.

"Chill?" Liv asked. "Are you serious? Chill? We are so far past chill, I can't even . . . I mean, don't you think I'd rest if I could? Don't you think I'm tired of seeing dead bodies, and learning how to stab things? I'm tired of living in this dark house with no electricity or air-conditioning, I'm tired of looking for some clue to help us all get out of this mess, and finding nothing. And now we finally, finally have some kind of idea as to what's happening to these Knights, and you want us to just take a break? There is no break! None of us gets a break!"

Liv didn't realize she was yelling until she'd stopped and the echo of her voice bounced around the walls of the dining room. Joe, Merek, and Peter all stared up at her as if she'd suddenly spewed pea soup from her mouth, *Exorcist*-style. It felt strange to yell, to let loose, to not be the calm voice of reason for once.

But she didn't know what else to do.

"Liv," Joe started, and his tone was so gentle, so placating, but it did nothing to help. Couldn't they understand? She wasn't just trying to fix the world, she was trying to fix the world that *she broke*. She'd opened that giant portal on the beach; she'd gone through it to save Peter; she'd been the one to make the clouds boil in the sky. And every person injured in the evacuation or the fires, every house looted and burned, every day that went by, racking up more death and damage—that was on her.

So she couldn't take a break. Not until she fixed this.

Joe was still staring at her, his expression a picture of calm. But Liv didn't hear whatever consoling words he'd been about to give her, because at that moment, there was a knock at the door.

"Expecting someone?" Merek drawled.

"Could be someone saw our lights, came to see if we have fresh water," Joe said, rising. "You guys wait here."

He grabbed a baseball bat—pretty unsteadily, Liv noticed—and went to answer the door.

"Liv! Better get out here," Joe yelled from the other room a moment later. "You have . . . a visitor."

The can of soda nearly slipped from Liv's hand. She stood, heart pounding.

Relax, she told herself sternly. *It's not* him*, it can't be him.*

Liv made her way quickly toward the front room, Peter and Merek on her heels. She ran through the list of people who might come searching for her at Daisy's Malibu beach house—other than the one person she hoped it would be. Her mind came up blank. No one else knew she was here. Only one person would come looking for her like this, only one person who could reasonably show up at exactly this moment.

Except it wasn't reasonable, was it? That after all these weeks of trying desperately not to think about him, of coming to terms with the fact that she'd never see him again, that she might turn the corner and see his face looking back at hers?

She turned the corner.

"Miss me?" Shannon asked.

Her hair was a little longer than when Liv had seen it last, its tips now muted pink rather than bright red. But she had her same Shannon-ish grin. Liv yelped, ran across the room, and hugged her best friend, hard.

"Guess that's a yes," Shannon said. "Okay, those are my lungs you're crushing."

Liv stepped back, a goofy smile still on her face.

Shannon looked around at the others in the dim light of the room. Her eyes fell on Merek, who stood stock-still a few feet away, his posture rigid. "I know, I know, you're way too cool to ever admit it, but I can see in your eyes you're glad to see—"

The rest of her words were muffled as Merek suddenly lunged forward in two giant steps and gathered Shannon to him, his arms almost swallowing her small frame.

Everyone, even Shannon, froze, unsure of exactly what was happening, but Merek still held on to her in a tight embrace. Finally, he pulled away, his face flushed. Shannon looked up at him, her eyes wide as saucers. For maybe the first time since Liv had known her, she seemed at a loss for words.

"Um," Shannon said.

Merek composed himself first. He shrugged, falling easily back into his lazy posture, though he kept his eyes on the floor. "It is too quiet without you here."

"Agreed," Liv said. But as she looked at her best friend grinning in the doorway, the dark orange sky looming behind her like a threat, the smile slipped from her face. "Except . . . why *are* you here?"

"Is everything okay? With your parents?" Joe asked.

"Oh yeah, they're fine," Shannon said. But there was a small hitch in her voice that Liv recognized. The Shannon-is-lying hitch.

"And they know where you are?" Joe asked.

"Of course!" Shannon said. "I mean, they will, as soon as they read the note I left them."

"Shannon." Liv beat Joe to a disapproving reply, crossing her arms.

"Hey, they left me no choice!" Shannon responded. "Do you know what's going on in Utah right now? Nothing, that's what. Even with my wrist healed I just had to sit there, day in and day out, making friendship bracelets with my thumb-sucking cousins, wondering what was going on out here. After you lost the internet in LA, I didn't even know if you were *alive*. I had to come back."

"So you just . . . left?" Liv asked, hating the scolding tone in her voice. "You left them there to worry about you?"

"Hey," Shannon said, sounding defensive now. "They know where I am. Not, like, the exact coordinates or anything, but I told them I was coming here to help you."

"How did you get here?" Joe asked. Liv was amazed by how calm he sounded.

"Stole the van, obviously. Driving into the city wasn't easy with half the roads closed, but I managed."

"Well, you have to go back," Joe said. He ran a hand through his hair, something he did when exasperated. Liv wondered how he had any hair left at all.

"No way," Shannon said, crossing her arms to mirror Liv. "It took me forever to get here. I'm not going back there. I'm not. Liv, come on."

Liv knew she should come to Shannon's defense. She should take her best friend's side, just like she'd always done. Just like Shannon had always done for her. But she couldn't help shaking her head.

"You were *safe*, Shan. Isn't that why you left in the first place? To get away from this whole mess and be safe?"

Shannon looked stunned, her cheeks going a bit red. "I went away because my parents were freaked after what happened . . . and maybe I was a little, too. But I'm all healed up now." She held up her arm, waving her wrist in the air. "And I made the decision to help before you even came back home, Liv. Now that I'm better and my parents are doing better, I'm sticking by that."

"And we are glad for it," Merek interjected, glaring at Liv.

Liv sighed. "But you're putting yourself in danger all over again—"

"So are you," Shannon retorted.

"I have no choice!" Liv exploded. "I have to fix this mess

because I started it. It's my responsibility. And besides, it's not like I have anywhere else to go. But, Shannon, you have parents. People who care about you and love you and want to keep you safe. Do you know how lucky you are to have that?"

"Of course I do," Shannon said, her eyes glittering in anger now.

"Then how could you do this to them? You can't just do whatever you want and not even think of the consequences!" The words poured out of her, hot and fast. "How do you think your parents will feel the next time you get yourself hurt?"

Shannon flinched, the red in her face deepening. She moved her healed wrist a little behind her back, and it was clear she was embarrassed she'd gotten hurt in the first place. Liv knew all that just by looking at her, and knew she should stop. But she couldn't. Things just kept getting worse, and no matter what she did, she couldn't control a single thing about the situation they were in. Every time she thought she had a handle on what was happening, something even crazier would pop up. Gravity would stop working. Men would turn into wraths. Things were spinning away from her, and there was no way to predict, let alone stop, what would happen next.

The one thing she'd been sure about was that Shannon and Daisy, at least, were safe and far away.

"I know what I'm doing," Shannon said.

"Oh, really? And what am I supposed to tell your parents if you get killed, huh?"

"Tell them it was my decision," Shannon responded, her dark eyes narrowing. "My decision to do what I can to help fix this. For them."

"Shannon is right," Merek said, taking a step to stand next to her. "We have all made a choice to continue on in this fight, despite the danger. Is that not what you told me, once, was special about this world? That everyone can make choices for themselves?"

"That isn't . . . That's not . . . ," Liv sputtered. She looked to Joe for help. "Please back me up on this one."

Joe sighed. "I'm on your side, Liv. If these were normal circumstances, I'd throw Shannon in the back of my car and drive her straight to her parents. But . . . these aren't normal circumstances. Even if we found the time to drive to Utah—"

"I'd just turn around and come right back," Shannon said.

"I can't believe this," Liv said, shaking her head. She looked at Shannon, who was wearing her most pissed-off expression, the one usually reserved for bouncers who wouldn't let her into nightclubs. Or for her parents. Liv could barely believe that the look was being directed at her. That Shannon would be against her. Or was it the other way around? Was it her against Shannon? But even as she thought about backing down, she remembered again the moment she'd learned Shannon had been hurt while she was in Caelum. And she imagined what worse things could happen to Shannon if she stayed in L.A. Worse than running into another Knight, worse than stumbling across a dead body. She pictured Shannon being torn apart by black-eyed wraths. Pictured her *becoming* one. Pictured her lying on the ground, her eyes staring up at nothing.

"I can't believe you'd be so . . . selfish," Liv said.

"And I can't believe you'd be such a hypocrite," Shannon spit back. "And kind of a bitch."

"All right," Joe said, spreading out his hands. "Let's just calm down. We'll go in the other room, take a breath—"

"No," Liv said. "We won't. Maybe you've all agreed this is okay, but I *don't*." She pushed her way past Joe, grabbing a set of moped keys from the side table and running out the still-open door into the stifling hot night air, her heart beating wildly in her chest.

⊱⊰

Two hours later, Liv still felt horrible. In fact, she felt more horrible, if that was even possible.

She kept running the conversation over and over again in her mind, wondering what could possibly have made her say those things to her very best friend? But no answers came to her. Yelling at Shannon was just one more mistake in the list of mistakes she'd made lately; though at least this one hadn't resulted in a near-apocalypse.

Above Liv's head, the sky was dark and burnt-looking, which was as close to nighttime as Los Angeles got these days. In the distance, beyond the rust-colored clouds, heat lightning flashed every few seconds. Liv dimly wondered if she should get inside, but there was nowhere to get inside *to*. In all her burning anger and frustration and shame, she'd jumped on the moped and taken off, not really thinking about where she was going.

And of course she'd wound up on the cracked cement banks of the LA River. She hadn't been here since—well, she couldn't remember the last time she'd been here. Her days had been so full of tracking down leads and missing Knights that she hadn't taken the time to come to what had once been her favorite place in the world. More than her favorite place, really; in a lifetime full of rotating houses, guardians, and foster siblings, this spot by the river was basically her only constant. The closest thing she had to home.

But now it was as broken and unrecognizable as the rest of her city. Looking down at the completely dried-up riverbed and then up at the lightless, empty blocks of the downtown skyscrapers beyond, Liv felt a sharp pang and hugged her knees to her chest.

She was homesick.

It was strange, particularly since she'd expected her homesickness to end the second she got back from Caelum, but there it was—strong and overpowering—the urge to go home.

But the place she'd been yearning for in Caelum—with its sprawl and bustle and dreamers and schemers, its cement and bridges and forgotten, beautiful spaces—was wrecked. Torn from her, like her parents, siblings, and first home had been.

But she could get it back. She had to get it back.

So what did it matter if Shannon helped her to do it? Surely she could use all the help she could get?

And if Shannon got hurt . . .

Well, she wouldn't let that happen. She'd train harder with Merek, get better at using the knives, be faster than the evacuation crews and police still scanning the city for stubborn citizens who'd stayed behind.

Liv had to get back to Malibu right away and apologize. She was just about to push herself up off the dusty ground when she heard it.

A voice. Clear as day. And impossible.

"Liv."

She didn't move. She didn't blink. She felt the speaker approach from behind, but she knew that as soon as she turned around, she'd be disappointed again. It wouldn't be him—it would be someone else. Merek had come after her, or maybe Joe. Her ears were playing tricks on her.

"Liv?"

More tentative this time. And much closer.

Liv slowly turned.

He was standing with his back to the bridge. And just like on the first night she'd met him, he stepped away from a swirling darkness in the structure's shadows—a darkness that closed down to nothing and disappeared. Unlike that night, he wasn't wearing nightclothes and a confused, frightened expression. He was in formal gear, the kind she'd last seen him wearing in the castle. And in his eyes there was disbelief and happiness, like he'd just stumbled across something amazing and was afraid to move a muscle it in case it disappeared in front of him.

Liv knew the feeling.

She jumped up, and he was moving toward her, too—they weren't that far away at all, practically nothing was between them, and she'd be at him in a matter of seconds.

Just before they could crash into each other, she stopped short, and Cedric did, too.

Liv had a million things to ask, a million things to say. But the words scrambled against each other in her mind.

"H-how?" she finally managed.

Cedric exhaled and motioned back to the now-closed portal under the bridge.

"Right," Liv managed, feeling breathless herself. "What I meant was . . . why?"

Cedric paused then, and it occurred to Liv that he was fighting for the right first words, too. That he was just as excited, just as nervous that they were actually, truly standing across from each other. And it suddenly didn't matter what he had to say.

"You know what? Forget it. I don't care why."

She launched herself at him.

Before he could move, her arms went around the shoulders she thought she'd never touch again, her fingers moved through the hair she thought she'd never feel again. Cedric's hands met around her waist, his fingers gathering at the small of her back. He pulled her in tight, and then her face was angling up to his, and their lips were a breath apart, and then that breath was gone.

She didn't think about it, or question it, or worry what would happen next. She just kissed him, and he kissed her back. Everything that wasn't his lips or his hands floated from her mind, and at the moment she didn't care if it ever came back.

Because Cedric was here. Finally, finally here.

When the ground started shaking, it knocked them off their feet. Just like when they'd first met, they fell together to the cement before they could catch their balance, though this time Liv barely felt it at all.

ATONEMENT

"So I messed up bad. Like really, really bad."

Cedric looked over at Liv's profile as she straddled the contraption that would supposedly take them back to Malibu. It was much smaller than a horse, but Liv assured him it was safe for them both—so long as he held on to her tightly. He didn't think that would be a problem.

"Did you hear me?" Liv asked.

"Oh, uh . . . yes," Cedric said, forcing himself to pay attention. "How did you 'mess up,' exactly?"

Liv took a deep breath and then went on to explain everything that had happened to her in the previous two months. She talked about how the changing city had caused everyone in it to flee and about her long quest for a remaining Knight of Valere who could help explain what exactly what was going on.

"I might know a bit about that," Cedric interrupted.

Liv looked at him, curious.

"It is the main reason I came back," he said.

"The main reason? So there were other reasons?" Liv's eyes

were on the road, but there was a smile in her voice that made Cedric's insides thump.

"There were," he responded. Then he told her everything he'd learned from Mathilde, and about his decision to come to LA. He skipped over the massive fight he'd had with Kat, which had mostly been about those "other reasons" for him to return to the other world. If Cedric had thought bringing Mathilde back with him to the castle would help convince Kat that he needed to leave, he'd been wrong. In fact, Mathilde's somewhat . . . quirky . . . ways did more to hurt than help her credibility.

"I just cannot understand," Kat had said back at the castle, her expression one of immense disappointment, "how you can put the word of one crazy old crone over the needs of our realm."

"I *am* thinking about our realm," Cedric had shot back.

They'd been alone in the parlor next to Cedric's bedchamber, pacing and arguing.

"No, you are not," Kat had replied. Her eyes were as still and hard as ice, and it killed Cedric that this look had come to be specially reserved for him. "You have been looking for any excuse to go back to Los Angeles for weeks—"

"That is not true. You know that I have been here, trying my hardest to be a good king."

"You let yourself be distracted."

Cedric whirled on Kat, his anger matching hers. "Worrying about Merek wasn't a *distraction*. Wanting to find Malquin, the man who *killed my father*, and bring him to justice—that was not a distraction, either. Those were legitimate concerns, Kat, and yet I still put them aside to do what was right. But this—this I cannot ignore."

Kat had shaken her head. "You believe this crazy woman because it is what you want to believe. Because it is easier to run back there than it is to face your duties here. Look outside, Cedric." Kat motioned out a window at the townspeople below. "Look at the people who need you now. *They* are what's important."

"But . . . the trees!" Cedric had yelled, throwing his hands in the air. Not exactly his best argument, but Kat's accusations were more piercing than he wanted to admit. He *did* want a legitimate reason to go back to Los Angeles, and they both knew it.

In the end, she couldn't stop him, so she agreed to cover for him in the castle until he returned, which he promised to do soon. An uneasy solution, but at least Cedric was here.

Now, Cedric got onto the back of the "moped" contraption behind Liv, holding on to her tightly as she drove down streets that looked radically different from when he had seen them last. But he could barely focus on the changed world as wind whipped past his face. As they got nearer and nearer to the Malibu house, Cedric knew he was facing another difficult interaction. With Merek.

The trouble was, Cedric had no idea what to say, or how to even begin to make things right. Liv assured him that Merek's injuries had all but healed and he'd been fine and even battle-ready for weeks, but every time he thought of how he would apologize to Merek—for not believing him, for never trusting him, for slamming his injured head into the ground—he could only imagine the last time he'd seen him. Then, Merek had been unconscious in a hospital bed, his face wrapped in bandages, his jaw swollen.

How could Cedric apologize for that?

In what felt like hardly any time at all, they were pulling up to the house, a dark silhouette against the ocean and the orange sky beyond.

"They might all be sleeping," Liv said as she made her way to the front door. "Unless they stayed up to curse my name."

She put her hand on the door handle, and Cedric reached out to touch her wrist.

"Wait," he whispered. "Just one moment more."

She took her hand from the handle and slipped it into his, looking up at him in the orange-y dark. After a brief pause, he nodded.

Liv sighed heavily. "It's grovel time."

She opened the front door of the house to the glow of very dim lights. In the living room, everyone was awake and sitting around a few flickering candles that were burning down to the dregs. They looked up as Cedric and Liv entered. Merek's eyes fell on Cedric immediately, and Cedric had to force himself not to look away.

"Look who I found!" Liv said, her voice unnaturally bright against the glumness of the room.

For a few seconds, everyone just stared at Cedric with wide, disbelieving eyes.

He cleared his throat. "Hello."

There was a brief moment of stunned silence before Liv broke from Cedric and rushed toward Shannon, apologizing so fast he could not understand half her words.

"I'm sorry, so sorry, I didn't mean—"

"No! I mean, I know! I'm sorry, too—" Shannon said back.

"You don't have to be sorry! I do want you here, of course I do—"

"But I never meant to call you a bitch. You're not a bitch, you're the opposite of a bitch, why can't I stop saying bitch?"

And then they were laughing and hugging, as Joe and Peter looked on with wide eyes.

Cedric looked to Merek, knowing his own round of apologies likely wouldn't take place in quite the same way. Which was probably for the best—if Merek ever hugged him, Cedric would know for sure the blow to his head had caused serious damage.

Merek didn't even stand as Cedric came forward. Before he could say anything, Joe intercepted him.

"Cedric! Not that it's not good to see you, but why . . . ?"

"I had to come back," Cedric said, glad for the interruption. "I learned about something that affects both of our worlds."

"If it's about the sky boiling up, we already got that memo," Shannon said.

"There's more," Liv put in.

Cedric went on to explain—again—everything he'd learned from Mathilde.

Joe responded first. "Well. That *is* bad news."

"So you want to close the portals entirely?" Peter asked, leaning forward.

There was a heavy pause. Cedric didn't look at Liv. Even

when they had caught each other up by the riverbed, they had talked quickly past this point, about the necessity of closing the portals. Because once the portals were closed for good, the two of them would be in opposite worlds. Again. Forever.

"That's assuming we even *can* close them," Joe put in.

"Mathilde seemed to think it was possible," Cedric said. "Even if she didn't know how."

"We have to keep looking for the Knight the professor told me about—Martin. Maybe he knows how we can close the portals." Liv's eyes opened wide, as if a thought was occurring to her. "Maybe that's why Malquin is killing the Knights—because he wants to keep someone like Martin from keeping our worlds apart for good?"

Joe shook his head. "Maybe. But it's still just a guess. We don't actually know John is behind those deaths. And if he was, why would he want to keep the portals open anyway? He already lost in Caelum, so there's no point in him going back."

"There's a lot we don't know, sure," Liv said. "But that's why we have to find Martin. He might be the only one with answers."

"Aside from John himself," Joe said. He bit his lip, and put one hand to his beard. His eyes were on the ground, as if he were working out a problem. "If I could only talk to him, reason with him—"

"Malquin does not understand reason," Cedric said, his voice cutting through the room. "He is a murderer. He killed my father."

Even saying the words out loud was hard. Cedric felt the rage and helplessness of that night, and he had to force himself to stand straight, to keep his voice firm.

Joe took a moment before replying. "I'm truly sorry, Cedric. I'm not defending John, but if there's anyone in the world who might be able to reach him, it could be me. If I could just find him—"

"If we found him, it would be to kill him," Cedric heard himself saying. It took effort to control the anger in his voice. "That is Caelum's punishment for murder."

Everyone was quiet.

"Speaking like a true king already," Merek finally said, not so much breaking as adding to the tension.

"Merek," Cedric said carefully. "Could I speak with you for a moment? Alone?"

"Is that a command?"

"A request."

Merek didn't say yes or nod, but he did stand. And he did follow Cedric (very slowly) out through the back door of the house. They stood a good distance apart from each other, both facing the ocean.

Cedric cleared his throat. "I know 'sorry' will never be enough . . ." He trailed off, hoping that Merek would at least look at him.

"Is that it?" Merek scoffed. "That is your whole apology?"

"No, of course not," Cedric replied, trying not to get frustrated by how Merek had to make everything difficult.

"I should not have so easily believed you would betray us," Cedric continued. "I should not have hurt you the way I did. There is no excuse for it."

Merek crossed his arms, staring over the water, stretching the moment to the edge of what was bearable, and then staying there for a few more seconds.

"Fine. Forgiven," he finally said. "So long as I do not have to refer to you as 'Your Majesty.'"

Cedric saw him smirk—for the briefest of seconds—but it was enough to know that things between them would be okay.

"I wouldn't think of it," Cedric replied.

"So we can just move on, then."

"Agreed."

After an awkward pause, Merek looked to Cedric. "I was sorry to hear about your father."

Cedric swallowed past a small lump in his throat. "Thank you. In truth, being a king is not what I expected it to be. I thought I would have . . . more time. To prepare. I am not sure I will ever be as good as my father was."

Merek looked shocked, perhaps at Cedric's honesty, and Cedric was a bit surprised at himself, too. He hadn't spoken those words aloud since the moment the crown was put on his head.

Merek finally gave a light snort. "That was possibly the least arrogant thing you have ever said. Maybe this place *has* changed you."

"Me?" Cedric couldn't help responding. "Look at you. I expected that as soon as your recovery was complete, you would come through a portal after us. But here you still are, well and fine—and seemingly content."

"I am not sure 'content' is the word I would use."

"All right," Cedric said, fighting the urge to roll his eyes. "But why did you stay?"

Merek shrugged lightly. "As it turns out, I wasn't really up for joining a revolution, fighting a wrath army, taking back the castle, all of that business. Seemed a lot of work."

Cedric shook his head, not buying it. "You are a lot of things, Merek. Challenging, sarcastic, irritating—"

"Can I take back my forgiveness now?"

"But despite all that," Cedric continued, "you've never been one to back down from a fight. Not ever."

Merek glanced once at the door to the house before shifting his eyes back to the ocean. "Maybe I found something else to fight for," he said, with a small shrug.

Cedric looked through the door, to where Shannon was sitting, and wondered how much she factored into Merek's sudden commitment to fight for this world. But he knew better than to ask about that. Instead, he followed Merek's gaze to the ocean.

"There *is* something about this place," he said.

"Do you know how enormous it is?" Merek asked, his eyes still on the distant waves. "Much larger than Caelum. Full of new things and opportunity. No overshadowing older brother, no disapproving father, no dreary destiny of almost-dukedom. Here, it is as if I were almost . . . free."

Cedric wanted badly to speak, but he didn't want to risk ruining this moment. How could it be he and Merek felt so similarly? Had things always been like this, with the both of them weighed down by similar burdens of a set future, so concentrated on their own problems they couldn't even see that their problems were the same?

"I suppose you couldn't understand that," Merek said, after a minute passed without Cedric responding.

"On the contrary, I do. More than you know."

After that, they fell into another silence, this one more comfortable. Then Merek asked after his parents and Rafe, and Cedric gave him a longer account of everything that had taken place in Caelum. When they went back inside, the others were preparing to go to bed.

As they made their way down the corridor toward the bedrooms, Liv and Cedric trailed just a bit behind the others. She reached a doorway and stopped before it. Without thinking, Cedric stopped, too.

From a few feet away, Cedric heard a cough. He looked up to see Joe watching them.

"You can sleep over here, Cedric."

Cedric nodded quickly. "Yes. Of course."

Liv bit back her smile and disappeared into her room. Cedric moved away from her door, half relieved, half disappointed. Part of him dreaded talking to Liv about closing the portals permanently and was anxious to put that conversation off for another day.

But another part of him hated to walk away from her, even for a few hours. Because if they did figure out how to close the portals forever, then a few numbered hours were all they had.

THE DARK KNIGHT

Teaching Cedric to drive a moped turned out to be much easier than teaching him to drive a car. The trickiest part was navigating where he would put his sword. This time, Liv knew better than to ask him to leave it behind. Getting pulled over and arrested by the police or an evacuation crew was possible, of course, but then again, having to use the sword to defend themselves was also a possibility.

That morning, Joe had consulted the list of leads he had left and divided the group into teams. Shannon and Merek were taking her van north to a doctor's office in Thousand Oaks. It was a slim lead—the doctor's office had been scribbled on a piece of paper left behind in a Knight's abandoned house, and might just as easily be the man's actual doctor as a clue to tracking down more Knights. Liv and Cedric were on their way to a home in Orange County that may or may not have been rented by a Knight at one point in the early 2000s, according to some old tax papers Joe had found in a former Knight's filing cabinet.

Joe's leads were definitely dwindling, and Liv had never felt farther from finding Martin.

Still, her spirits weren't exactly low as she motored south along an empty highway, Cedric at her side. It was still hard to believe he was actually back, and she had to look over at him every few moments just to confirm he was still there.

Cedric caught Liv looking at her and smiled. He yelled something out, but his voice was swallowed by the wind.

"What?" Liv called.

Cedric shouted again, but again, she couldn't hear. But she could tell from the excitement on his face that he liked riding the moped. He was taking to it much better than Merek, who scowled every time he had to approach the bike's thin seat.

As they neared Orange County, the orange-ish color in the sky started to thin out, looking first yellow, then fading into a more normal blue. The lead they were chasing was firmly out of Apocalypse Zone, and the OC hadn't felt many of the effects of the earthquakes. Still, the city roads were much emptier on a weekday afternoon than normal.

Unlike Los Angeles, with its twisty-crowded streets and buildings spanning from 1970s bungalows to modern skyscrapers to actual glass houses, Orange County was almost entirely uniform in its design. Its streets were wide and clean, and its neighborhoods were orderly. The buildings in the strip malls were all painted the same shades of white and tan, and they all had the same red tile roofs. Even the KFC looked classy.

"Weird," Liv murmured to herself, looking around. Orange County seemed as different a world from LA as Caelum had.

Liv motioned with her head for Cedric to follow her, then pulled over into a giant parking lot surrounded by well-manicured shrubs and palm trees. Cedric pulled his moped over next to her.

"These are so much better than horses," he said, grinning.

Liv couldn't help but smile back. "Thought you might like it. We should be pretty close to the house from here. Snack?"

She motioned to the pack on her moped, but Cedric shook his head. "No, but a moment's rest would be good. I feel as though my legs are vibrating."

They both straddled their mopeds, only a couple feet apart from each other. It would be nothing for him to lean over and close the gap between them, nothing at all . . .

Instead, Cedric leaned back a fraction. "Liv."

She tensed and looked away, not sure she was ready to hear what he was going to say. Emotional reunion make-outs aside, he was still a king in another world, and she was committed to staying in this one. There were so many things she wanted to tell him, but the second they started that conversation again, she knew where it would lead. Whenever they were honest with each other, it seemed to close doors rather than open them.

And she wasn't ready for that yet. Not so soon after she'd gotten him back.

So she pretended she didn't hear him, instead looking quickly away to check the map in her pack. Without the use of GPS, she'd had to pull over every twenty minutes or so to make sure they were still heading in the right direction.

"Looks like the house is just on the next street up," she said, pointing to the starred location on the map.

He looked a bit startled, but then nodded. And when she started her moped up again, he did the same, following just a few feet behind. Liv led him down a wide and perfectly manicured side street, where white stucco houses lined the road like a row of sturdy wedding cakes. She tried to get her mind back to the task at hand as she stopped in front of their destination, noting its functioning sprinkler system and the Lexus in the driveway.

"That's strange."

"Water spraying from the ground?" Cedric asked, eyeing the sprinklers with suspicion. "Definitely strange."

"Yeah. I mean, no, sprinklers are normal. But every other lead we've chased down has led to abandoned properties or . . . worse. It looks like someone's actually home here."

"Is that not a good thing?"

"Maybe. One way to find out, I guess."

She hopped off her moped and made her way up the front walk. What would she say if someone answered the door? In all their searching over the past two months, she hadn't yet encountered a living person, one who might actually know something helpful.

Liv stood in front of the door, her hand poised near a brass knocker. Cedric raised his eyebrows. "Well?"

"Give me a sec. And also maybe hide your sword?" He quickly stashed it behind a bush near the front door. Now there was nothing left to do but knock.

The man who answered the door was not at all what Liv was expecting. He looked to be in his mid-sixties, and he wore an old newsboy cap and a bow tie along with a freshly pressed shirt. His eyes narrowed under bushy white brows as he peered out the door.

"Yes? What?" he asked, though his gruff voice sounded more like a demand than a question.

"Um, hi?" Liv said, immediately cursing her shaky voice. She tried to sound more serious. "My name is Liv, and this is Cedric. I was wondering if we could ask you a few questions?"

"I'm not interested in buying anything," the man said, already starting to shut the door.

"Right, well, we're not selling anything," Liv answered quickly. "We're actually looking for someone who used to live in this house. Maybe ten or fifteen years ago?"

"Can't help you there. Just moved in myself."

"Really?" Liv asked. She looked down to the welcome mat under her feet. It was faded, its edges covered in dirt. It looked a lot like the mat that Liv's most recent foster mom, Rita, had had outside her front door for years.

The man's eyes narrowed again. His liver-spotted hand trembled a bit on the doorknob. "Yes," he said. "Really. Now, I am quite busy this morning, so—"

"It's just . . . ," Liv said, stepping just a bit closer to keep the man from closing the door on her. "We've come a long way, and we only have a few questions. They're about what's been going on in Los Angeles. We're looking for a way to help."

The man gave no reaction to Liv's words. When she mentioned Los Angeles, he looked as blank as if she'd said she needed to get a haircut.

"I wouldn't know anything about that," he said. "And like I

said, I can't help you."

The man avoided her eyes, and Liv knew, in her gut, that she was missing something important here. She decided to just take a stab and see—

"We're looking for a Knight of Valere."

For the briefest moment, the old man flinched. And Liv knew.

"You've heard of them, haven't you? Did one used to live here?" Liv asked, unable to keep the excitement out of her voice. "Or maybe, are *you*—"

"Who are you? What do you want?" the man barked. His hand gripped harder on the door edge, and Liv got the impression he was much stronger than he seemed. "Answer me now or I call the police."

"We just want to talk," Liv said, stepping forward, and Cedric moved to put his own arm and shoulder against the door.

"I will call 911, I swear," the man said.

Cedric turned to Liv. "You are sure about this?"

No. But it was worth trying. She nodded.

Cedric pushed his way into the house, forcing the old man to take a few steps back. Liv followed, watching as the man's expression morphed from confusion to rage. His cheeks turned red. She felt guilty, but she still followed Cedric inside. She couldn't just walk away from the first lead that might have actually *led* to something.

"Please," Liv said, trying to sound as nonthreatening as possible. "It's like I said—we just want to ask you a few questions. Questions that might help save the world."

The old man just stared at her from under his bushy

eyebrows, his mouth opening and closing slightly.

"Liv," Cedric said, his voice low and near her ear. He motioned to the living room behind the old man. Liv looked around the room with its tasteful pink couches sitting on a spotless rug. Above the mantel was a row of framed photos—all of a man and a woman, both fair-haired and in their mid-thirties. One of the man and woman together, one of the man holding a diploma, one of the woman petting a dog. Liv looked all around the room at the various framed photos—all of them had the same couple. In front of her, the old man was following her gaze, his face now going white.

"Whose house is this?" Liv asked.

"Now . . . now just a minute," the man said, pointing a finger at Liv. "You can't just come in here and . . . and . . ."

"What happened to the people in those photos? Where are they?"

"I'm not saying anything. Not till you tell me who you are."

"I'm Liv, like I said. Liv Phillips."

"That means nothing to me." The man jutted his chin up. Liv made a quick calculation—on the one hand, there was something shady about this old man being in a house that was clearly not his. But on the other hand, if he had information . . . . She had to take the risk.

Liv looked to Cedric once, but there was no way to warn him what she was going to say.

"I'm a scroll. Does *that* mean anything to you?"

The man's eyes widened, his eyebrows shooting so far up they almost met his hairline.

"See?" Liv turned around, pulling down the back collar of

her shirt so the man could see her "tattoo."

"A scroll," the man whispered, staring at Liv in something like awe.

"So you have heard of them, then," Cedric said.

The man hesitated a moment, as if he were debating whether or not to be as honest as Liv had been. But then he nodded. "I have not seen a scroll in a very long time."

"We're here because we need to find the Knights of Valere," Liv went on in a rush. "They might have some of the answers we need to fix what's going on in LA. But everywhere we look for them, we find—"

"Bodies," the old man finished. "Yes, that's what I have been finding, too."

This time, Liv was the one to look confused. "You've been looking for the Knights?"

The old man sighed, then sat heavily on the couch. He looked around the empty, sanitized living room. "I knew a portal must have opened—maybe more than one—with what was going on in the city. I started looking for the Knights again, after all this time, just to see what was really happening. But everywhere I went, I came across this instead"—he gestured around the room—"abandoned houses. And dead bodies."

"We must have been on the same trail," Liv said. "So the people who own this house . . ."

"Were Knights, yes. Though not as active as most. And they were gone before I got here, a few days ago," the old man said. "Left in a hurry, too, it looks like. No sign of a struggle, but some lights were left on; the mail keeps coming. The sprinklers keep turning on. Like they just walked out in the middle of the day and kept going."

Goose bumps rose up on Liv's arm. She looked to Cedric, but he was staring at the man intently. "What did you mean when you said you were looking for Knights 'after all this time'?" he asked.

The old man waved a dismissive hand. "It doesn't matter."

But Liv was starting to pick up on Cedric's train of thought. "It might," she said. "We're looking for one former Knight in particular—one who knows about the portals. Someone called Martin."

The man's mouth fell slightly open, and his shocked expression was all the confirmation Liv needed. She felt a rush of excitement. Finally, after all these weeks, the man she'd been searching for was right in front of her.

"Where did you get that name?" he asked.

"From another Knight," Liv said, her voice shaking a bit as she thought of the professor, dead in another world. "One who said Martin could help us fix what was broken. What *I* helped break."

The man studied Liv.

"So can you help me?" she asked. "Martin?"

After an agonizingly slow beat, he nodded. "Yes," Martin said. "I think I can. And it's Henry. Henry Martin."

The relief Liv felt was so overpowering, her eyes actually closed for a few seconds. She'd found him. Martin was here. And now she'd be able to fix everything she'd broken.

"Do you know how to close the portals?" she asked.

Henry shook his head. "It's too late for that."

Liv's heart sank.

"The magic from the other world is already here," Henry continued. "Our world's already fighting it. Closing the portals won't stop what's already started."

"So what can we do? We were told you could help us."

Henry's thick eyebrows drew together. "When I was a Knight, there were certain theories I was interested in. Research into historical legends most Knights had long forgotten. I started to look into them after . . . well, it's not worth getting into."

"After you killed a child," Liv said. Her words sounded blunt, but she didn't think it was right for him to gloss over that part of his story—that part of Joe's story as well.

Henry looked momentarily shocked at her words, and then he shrank back against the couch cushions. "There is no excuse for what I did," he continued. "I could argue how much we believed . . . as Knights, we truly thought we had to eliminate the scrolls to save the world. It wasn't until I actually had to do it that I questioned everything. . . ." He trailed off, though his lips kept moving silently, searching for the words that would never be enough. "I still see his face every day. Every minute." Henry kept his eyes not on Liv, but on the ground. But she didn't want to hear his apologies. They were for Joe, not her.

"That was when I left the Knights. I wanted to search for another way to end the threat that portals and magic posed to Earth."

"And you found it?" Liv prompted. "A way to keep portals from hurting Earth?"

"It's a long shot. All those years of research, and all I have is a theory. A hunch. It's the magic. We can't overlook the magic."

"Trust me, we're definitely not," Liv said.

But Henry went on as if she hadn't spoken. "Our world's not used to magic anymore, and that's why it's causing so much destruction."

"Right, because it's sneezing," Liv said, remembering how the professor had described it to her. "We already know that."

Henry and Cedric both looked at her with puzzled expressions, but she just motioned for the older man to continue.

"But what if the Earth didn't view magic as a threat? What if there was a way to properly restore the balance between nature and magic that once existed here?"

He paused to let this idea sink in.

"So . . . keep the magic here? Like, for good?" Liv asked. "What would that even look like?"

Henry shrugged. "I don't know. All I have is a theory on *how* to do it. And now that we have you, an actual scroll, we might truly be able to stop what's happening before it gets worse—"

Henry stopped talking, his body going tense. Liv followed his gaze to the door on the other side of the room, where Cedric was already headed.

"What?" she asked.

But Cedric raised his hand, cutting her off. He walked quietly, pausing in front of the mostly closed door. Beyond it, Liv could just make out the edge of what looked like a kitchen counter.

And then she heard the noise.

It was a light scraping, the sound of a door handle turning.

Once again, she felt goose bumps rise on her skin.

"You brought more with you?" Henry asked in a whisper.

Liv shook her head quickly. Before they could do anything—before they could say another word—loud footsteps made their way across the kitchen. Just as Cedric put up a hand to push the door closed, it was slammed open from the other side, knocking him backward.

A man stepped into the doorway, so large he blocked their view of whatever might be standing behind him. But it wasn't just his size that caught Liv's attention. It was his eyes—all black.

"Well, look what we got here," the wrath said. For a moment, Liv thought he was talking to them. Then she heard more footsteps moving through the kitchen. How many wraths were in the house? Two? Three?

Before Liv could think to move, Cedric was darting toward the front door. Belatedly, Liv remembered the sword he'd left just outside. She knew that as long as Cedric could get to his weapon, they might be okay. She'd seen him take on three wraths before.

Cedric ripped the front door open. Standing there, filling up the main doorway, were two more wraths. The one standing closest held a long, silver blade in his hand—Cedric's sword.

"You were right," the wrath at the front door said to the creature standing behind him. "Wife did come back."

The second wrath stepped up, his added bulk blocking out the light from the outside. His eyes narrowed as he took Liv in, his mouth twisting up in a sneer. She recognized him just before he spoke.

"That's not my wife."

The second wrath was tall, with fair hair and a thin face. The same face that was framed in dozens of places around the living room. Just inches away from Liv, on the side table, was a picture of the fair-haired man on a beach with his arm around a blond woman.

He'd lived here. As a man. But he wasn't a man anymore. Just like the Knight in the Ralphs's parking lot, he'd somehow been turned. His black eyes flashed as he tilted his head at her and stepped into the house.

"Course it's not the wife, idiot," scoffed the wrath by the kitchen doorway. "Don't you know anything?"

The first wrath at the front door trained his black eyes on Liv. He smiled. "It's *her*, isn't it?" He smiled. "That's even better."

Cedric turned to Liv, but she was already running before a word could come out of his mouth.

Not that there was anywhere to run *to*. Both doors were blocked. She raced for a window, but the fair-haired wrath grabbed her by the back of her shirt and yanked her off her feet, throwing her down. As she hit the ground, Liv scrabbled for the knife she'd hidden in her boot. She pulled it out a little too quickly, scraping the skin of her ankle. She crawled forward, slicing the knife at the wrath's calf. He jumped back, clearing the blade by inches. Then he pulled his leg back and kicked out at Liv. His foot hit her shoulder with a painful jolt, and she went flying backward. Her head smacked hard against the wall.

Black dots swam before Liv's eyes.

"Don't kill her," she heard another wrath growl. "Orders."

The voice sounded fuzzy to Liv, as if it were coming from far away. She looked up, but could barely see Cedric grappling with another wrath, trying to get his sword back. Henry was still on the couch, his hands in the air as if they could protect him from the creatures in the room. As a wrath approached him, she saw Henry reach for a poker from the fireplace and hold it out before him, shaking.

Not that Liv was faring much better with her own weapon. The small knife in her hand felt flimsy, and she suddenly realized that all of her weapons training had been a joke. These creatures were bigger than her, and stronger. And though they weren't the seven-foot-tall, horned monsters of Caelum, in some ways they were even worse. Because they walked around like men, hiding their true natures underneath. And Liv knew she couldn't beat them.

Her head felt fuzzy and thick as the fair-haired wrath leaned down to grab her. For a moment it looked like there were two of the same wrath, bending down, getting closer and closer. Only when he was inches from her face did the wrath morph back into one being. Liv heard grunts and a cry, but the shapes behind the wrath were too hazy to make out. She tried blinking, but things weren't getting clearer.

As the wrath started to haul her up, Liv thrust her hand out one more time, plunging the knife wildly. But it was hard to see where she was aiming. The wrath tried to smash her arm against her side, and then he tried to take her knife. But she wriggled her hand free.

Merek's words rang, suddenly, in her ears. *You have to mean it.*

Liv took a deep breath and stabbed toward the wrath's hand as it reached for her. *Stab him*, she thought. *Mean it*. The wrath made a sharp hissing noise, drawing his hand back. She'd done it—she'd hit him.

That's when she heard the scream.

It wasn't from the fair-haired wrath she'd stabbed—it was coming from across the room. She looked up just in time to see another wrath twist the fire poker from Henry's hand. He raised the iron bar high. Liv called out for Cedric, but he was too far away, busy fighting the other three wraths near the kitchen doorway. Liv could only watch as the wrath with the fire poker swung it out wide and brought it down hard over Henry's skull.

"No!" she screamed. The effort of it caused black dots to swim again before her eyes, so she couldn't see Henry as he fell—she only heard him hit the ground.

She took one shaky step toward him, but the fair-haired wrath was waiting for her. He grabbed her up, hauling her over his shoulder. Already woozy, Liv's stomach dropped at the movement. She thought she might throw up. Then the knife was wrenched from her fingers and thrown across the room.

Liv heard Cedric yell her name. She knew he was still in the same room with her, but he sounded so far away. There was movement, so many arms and legs and torsos blocking her line of sight. If she could just *see* him. If she could just get clear of these wraths, if they could just get back to their mopeds and get away from here . . .

But they were too outnumbered; they had too few weapons. Liv had trouble lifting her gaze up off the floor as her head bounced against the wrath's back with every step. Soon the wood of the living room changed to the stone of the front steps and then the grass of the front lawn. The grass looked much darker than it had when she'd walked across it not twenty minutes earlier, and it was getting dimmer with every step.

"Liv!"

Someone was shouting. Cedric? Yes. But where was he? She couldn't see him. She wanted to shout, but her mouth wasn't working. The grass looked darker, darker, darker still.

She heard her name being screamed—over and over and over—and then everything went black.

TAKEN

Two wraths lay at Cedric's feet, but he didn't have time to make sure they'd stay down. He left the creatures behind and, still panting from the fight, raced outside.

He'd managed to get his sword back, though one of the wraths had given him a bad gash on the thigh. But none of that mattered, because they'd taken Liv. Just taken her.

Cedric ran across the grass and toward the street where three wraths were shoving Liv into the back door of a large, boxy vehicle, one he remembered Liv calling a "van." This one was all white, with words that Cedric didn't recognize printed along its side. Cedric's feet slapped against the pavement, the gash in his leg burning with every step. The wraths were getting into the van now, shutting the doors. It started moving forward just as Cedric caught up to the rear end. All Cedric could do was slap one futile hand against its backside before it outpaced him. For just a brief moment, he stared after it—after Liv—and knew she was lost. There was no way for him to track that van once it disappeared around the corner, no way to know where in this very large world it was going.

Stop, Cedric thought to himself, gripping his sword handle tight. *Think*.

She's not lost yet.

Cedric spotted the mopeds over near the curb and raced to them, jumping on one. He didn't even bother to sheathe his sword, but kept it dangling from one hand as the other hand gripped the front bar. Remembering what Liv had taught him just that morning, Cedric turned the key and took off down the street.

The van was faster than the moped, and Cedric knew if he didn't catch up to it soon, Liv really would be gone. He bent forward, keeping to one side of the road. As the white van slowed down to turn onto a cross street, Cedric knew he had his chance.

He pulled up to the large van's bumper, then its doors. He was less than a foot away from its side, moving at nearly the same speed.

Then he was moving past it and just barely in front of it. The wrath at the wheel would have no choice but to stop, swerve quickly, or hit Cedric's moped. Cedric wasn't quite sure which option it would choose. But he'd find out in a few seconds, when he either cleared the vehicle or was hit by several hundred pounds of screaming metal.

Cedric kept his eyes open as his moped cut directly into the path of the wraths' van. He gritted his teeth as he heard the sound of squealing, then smelled something acrid in the air. The van was turning quickly, its wheels dragging sideways against the pavement as its front end missed Cedric's moped by inches.

Cedric had to swerve before he hit the shoulder of the road.

He didn't quite make it in time. One second he was on the bike's seat, and the next he was flying through the air.

Cedric hit the ground hard, landing on his shoulder and hip and then rolling once, twice, three times through the grass. He pushed himself up off the ground to see the wrath's vehicle skidding sideways on the road, leaving behind a light trail of smoke and black marks on the pavement.

With a grunt, Cedric got to his feet. He could feel that the entire left side of his body would be black and blue in a few hours, and the gash in his leg was still bleeding. But he could take care of those things later. He ran as quickly as he could on his injured leg toward the back of the vehicle.

It was only as he got nearer that Cedric realized he no longer had his sword on him—it must have fallen clear when he'd been thrown from the moped. He whirled quickly, looking for its silver shine, but couldn't see it in the tall grass lining the road. There wasn't time to search for it. He might only have a matter of moments before the wraths straightened the van and took off again.

But just as Cedric reached the back door of the vehicle, it opened. Cedric stopped in a fighting stance, ready to face whatever creature jumped out at him. Instead, it was Liv who tumbled out of the seat and onto the ground. She looked up at him blearily, her pupils nearly overtaking the green-brown of her eyes.

"Ced . . . ," she started, blinking heavily.

He knelt down to her. "It's okay, I've got you."

"Cedric, there's . . . there's . . ." Her eyes closed again, almost as though she'd fallen asleep mid-sentence.

The two front doors of the van burst open, a wrath jumping out of each side.

Cedric was just barely able to move Liv behind him and face the wrath nearest to him as it punched out with one hand. Cedric blocked the punch with difficulty. His whole body felt tired. And there were three wraths in the van, and he had no—

"Weapons," Liv whispered from the ground. She struggled to sit up as Cedric dodged another blow. The other two wraths were rounding the other side of the boxy vehicle.

"Inside." Liv pointed toward the interior of the vehicle. Cedric looked inside the van and saw a stack of gleaming, shining metal sitting there just beneath the fabric seat. It felt like looking into a mirage, or a dream. There were swords and axes and knives. All he needed to do was reach one.

Cedric dove inside the van and shut the door behind him just as the three wraths all converged where he had been standing. He reached into the pile of weapons that were strewn across the seat and picked one up at random—a thick sword as long as his arm. It would have to do. Quickly, he opened the door on the other side of the van and jumped out again, racing around the front to meet the wraths head on.

They were already there, anger twisting up their faces.

But Cedric had a weapon now. He swung back his arm and slashed it down toward the first wrath's neck—

Only to watch it bounce right off.

Almost as if the creature's neck were made of rock, or as if the sword were made of . . . what was it called? Plastic?

Cedric looked down at his weapon with a sudden under-standing. It wasn't real metal, but a fake. Completely harmless. Completely useless.

Why in hell would wraths have fake weapons?

But there wasn't time to think about that. All three of the wraths were circling Cedric now, the nearest one grinning at the plastic sword in his hand. It reached into the leather holster at its side and pulled out a very sharp, very real knife. One that could cut through Cedric's fake weapon—and his skin—in half a second.

The wrath with the knife smiled as the others closed in on Cedric. He gripped his ridiculous weapon tight in one hand. It might be worth less than a twig, but it was all he had.

The first wrath lunged at Cedric, and he ducked low, jab-bing his fake sword up into the creature's midsection. The plastic edge bent in half, but it still slowed the wrath in his tracks. The only problem now was the other two. . . .

A buzzing noise distracted Cedric, and he looked up quickly to see a dark shape come sailing toward him. It was Liv, hunched down over the handlebars of Cedric's moped. She was coming straight for their group.

The wraths spun to face Liv as she got closer. One jumped out of the way to avoid being mowed down, but another charged right for her. She was close enough that Cedric could see her grit her teeth and scrunch her shoulders before turning the moped slightly and running it over the wrath's blocky foot.

The moped squealed and stopped, and Liv wobbled a bit on top of it.

"Cedric," she gasped. "Get on!"

He didn't have to be told twice. He got to her in two large leaps, just barely missing the grasp of the wrath with the knife, who reached out to catch him. Instead, the wrath got hold of the sleeve of his shirt, tearing it completely as Cedric wrenched himself away and threw himself on the moped behind Liv. She turned the bike and sped off just as Cedric felt a knife whiz past his ear.

The moped sputtered as it moved, carrying them down the street at a speed barely faster than running.

"They will catch up to us," Cedric said, his mouth up against Liv's ear as he tried to lean forward, as if pushing ahead with his own weight could make the bike speed up.

"Something's wrong with it," Liv said.

She was right; the moped was making a loud, clunking noise as they moved at half speed over the pavement. But the bike wasn't the only problem. Liv was less steering the moped than hanging on for dear life, her shoulders slumping down lower and lower. The bike wobbled as her head dropped down onto one shoulder. Cedric had to press himself up against her back and put his hands over hers on the handles, straightening the bike and keeping it moving forward.

Over the clangs of the bike, Cedric could still hear the wraths in pursuit behind them. He looked over his shoulder to see one wrath chasing him, while the other two were piling back in the vehicle. The moped was just barely outpacing the wrath on foot, and Cedric whirled back around, leaning forward to will the bike to go faster. He took a corner onto a side street, and when he looked around again, the wrath behind him was circling back to join the others. The vehicle would be able to catch up to them in a matter of moments.

Liv's head drooped and snapped up, the weight of her body leaning dangerously to the right. The cage of Cedric's arms was the only thing keeping her upright on the moped. They wouldn't make it much farther.

That's when Cedric saw it—a small row of bushes lining the front of someone's yard, protected by a set of black and blue bins. He quickly maneuvered the bike off the road and behind the bins, lifting Liv off the seat and dropping them both to the ground beside the bushes.

Cedric moved as close to Liv as he possibly could, hunching his shoulders down low over her body and hoping against hope the bins were sufficiently blocking the moped from the road. It was only a few seconds before he heard the van speed around the corner with a squeal. He held his breath as it got nearer and nearer, trying to see through the thick green and brown of the hedges. The van was right in front of them, then passing by, then moving quickly down the street.

Cedric let out a long, jagged breath. But he knew they weren't totally safe. The wraths would figure out that the moped couldn't have gotten away from them so easily, and they would probably double back. Still, he couldn't find it in himself to get up. One entire side of his body was throbbing, the cut on his thigh still bleeding. Inches away from him, Liv's eyes fluttered. She turned just a bit, rotating her body so she was facing Cedric.

"There you are," she whispered.

"Here I am," Cedric replied, reaching out one hand and gently resting it against the side of her head. "You're hurt."

Liv nodded. "My head hit a wall."

Her eyes found his, and she seemed to struggle to focus them. Her pupils were still unnaturally large, but at least now Cedric could make out the color around them. "You saved me," she said. "Again."

Cedric smiled. "And you saved me. Again."

"Anytime," she said, slightly slurring the word. Then the smile slipped from her face, and her eyebrows pulled together. "The wraths said something . . . they were going to take me to the castle? Or *a* castle? It was hard to hear because my ears were all fuzzy." Liv gave a sloppy, too-loud laugh. If Cedric didn't know any better, he might have thought she'd spent the whole morning drinking mead.

"Fuzzy ears," she repeated, giggling.

"Shh, we can talk about this later—"

"But they were going to take me back. To your world. They said 'castle.' What would Malquin be doing back there?"

Cedric shook his head. Every time he thought about Malquin, rage buzzed through him, making it hard to think of anything else. Could Malquin really be back in Caelum? He had no more army there, no more power . . . He stopped himself from wondering. Thinking of Malquin clouded his mind, and he had too much to focus on right now—trying to listen for the wraths' van turning around, and trying to keep Liv quiet in case they did.

But delirious Liv had other ideas.

"Cedric," she continued, her eyes going wide as she looked up at him, "Your face is *so* close right now."

"That's because we are hiding for our lives."

Liv sighed. "We're always doing that. But now that you're right here . . . I mean right *here* . . ." She put one hand up to the side of his face. Cedric froze, looking down at her suddenly still expression. "I maybe shouldn't say this right now, 'cause I'm a little woozy and also I think there might be two of you, but . . . I can't keep not saying the things I want to say 'cause I'm scared of what you'll say back, you know?"

He did know. Even though her words were slipping into nonsense, every part of him wanted to hear what she had to say. His heart beat rapidly, and he was torn between his need to keep watch and his desire to focus on nothing but her.

"You don't have to say anything right now," Cedric forced himself to say.

"I do," Liv responded. She blinked hard. "We've been avoiding talking about it, about the portals . . . and what happens when we close them forever."

"Liv—"

"I don't want to never see you again," she said, putting some force behind her words so they'd come out clearly. "That sucked so much, saying good-bye to you in Caelum. When I came back here, I thought I saw you everywhere."

Liv's hand was still against Cedric's face, and her thumb made a small circle over his cheekbone.

"Did you see me everywhere?"

Cedric put his hand over hers, his fingers touching against

her finger near his temple. "I saw you here," he said, tapping the side of his head. "Every minute."

Liv smiled. "And now you're here. You came back. And I don't want you to tell me you have to go again." Her words were slurring more now, despite her obvious effort. Her eyes began to droop. "I know it's selfish, and I shouldn't say it . . . but I'd rather hide behind these garbage cans with you forever than have to say good-bye again."

Her eyes sank lower as her voice faded off.

"Liv?"

Her eyes popped open again. "Do you hear that?"

Cedric lifted his head slightly, and he did hear it—the sound of a vehicle getting closer. Were the wraths doubling back?

"We have to go," he said. "Can you stand?"

"Maybe. But what happens after that?" she asked, her voice fading away again.

Cedric's mind raced. There was no way he'd get Liv all the way back to Malibu on a moped, not with her like this. He suddenly remembered the car in the driveway back at the house where they'd met Henry Martin. Maybe the keys were somewhere inside. . . .

The sound of a car motor was getting nearer. It was going slowly—probably looking for them.

"We'll have to slip behind the houses. Come on."

With some difficulty, Cedric hauled Liv to her feet and walked her quickly behind the nearest house, leaving their hiding spot and everything they'd said there behind.

MISSION: IMPOSSIBLE

Henry Martin was dead.

He was lying on the living room floor of the OC house, his body half on the rug, one foot extended into the fireplace. A pool of blood was congealing under his head.

Liv stared down at him, a wave of nausea overtaking her. If she didn't sit down soon, she was definitely going to throw up. But she couldn't move. For two whole months, her mission had been clear: find the Knight called Martin, then save the city. Maybe the world. And after all that searching, she'd finally found him. He'd been on the verge of giving them the answers they needed, and now . . .

He wouldn't be giving them anything now.

Liv had hit a wall—in more ways than one—and she didn't know what to do next. Her whole body was still as she stared at the unmoving form of Henry Martin. Or what *was* Henry Martin. Another dead Knight. So many dead Knights.

"What do we do now?" she whispered, then swallowed

against the bile rising in her throat. She sensed that Cedric was moving behind her, but she couldn't remember what he was doing. Looking for something? She should help him, but she couldn't move, couldn't tear her eyes away from their last chance to fix things, lying dead at her feet.

"Liv." She heard Cedric behind her, urgent, low. "We have to find those car keys. The wraths will be back at any second. Where are keys generally stored?"

Liv's mind spun. It felt like her thoughts were whirring around her, and she was unable to catch and hold on to a single one. Her tongue felt thick. She really needed to sit down.

"Liv?" That urgent voice again. More footsteps. Out of the corner of her eye, Liv saw Cedric pick up a vaseful of fake flowers and empty it, then look inside.

"The keys, Liv. We need those keys."

Liv swayed on her feet. She was going down. She lowered herself, as gently as she could, to her knees. She was careful to keep away from the pool of blood. Her eyes stayed transfixed on Henry Martin, on their last hope.

"Please," Cedric said, kneeling down low across from her, on the other side of the body. "I know you're upset, but we *have* to leave."

Liv knew she had to focus, had to concentrate. . . . Her hand went to the edge of Henry Martin's pants pocket, and she realized she wasn't breathing. If she exhaled now, she would definitely throw up. Carefully, keeping her line of sight just a few inches above the spot where Henry Martin lay, she reached her hand into his pocket. Her fingers closed firmly over a thin piece of metal, and she forced herself to pull them out again.

She splayed her palm, holding the keys up to Cedric. He looked down at them for a moment, eyes wide now with amazement.

"Let's go," he said, gently. "Can you stand?"

She could.

⊁+⊹⊰

It was barely nighttime, but the Malibu house was already dark. Or maybe it just *felt* dark. Liv's nausea had been gone for a few hours, but she couldn't shake the feeling of low-level dread that had crept in just under her skin.

She'd managed to stay awake enough to guide Cedric back to Malibu, even stopping at a pay phone to call the police in Orange County and give them an anonymous tip about Henry Martin.

As soon as they got back to the house, Joe and the others had immediately taken out the first-aid kit and seen to Cedric's and Liv's wounds. Fortunately, the gash on Cedric's leg wouldn't need stitches, and Liv had only suffered a bump on the head. After some aspirin and water and a few hours' rest she was feeling physically better, though Joe told her she'd have to stay awake for the next twenty-four hours just in case she had a concussion.

Which gave her plenty of time to think of all the ways they were screwed.

"Did Henry Martin have anything with him? Any papers or books, anything that might help us?" Joe asked. He was sitting in an armchair in the Malibu house. Liv, Cedric, Merek,

Shannon, and Peter sat scattered nearby.

Liv shook her head gently. "We didn't have time to look."

"The car we took was his," Cedric added. "But there was nothing inside apart from an old bagful of clothes."

Joe's shoulders fell as he leaned back against his chair.

"Henry Martin talked about a way of bringing magic back to Earth permanently—restoring the balance to stop all this destruction," Liv said, repeating the information she'd already told them all. "He just didn't get a chance to tell us *how*."

"The how is kind of important," Shannon put in from her spot on the floor, where she was eating from a can of cold SpaghettiOs with a spoon.

"Kind of very important," Liv said.

"Did he say anything else? Anything at all?" Joe asked.

Liv tried to remember. She still wasn't thinking as clearly as she could; her head felt like it was wrapped in gauze, her thoughts muted. "We need to use the magic to do it, that's all he said."

"He also mentioned that Liv is a scroll," Cedric said, leaning forward from his spot next to her on the couch. He hadn't left her side since helping her out of Henry Martin's house. "He said it as though . . . as though she would be important in fixing things."

"Hold on." Peter said. "Didn't Malquin tell you before, Liv, that there's a little bit of magic *inside* of us? The Knights put it there in our markings to open the first portal. And maybe there's a way they can use it now, manipulate it somehow . . . ?" Peter's voice trailed off. He didn't have the answers they needed—the only person who had those answers was gone.

"Manipulating magic . . ." Cedric's voice was low, almost as though he were talking to himself. "Mathilde said something like that to me. She said that when the Knights first created the portal to Caelum all those generations ago, they did it by manipulating magic. It took hundreds of them, she said, and they accidentally created a whole world instead of just opening a portal to one, but they were able to use their belief in magic to get it done."

"Well, if Knights hundreds of years ago could use magic to do what they wanted, why can't they do it now?" Shannon asked. "I'm sure they'd help us if it meant keeping the world from being destroyed."

"You mean the Knights who've been mysteriously disappearing and showing up dead for the past two months?" Merek asked.

"Oh . . . yeah."

"Malquin is definitely behind that," Liv said. "Those wraths who showed up were looking for one of the Knights of Valere who lived there, a woman. They'd already . . . turned . . . her husband."

She fought back a shudder, thinking of the fair-haired Knight with his black eyes. It was hard to believe he'd been a man just recently.

"We still do not know how Malquin is managing that. Turning humans into wraths?" Merek asked.

"I think the *how* is less important than the *why*," Cedric said.

"He's right," Liv added. "It's not just one lone Knight they've turned anymore—Malquin's up to something. And it can't be something good."

"I can ask him," Joe said, his voice ringing out clear in the stifling room.

"Joe, you can't," Liv said. "We don't even know where he is."

"He might even be in Caelum," Cedric put in, his voice still tight.

"That's true, I forgot," Liv added. "The wraths . . . my head was kind of fuzzy at the time, but right after they took me, they said something about going to a castle . . . Malquin might not even be in LA anymore."

"He still has wraths here looking for you . . . and he knows I'd stay with you, which means they'll be looking for me, too," Joe said. "My old apartment, my work—if they're tracking me at all, I can find them, and get to John—"

"Even if you could, Joe, we have no idea how many wraths are working with him," Liv said. She felt her voice growing louder, more anxious. She just couldn't risk it, losing Joe to Malquin. "The ones we came across today, they weren't messing around."

"We barely got away," Cedric replied. "And Henry Martin didn't."

Joe sucked in a breath, but pushed on. "I hear what you're saying, but . . . I might be able to reach him. I'm his brother."

"And he's a killer."

"So was Henry Martin, and we were going to trust him," Joe said.

"It's not the same, Joe," she said gently. "What Henry did was a horrible thing, but Malquin . . . he has no remorse for anything. He'll never help us, and he'll kill again; I know he will. He could kill *you*."

For a moment, Joe looked like he was going to continue arguing. But finally, he sighed and ran a hand through his hair. "You're right. It's not worth it."

A tense silence fell over the room.

"Okay," Liv said slowly, trying to get the conversation back on track. "So Malquin is turning the Knights into wraths. And we need the Knights—maybe hundreds of them—in order to manipulate magic. In order to, somehow, create a spell or something that will stop the Quelling, turning off the planet's giant immune system and saving both worlds."

Liv paused to look at the others.

"I'm following you," Peter said, nodding.

"Okay, so . . . let's say we somehow manage to find that many . . . we track down those who haven't been killed or kidnapped or turned, and we get them to help us."

"Right," Shannon said.

"Then what?" Liv asked. "How would we actually *do* this?"

Once again, silence fell over the room. No one had an answer.

As they sat in the darkness, the heat seemed to press down on them more with every passing second. The orange sky turned darker and more sickly-looking outside. They'd already run out of answers.

And soon, they would run out of time.

LET THE RIGHT ONE IN

The mood in the house was still pretty low when everyone decided to call it a night a few hours later. Shannon had volunteered to stay up with Liv and keep her from nodding off. The only problem with that plan was that Shannon kept dozing off herself.

Liv sat on the twin bed across from her as light filtered in from the window, casting the room in a burnt-looking glow. Both girls had flashlights in their hands, but Shannon's light kept drooping lower and lower as the muscles in the hand went limp—

"Shannon!" Liv called out.

Shannon's head snapped up, the flashlight beam flicking wildly around the walls. "I'm up, I'm up."

But almost immediately, her eyelids started droop again.

"You don't have to stay up with me all night," Liv said. "I'll be fine."

"No, no, no, I'm up," Shannon said, her words slightly slurring. "I'm a good friend."

"You definitely are. But I'll really be okay. Just lie down for a bit."

"No, I'm good," Shannon said, even though her body was already leaning nearer and nearer to the pillow. "If I can fight off monsters, then I can certainly . . . keep my eyes . . . open . . ."

Liv smiled and shook her head as Shannon slumped over on the bed.

Honestly, she didn't mind having a few minutes alone to think about things. Now that her mind felt clearer, it whirled around the million problems and questions that had been stacking up in it. For so long, she'd had a single mission to focus on. In Caelum, it was to find Peter and get home. Then back in LA, it was to find Henry Martin. But now—now she'd hit a dead end. Literally.

And then there was the hazy memory of what she'd said to Cedric while hiding from the wraths. She'd almost be able to write it off as something she'd dreamed, or maybe even hallucinated in her half-concussed state, but . . .

She knew better. She cringed as she remembered some of the things she'd said, the naked, unfiltered truth of them, and she tried hard to remember how Cedric had reacted to her spilling her guts. She pictured his face, hovering above hers . . . had he been happy to hear how much she'd missed him? In her memory of that moment, his face was a frustrating blank. Like her brain was missing that piece.

He'd asked her to be quiet more than once, she remembered. She'd brought up the portals, and not wanting to say good-bye when they closed them forever . . . except . . . Henry

Martin had said closing the portals couldn't fix things. Which meant . . .

Stop. Liv told herself, leaning up against the wall. She couldn't think about what would happen *after* they fixed things. First, she had to figure out how to fix them at all. Which meant running up against that dead end again and again until something started to give.

Liv started tallying up the list of possible actions to take. That usually helped her figure out how to make a decision, even when the world continued to take her choices away one by one. As a foster kid, she'd always had little say over what happened in her own life, but making a list of those things she could control had always seemed to help, even if just a little.

So, number one: gather an army of magic-believing Knights to help bring balance back to the world(s) . . . somehow. This would involve not only finding all the Knights left in existence, but getting to them.

And number two—there was no number two. If they just did nothing, or ran away, Liv would be giving up Los Angeles as a loss. And what would happen to Caelum if they didn't bring some sort of balance back to the two worlds, allowing magic to flow freely between them? Would Cedric's home just wither up and die? So no—there was no second option. Liv's headache was coming back with a vengeance. Her brain was running in circles. She needed to get out of this bed, she needed to talk this all through with someone . . .

No, not just someone.

Liv crept out of bed, careful not to wake Shannon. She

walked quietly down the hall to the farthest room on the right. She smoothed down her sweat-dampened hair and opened the bedroom door.

Cedric was awake.

He sat up in bed the moment Liv stepped into the room, his shoulders, head, and stomach a dark outline in the gloom. His posture was tense and alert, until he saw it was Liv who moved quietly into his room and shut the door behind her.

"Hi," Liv whispered.

A pause stretched across the small room.

"Hi," Cedric responded.

Liv knew he was looking at her, though it was difficult to make out his face. It was less difficult to make out the fact that he wasn't wearing a shirt. Shadows played over his muscles as he moved, and Liv could alternately make out bits of his shoulders, his stomach, the taut area of skin right where he held a single sheet bunched up near his hips.

Liv cleared her throat.

"Did you . . . need something?" Cedric asked.

"Shannon fell asleep."

"Ah."

"And I figured if you were up, maybe you could help to, uh . . ."

"Keep you awake?"

"Um, yeah . . . ," Liv replied, at the same moment Cedric said, "With talking. Keep you awake with talking."

"Yes, talking is definitely what I meant," Liv said, giving a little laugh.

"Did . . . you want to sit?" Cedric asked, gesturing to the edge of the bed.

Seeing Cedric half naked and tangled up in bedsheets had the effect of scrambling Liv's thoughts even more.

"Uh," Liv started, her train of thought completely pulling out of the station and leaving her behind on a platform of hormones. Cedric stared at her, expectant. He moved slightly over on the bed, making space for her. He didn't pull the sheet up, though, damn him.

Liv hesitated—for about a half second.

"Okay."

She moved to sit next to him, her head against the backboard. She was wearing only a tank top and sleep shorts. And who knew what Cedric had on under that sheet. This close, she could feel the heat coming off of him, the slight dampness of his skin.

"What did you want to talk about?" Cedric asked.

Liv swallowed. Just that morning, she'd wanted to avoid having a real conversation with Cedric at all costs, afraid of where that conversation would lead. But now, all she wanted to do was talk to him—not just about everything they were facing, or what would happen in the future, but everything in the world. Whether he'd go with her to Six Flags. His opinions on thin versus thick pizza crust. His favorite color. What he'd really been thinking when she spilled her guts out to him behind that bush . . .

Focus, Liv, she commanded herself.

"Remember in Caelum, when we got into that fight and I

took off into the woods with Rafe?"

Cedric gave a small laugh. "That is not the type of thing one forgets."

"Right. Well, I think my mistake . . . I mean, one of my mistakes, was in thinking my own plan was better than anyone else's. I should have just been honest with you, talked it out—"

"I was not exactly ready to listen," Cedric admitted.

"Sure, but still. I've had enough of keeping things to myself. We're better when we work together, right?"

"I believe so," Cedric said. When he exhaled, his breath hit Liv's arm.

"Okay, good," Liv said. She struggled to keep her breathing steady. Could Cedric hear her heart pounding from where he sat? "So . . . let's talk it out. This whole mess. Maybe we'll come up with an idea if we just keep working on it. We'll stay up all night if we have to, which, technically, I do."

A pause, then Cedric's breath again on her arm. "I would like that."

Liv looked away, glad the darkness between them could hide the color she knew was rising to her face.

"It just feels like there's a piece of the puzzle still missing," Liv said slowly, refusing to be distracted again. "So we know how the portals were first created. That old lady in Caelum knew that if we opened too many of them, bad things would happen to both of our worlds. And Henry Martin believed— maybe—that there was a way everything could be fixed with magic. But what we're still missing—"

"Is how," Cedric filled in. "How to find enough people who

believe in magic like the Knights did centuries ago."

Liv sighed and looked out the window. "You'd think that if there were a time to believe in magic, it would be now."

"Is it possible," Cedric asked, "to convince people that magic is responsible for what is happening outside?"

Liv thought about it a moment, then shook her head. "I don't think so. I mean, climate change has been affecting our world for years, and lots of the people in this country don't believe in it. And that's *science*. Trying to get enough people to believe in magic so we can do . . . whatever it is we have to do? Even if it was possible, even if I knew how, there's no way they'd listen to me. I'm just some nobody teenage girl. I mean, I barely even have fifty Twitter followers—"

"You're wrong," Cedric whispered, cutting Liv off.

Her eyebrows furrowed. "No, seriously, last I checked it was, like, forty-seven—"

"I mean, you are wrong when you say you're nobody. You are several hundred things, Liv, but you could never be nobody."

Liv's breath caught in her throat. When she looked over at Cedric, he seemed even closer than he had been before.

"You must know that," Cedric said.

Liv smiled. "I guess. But it's still nice to hear it." She took a shaky breath. Why be shy now? "And it's nice to sit here with you, like this, even if it's a million degrees in this room."

"Agreed."

"We should . . . do this more often. While we can, I mean."

His face was closer now, close enough to blur around the edges. She could still see the brightness of his eyes, and how his pupils dilated as he moved closer.

"Talk?" he asked.

She inched nearer to him, so her arm pressed against his. She could feel his legs through the sheet.

"Right. Talk . . ." Her voice grew faint. "Or . . ."

His skin was so hot that she wondered briefly if he had a fever. But no, she was just as warm as they moved closer together, eliminating the space between them. As her mouth found his. As his fingers curled around the back of her neck and held tight there. As all of the problems she'd been worried about slipped away one by one.

Liv barely had time to notice that not only was Cedric's chest bare; his neck was, too. His golden betrothal ring no longer hung there from a chain. Then even that observation flitted out of her mind.

And once again, they were done with talking.

NIGHTCRAWLER

Deep into the early hours of morning, Liv was having trouble keeping herself awake. The temperature in the small bedroom seemed to only be going up, and even though she'd kicked the sheets off long ago, her tank top and shorts were stuck to her body. Part of her longed to get up, but a bigger part wanted to stay exactly where she was—curled up on her side with Cedric lying at her back. One of his long arms stretched over the space between her ribs and her hips. The weight of it was immensely comforting, like hot cocoa on a rainy day, but times a thousand.

Even though he'd tried—pretty valiantly—to stay awake, Cedric had eventually faded. Liv had meant to wake him, but she didn't want to move, didn't want to stop feeling his long, even breaths hit her skin at the exact place where her hair met her neck. She wanted to just lie here like this, safe, until the sky turned back to blue and the world turned back to normal.

And then maybe a few days more.

A bead of sweat dripped down her forehead, and Liv very

gently moved her arm to wipe it away. That's when she saw a flash of yellow light come through the window and scan across the wall. It almost looked like—headlights?

Joe.

The thought came to her instantly, and she knew it was true before she sat up carefully to look out the window to see the familiar Jeep in the driveway, lights on. Liv couldn't see through the darkened windshield, but she knew it was Joe in there. And, in a flash, she knew where he was going.

Idiot, she thought. How could she have believed that Joe would give up on his plan to find his brother and talk some reason into him? Joe thought every problem in the world could be solved by talking reasonably. She thought back to how easily he'd given in when they'd tried to convince him not to find his brother. Of course he was going to do it anyway. Wouldn't she have done the same reckless thing if one of her own siblings were on the line?

She carefully and quietly slipped off the bed and toward the door. Cedric rolled over once, snorting as he did so, and Liv wanted to smile at how innocent and *ordinary* he looked, lying on a tiny twin bed under a video game poster. It was hard to believe the boy lying in that bed was a king. Harder still to believe he could in any way be hers.

She thought for a moment about waking him up, but she knew the only person who could stop Joe from leaving was her.

So, tearing her gaze away from Cedric, Liv opened the door and sped lightly through the house and out the front door.

The Jeep's headlights were focused directly on her, so she

had to lift her hand up to her eyes to try to see through the windshield. She knew that, inside, Joe could see her. After a few seconds, the door opened and he stepped out.

"Joe," Liv said, moving forward carefully on bare feet. "Please don't do this."

She could only see Joe's frame silhouetted against the rust-brown sky. His head dipped down, but he didn't come closer.

"I can't imagine what you must be feeling right now," Liv went on. "And I know that you want to reach Mal . . . John. I know that because it's what you do, every day. You try to save people. Like you always saved me."

Liv's voice broke as she thought about how in the past ten years, after all the stupid stunts she'd pulled—running from foster homes, living on the street, lying, taking off to other worlds—Joe had never given up on her. Even in a foster system that seemed so impersonal, he'd always been a caring force. He'd always understood why she hated getting new placements and having to change schools, why she hated having every decision made for her.

So how could she turn around and tell him that he should ignore every instinct that made him . . . him? How could she try to make this decision for him, when she knew exactly how terrible that felt?

And yet, how could she let him go after Malquin and get himself killed? Even if it wasn't fair, she had to try. She had to beg.

"But, Joe . . . we can't lose you from this fight. *I* can't lose you."

Liv took another step forward at the same time Joe sighed. He looked off in the distance past Liv, as if he were looking for answers in the ocean waves, and then he nodded. Hope flared up inside of her. But as she took another step closer, Joe moved back, reaching a hand toward the Jeep's door handle.

"Please," Liv said, hearing the desperation in her voice. "Please, Joe, please don't try to find him."

That's when Joe froze. Liv moved around the front of the Jeep, finally out of the glare of the headlights. Joe turned toward her, one hand still on the door handle.

"Too late," he said.

Despite the sweltering heat, everything in Liv's body turned to ice. That voice—it wasn't Joe's voice. It might have sounded like him, but it was—empty. Like it was lacking a key element. The element of Joe.

Without breathing, Liv took one more step forward, and that's when she saw his eyes. Not the warm brown eyes she'd known for years. These eyes were hollow. Vacant.

Pools of inky black.

Liv felt like her brain was short-circuiting. She couldn't move to run, she couldn't remember to breathe. Her mouth opened, and she thought she might scream. But that's when heavy arms circled her from behind, clamping a large cloth over her mouth. She tried to fight back, kicking and yelling and scratching, but the arms were too strong.

As she struggled, the thing in front of her that was no longer Joe calmly opened up the back door of the Jeep.

⊱┼┼⊰

Liv stayed conscious during the entire ride through the abandoned, darkened streets of LA. Her mouth, hands, and feet were tightly bound. The creatures in the Jeep hadn't thought to cover her eyes, though, and she could see every turn they took as they made their way slowly through the city.

Joe sat right next to Liv, and she couldn't stop herself from trying to look into his eyes. He had to be in there somewhere, still . . . didn't he? She willed him to look at her so she could see something, anything there she recognized. The disappointment when she did something stupid, the anger when a foster family treated her poorly, the guilt when he'd first told her about his past. But there were no emotions in Joe's eyes—there was nothing.

How was this possible? How could this monster be wearing Joe's face? Liv thought she'd already felt the worst pain in her life the day her parents were killed. But this, to see Joe sitting next to her, there but gone, that was a new kind of pain.

If her mouth hadn't been gagged, she would have screamed herself raw. But instead, all that came out was a muffled, moaning noise. Not-Joe had to have heard her, but he made zero reaction. He sat, stiff, eyes forward, for the entire ride.

Liv couldn't remember ever feeling so alone.

And the others were sleeping in the house, maybe for hours. No one even knew she'd gone. She imagined Cedric waking up to an empty spot next to him, going to look for her, finding nothing there. What would he think?

Eventually, the Jeep turned onto Melrose Avenue. It made its way past darkened and shuttered boutiques and vegan restaurants, past abandoned cars and tipped-over trash cans. Down one side street, Liv could see another Gravity Incident, marked off with caution tape. She could just barely make out a park bench floating in the air before they passed it.

The Jeep slowed as it neared a tall green hedge lining the side of the road and then turned into a business driveway. In front of them was a small guard hut with a long wooden arm that was meant to raise and lower to let people onto the property. Only the arm had clearly been smashed through, and was now just a broken piece of wood dangling onto the pavement. The car made its way toward the guard hut quickly, driving under a large double-arch bearing a familiar sign in cursive: "Paramount Studios."

"What the—?" Liv mumbled into her gag.

No one answered her.

Just months before, it would have been a dream come true for Liv to finally be on the grounds of an actual movie studio. But now, the moment barely counted as surreal. Just like everywhere else in the city, the studio lot was abandoned. Liv highly doubted anyone would have stuck around a semi-apocalypse just to finish up reshoots on the latest *Teenage Mutant Ninja Turtles* sequel.

Some golf carts were strewn along the side of the street, and a giant parking lot sat mostly empty, the Paramount water tower standing tall like a defunct sentinel. They made their way past tan-colored buildings and an entire backlot designed to look like a New York City block before stopping in front of a massive building labeled "Stage 18."

Joe barely looked at Liv as he hauled her out of the Jeep, the other wrath following behind. He pushed her through a small side door in the soundstage.

The interior of the stage was enormous, one large room that was three stories high, with metal rafters barely visible in the ceiling. But what caught Liv's attention wasn't just the scope of the room, but what was *inside* of it.

A castle.

It sprouted up in the middle of the room, its tallest spires reaching nearly to the top of the ceiling. With its stone walls, battlements, and thick wooden doors, it looked like it belonged in Caelum. It could practically pass for a mini replica of Cedric's home.

That is, until Liv looked closer and was able to take in more detail—how some parts of the castle ceiling were completely gone, revealing the sets in the rooms below, and how other parts of the ceiling were covered in cardboard. How the blue sky surrounding the castle was painted onto a backdrop. How one of the giant wooden doors was ripped in half, revealing its white Styrofoam center. Up close, it was easy to see how fake everything really was. Not that it mattered, really—the danger was just as real.

The room teemed with wraths, more than Liv could count. Some stood apart; some stood in groups. Some chatted with one another; some scowled alone. A few sparred while others tore into the bags of potato chips that covered a table at the far end of the room. Liv's heart dropped. Even if Cedric and the others had realized she was gone by now (which seemed unlikely, given that it was still the dead of night), and even if they could figure out where she was (unlikelier), they would never be able to take on this many wraths themselves. They'd be massacred.

Just as Liv was getting her bearings, Joe threw her down to the cement floor, hard. With her hands still bound, her elbows took most of the hit, and she cried out against her gag as a sharp pain shot up her arm. Her head landed on something crinkly, and she turned to get a closer look.

It was a script, crumpled and half-torn. The title page read "KING ARTHUR VS. THE UNDEAD." Liv vaguely remembered reading about the project on *Deadline*—some sort of zombie retelling of Camelot. She had thought it sounded kind of cool at the time.

Suddenly, the script was pulled out from under Liv's head. She tilted up as far as she could to see someone walk past her.

It was Malquin. He barely cast her a second glance, instead sneering at the script's title page with disdain.

"Can you believe this garbage? I suppose it makes sense, given that its executive producer was secretly a member of a fanatical cult bent on killing magical children. That kind of multitasking leads to shoddy work," he said, throwing the script back to the ground. "At least he let me know about this place. Before he died."

Liv tried to yell against her gag, but Malquin just talked over her.

"But honestly, I can't *believe* what's happened to cinema in the years I've been away. As if the glut of superhero movies wasn't enough, now there's all this zombie tripe. It's almost enough to make me wish I'd stayed in a medieval dimension with no plumbing."

Liv scoffed. Malquin tipped his head toward Joe, who knelt down and undid the knot of the fabric tied around Liv's jaw. She carefully kept her gaze averted as Joe knelt down, knowing that if she looked into the blankness of his eyes, she'd start to cry again.

Instead, she forced herself to look up to Malquin. "Of course you'd be a movie snob. You're evil."

Malquin gave a tinkling little laugh. "Evil? I guess I understand how you'd believe that, what with you being tied up on the floor at my feet. But, Liv, try to see things from my side, would you? 'Evil' is a bit strong. Just look at everything I've done for these wraths! I brought them to a whole new world, and I even set up base in this falling-down joke of a prop to make them feel a little more at home. Because I care."

Liv gritted her teeth. "And what you did to Joe? He's your *brother*."

Malquin shrugged. "My brother is perfectly fine. He's standing right there, as you can see."

"That's not Joe," Liv whispered.

"Well, that's a matter of opinion," Malquin replied. "I could have killed Joe after how he abandoned me. I *should* have. I knew he would come crawling back eventually, looking to apologize, looking to 'save' me. Took longer than I thought it would, honestly. I was just about to tell the wraths staking out his apartment to give up. And then he shows up tonight, sure enough, looking for me. Like I knew he would. All these years

317

later, and I still know exactly what my little brother will do to ease some of his own guilt. It was my right to do whatever I wanted with him, and I showed him mercy. Which, again, supports my *not* being evil."

"Joe had—has—nothing to feel guilty for," Liv said, again carefully avoiding looking in Joe's direction. As long as she kept *her* Joe and whatever this creature was separate in her mind, she'd avoid dissolving into a useless mess.

Malquin's eyes narrowed. "You have no idea what you're talking about," he said. But he was angry now—and talking. Liv knew how he loved to talk. As soon as Malquin looked over at Not-Joe, Liv tried quietly shifting her hands around, hoping there was some way to get a finger or two free from the ropes that bound her without drawing the attention of any nearby wraths.

Malquin was still looking at Joe with disdain. But the thing that used to be Joe stood, solid and indifferent, under his brother's glare. "Things would have been so different if he'd just come with me when he said he would. The two of us together in Caelum, looking out for each other, helping each other . . . but he left me to go alone."

Malquin glanced at his own withered arm, and his expression turned stony. But in a blink, it softened, and he shook his head as if shaking off a negative thought.

"But that's not even the worst of it. An instant of cowardice? That, I could maybe forgive. But he knew what was happening here. He knew the Knights were bent on killing more scrolls. Just like they killed Eric. And he did nothing to stop them."

Wrath Joe continued staring forward. If any of Malquin's words were affecting him, he didn't let it show.

"That's not true," Liv spat. If Joe couldn't defend himself, the least she could do was speak up for him. "He saved me and my brother and sister—"

"Did he?" Malquin said. "He separated you, lied to you, put you into different homes. And how did your life go then, Liv? What was it like growing up without parents?"

Liv stopped pulling against her bindings, her whole body going still.

"Do you know they might still be alive if Joe had just fulfilled the promise we made to each other?"

Malquin was watching her with a kind of burning intensity that made her feel pinned to the ground, like an ant struggling under a magnifying glass in the heat of the sun.

"After Eric died, Joe and I made a promise that nothing like that would ever happen again. We wouldn't let the Knights hurt us—us or anyone else. But after I went through the portal, Joe let that promise die. Instead of eradicating the Knights, he hid. He kept them a secret, even when they kept killing. So every single body the Knights have piled up since is on his head." Malquin swiveled to Liv. "Even your parents'."

Liv's breath caught in her throat, and she struggled to find a response.

"You still think *I'm* the evil one?" Malquin asked.

Liv shook her head. "That's not . . . it's not his fault." But her words came out shaky, and she avoided looking at Not-Joe.

"Maybe it was, maybe it wasn't," Malquin continued. "But

I won't let the Knights live to hurt a single more person. I'll admit it took years—and a lot of mistakes—but I finally have the power necessary to eradicate their organization entirely. And to make sure it never returns."

Liv looked at the looming shadows against the walls of the castle set. The wrath army.

"I will get payback for Eric and for everyone else they ever hurt. Every family they destroyed."

This time it was Liv who kept her eyes trained on the floor as Malquin peered at her. She wanted to block out his words as much as she wanted him to keep talking. The Knights had killed her parents. And they deserved . . .

She thought of the professor, lying cold and dead on the floor of a cave. Did he deserve that? For being part of an organization that killed children, that killed her parents?

Yes, came the voice from inside of her. An angry voice. She physically shook her head to keep it away.

Malquin still frowned down at her. "As you know, my original plans to bring the wraths through a giant, permanent portal and have them destroy the Knights . . . went awry." Malquin waved a hand. "But my actions had a rather exciting side effect, as it turns out. The second I got back to Caelum, I made my way to the castle portal. I came through again to check on my scattered army here, and saw instantly what had become of Los Angeles—what we had done together, Liv. We've changed the entire world! And finally, *finally*, the power I sought all those years ago in Caelum—it's here. It's all around us."

This time, Liv shook her head in confusion. Malquin

seemed disappointed that she wasn't catching on to what he was saying.

"Don't you see?" he asked, his voice dripping more with condescension than excitement. "It's the magic, Liv. Magic that we brought back to Earth, you and I."

"You mean the magic that's ruining the city, throwing off the balance, destroying the world? How is that going to help you against the Knights?"

"How?" Malquin asked. "However we want. It's *magic*. As a scroll, I thought you'd have a bit of imagination. Don't tell me you're just as bad as every terrified Angeleno who ran at the sight of anything new or different."

"New or different?" Liv retorted. "The sky is practically on fire. There's an earthquake every few hours. Gravity's just . . . not working—"

"I know!" Malquin yelled. "Isn't it amazing?"

Liv just shook her head, at a loss for words. She knew Malquin was crazy, but this . . . this was *crazy* crazy.

"Anything could happen! Magic is back in our world, Liv. Which means that anyone who figures out how to use it might have power. Real power. Not just the power to find and destroy the Knights—though that's certainly been my first priority. But now we have the power to really change, well . . . everything." As he spoke, Malquin gestured to Joe and the wraths around him.

"So it's true. You used magic to do this to them. To turn men into monsters."

"And they're just the beginning. Just the start of what I can do. I'm going to remake the whole world, Liv. Into whatever I want it to be, into what it *should* be. And you're going to help me."

Malquin looked at Liv, his face lit up like an overzealous TV game show host. He looked almost insane. Except Liv knew he *wasn't*—everything he was talking about was possible. Magic was back on Earth, and Malquin had figured out how to use it first. And Joe was standing there, his black eyes proof of everything Malquin could do.

And, as if to highlight his point at just that moment, the world around Liv started to shake. Malquin lifted his arms above his head, as if he were an orchestra conductor leading the earthquake. He closed his eyes, almost serene, and smiled.

THE DEPARTED

S hannon woke up, again, to an earthquake.

She really should've been used to them at this point, but still—it's not easy to train your mind to stay unconscious while the whole world thrashes around it. She pulled herself over to the doorway with a yawn and waited for the shaking to subside. That's when she noticed the other small bed in the room was empty. Crap. She'd fallen asleep, and Liv was— where was she?

"Liv?"

The only response was the shaking of the walls, the rattling of the windows. Liv and the others had long taken down the knickknacks and breakables that might crash to the floor in an earthquake.

"Liv?"

A crashing sound from down the hall. Shannon turned her head just as the shaking began to die down. The crashing hadn't been something falling over—it'd been a person barreling down the hallway, thudding on the wood floors. Cedric.

He skidded to a stop in front of Shannon, shirtless and out of breath.

"Is she here?"

"I'm also okay; thanks for asking—"

"Is she here?"

"Geez, no. She must be in the kitchen or something."

Cedric looked toward the kitchen, his eyes full of concern. "When I fell asleep, she was with me, and then—"

"Wait. Liv was with you? In your room?" Shannon's mouth split into a wide grin, which only got bigger as Cedric's face began to turn several different shades of red.

"That is not—she—I have to find her."

"Mm-hmm. I bet you do."

Cedric looked too flustered to reply, but was saved when Merek sauntered down the hallway, yawning.

"These earthquakes are hell on one's ability to get a good night's rest," he said.

Cedric whipped around to face Merek. "Have you seen Liv tonight at all? Did she go by your room?"

Merek raised an eyebrow and smirked. "Jealousy this early in your courtship does not bode well for you."

Cedric just shook his head, pushing past both Merek and Shannon. "Never mind. I will find her myself."

"I'm telling you, check the kitchen—Liv loves late-night snacks," Shannon called after him.

Merek leaned back against the opposite wall, looking at Shannon.

"It's gonna be hard to get back to sleep now," Shannon said.

"The earth should not shake again for a few hours, at least."

"You've really gotten used to this place, huh?"

"It has its charms."

He kept his eyes focused on her, and Shannon felt her face growing hot. Sarcastic flirting was one thing, but somehow, at some point, she'd started to think about him in a different way. When she'd been bored in Utah, she'd find herself imagining the snarky comments Merek would have made—about the bland food, her parents' rules. It helped keep her a little sane when she felt suffocated by boredom and worry. But she had no idea if he'd spent any of those weeks thinking about her. She only had one clue—

"Liv told me that you hunted down that Knight, the one who knocked me over," Shannon said, gently touching her recently healed wrist. "Even though I specifically remember telling you not to."

Merek cocked his head, smiling. "Did you? I do not recall . . ."

"Liar," Shannon said. But she was smiling, too. "So . . . why go through all that trouble?"

Merek's eyes burned into hers. "Some trouble is worth it."

Shannon opened her mouth to respond, but at that moment, Cedric came running back past them. "I cannot find her anywhere."

Shannon stood up straight, snapped out of the moment. Wisps of worry stirred in her stomach as she tore her eyes away from Merek toward Cedric.

"We'll look outside. She's gotta be here somewhere."

Except she wasn't.

They searched every room in the house, waking up Peter to help, but Liv was missing. And so was Joe. And so was the Jeep.

"What could possibly make them both take off like that?" Shannon asked as they all stood in the living room a few minutes later. "I mean, let alone making us worry—and not even leaving a freaking note—what could they possibly be after at four in the morning? What, did they go on a late-night Fatburger run? In the next county? Without even having the decency to wake us up and see if we wanted anything too?"

The others just stared at her.

"I think we all know where Joe might have gone," Cedric said, his voice ridiculously sure for someone who'd been running around the house barefoot in a panic just minutes before.

"We do?" Peter asked.

"He wanted to find Malquin. And now he's gone in the middle of the night . . . he would only do that if he did not want us to try and talk him out of it again."

"But what about Liv?"

"Maybe she went with him. Alone. Even though she promised—" Cedric cut himself off, shaking his head. Shannon wanted to stand up for her friend, but honestly, she was kind of ticked, too. Why would Liv leave without saying anything to her? If only she hadn't fallen asleep . . .

"But how would they even know where to go?" Peter interrupted. Everyone stared at him—it was a good question.

"Maybe Joe figured it out," Shannon put in.

"Well, if he can, so can we," Peter said.

Merek crossed his arms. "So we plan to go after them, then."

"Obviously," Shannon said.

"I only mean, if they had wanted our help, they would have woken us up to go with them. Or better still, they would have waited until morning."

Cedric bit his lip, as if considering Merek's words. Shannon thought she recognized hurt in his eyes. Then he shook his head. "It does not matter why they left alone. We have no idea how many wraths they will face or what will happen to them if . . . we have no choice. We have to find them."

"Agreed," Shannon said, cutting a sharp look at Merek. He just shrugged in response.

"Right," Peter said, sitting down on a nearby chair and stretching out his still-healing leg. "So we're going. We still have the main problem of *how* to find them. Cedric, didn't Liv say something about a castle last night? That the wraths were taking her there?"

"Yes," Cedric responded, furrowing his eyebrows. "But the only castle I know is back in Caelum."

"And why would Malquin take her to our world, if he no longer has any hold there?" Merek said. "It makes no sense."

"There are castles here, too," Shannon piped up. "Like, at Disney in Anaheim, or the Magic Castle in Hollywood. They do magic there. Not like, the-sky-is-turning-orange magic, but with cards and rabbits and stuff."

"Rabbits?" Cedric asked.

"I mean, I've heard," Shannon said with a shrug.

"Maybe," Peter said. "But we have to narrow it down.

Cedric, is there anything else you can remember? At all? What about the van the wraths put Liv in—did you see the license plate?"

Cedric shook his head, but then straightened suddenly. "It had lettering on its side, though. It was, ah . . . um . . ." He made a motion with his hand like writing.

Shannon ran and got a pen and paper from the kitchen counter and handed it to him. "Here, try to get it down."

Cedric bent over the paper, his hand curling around the pen. "I do not know the word, but there was a *P* first . . . and then . . ." He looked up into the distance, as if remembering. "Another word . . . study . . . studo . . ."

"Studio?" Peter asked.

"Yes!"

"P Studio, P Studio . . ." Peter trailed off. Suddenly, his eyes lit up. "Oh, of course!"

"What is it?" Shannon asked, trying to keep the irritation from her voice.

"The fake weapons. The van . . . it belongs to a studio. Like, a movie studio. And what's the only movie studio that starts with a *P*?"

"Paramount?" She almost clapped.

Cedric nodded eagerly. "That's it—the word on the van."

"I know where that is, too. It's not that far from our high school," Shannon said.

Peter grinned, while Merek and Cedric still looked confused. "But what is a studio?" Cedric asked. "Do they have castles there?"

"Maybe. They have lots of sets there," Shannon said.

"So we know where we are going," Merek said. "But we have to assume we will be outnumbered on unfamiliar ground. So what are we going to do once we get there?"

Peter tilted his head, considering. "You're right. We should probably plan for the worst-case scenario."

"Considering the best-case scenario is two fighters and a handful of weapons against what very well may be an army, I would hate to see what the worst-case scenario is," Merek said. "How are we supposed to fight them all?"

"Any way we can," Cedric said, his jaw tight.

"Or . . . maybe we don't," Peter replied, pushing his glasses up his nose, "Maybe the way to get Liv back isn't by fighting off the wraths. Assuming the worst—that they have her and Joe—maybe we just need a way to distract them so they can get away themselves."

"What kind of distraction?" Cedric asked.

Peter thought about it for a few moments, and then his eyes lit up behind the frames of his glasses. He stood up straighter. "The wraths aren't from this world, right? So there's a lot about this world that they don't know. A lot of things that wouldn't faze a regular person would really freak out a black-eyed monster who's only playing at being human."

"What things?" Shannon asked.

Peter grinned. "Exploding things."

Shannon leaned forward, eager to hear more. But at that moment, there was a sharp rapping sound on the door. Everyone jumped and exchanged quick glances.

"Could that be . . . ?" Shannon started, making her way toward the noise.

But Cedric was quicker. He flung the door open in one movement. Two figures stood in the dim orange glow—one male and one female.

"Liv?"

"Sorry to disappoint," the girl said, stepping into the foyer.

"Kat?" Cedric choked out.

Kat strode gracefully into the room, wearing not the Salvation Army T-shirt and jeans Shannon had seen her in last, but instead loose trousers and knee-high boots. And a tight-fitting leather vest, of course. She had a sword at her side, and her dark hair was pulled back into a braid. Basically, she looked like some bad-ass elf who crawled her way out of a video game, ditched the giant ears, and set about conquering the world.

Shannon unconsciously stood up a little straighter.

Someone else walked in behind Kat, tall, handsome, and in similarly ridiculous clothing. He looked around the living room with wide eyes.

"R-Rafe?" Merek spit out. His voice sounded scratchy and unsure—very un-Merek-like.

The tall guy walked over to Merek and clapped him hard on the back. "Hello, little brother. I had heard you were in dire straits, but you seem in fine health to me."

Merek's mouth opened like a fish and snapped closed again.

Before Shannon had time to truly reflect on that development, Kat was addressing Cedric.

"You were expecting Liv?"

"We were just formulating a rescue plan," Cedric responded, looking a bit sheepish. "She has . . . ah . . . gone missing."

"Of course she has."

"What are you doing here?" Cedric asked, still thrown. "Is everything all right in Caelum? Emme? My mother?"

"Your family is fine," Kat said, her voice taking on the gentle note she really only used with Cedric. "But Caelum . . ."

"What is it?"

Kat sighed heavily. "You were right about the woods. I am sorry I did not believe you, but that ridiculous woman you brought to the castle kept pestering me, so I went to investigate myself, and it is undeniable. The trees are dying at an alarming rate. Caelum is in danger."

Cedric just nodded, urging Kat to continue.

"If the only way to fix things is from this world, then I need to help. So I found the portal in the woods that we came through with Liv. I knew it would lead to this beach, and I hoped you might still be at this house."

"That explains the earthquake," Shannon muttered.

"Oh, and Rafe wanted to come as well." Kat said, almost as an afterthought.

"I could not miss the chance to see this," Rafe said, turning in a slow circle around the room and taking it all in. He walked across the room, tapping his finger against the flat-screen TV in the corner.

"We cannot linger for long," Kat said. "We need to fix what was broken and return to Caelum as soon as possible. Rafe still has an army to rebuild, and we need to regrow crops, feed the hungry, rebuild the wall . . . there is still work to do. For all of us."

Kat might have been talking to all of them, but her eyes were focused only on Cedric. A heavy tension filled the room. Peter quietly slipped out into the hallway, and Shannon sidled over to Merek.

"Maybe Peter's got the right idea . . . should we give these two a minute?"

But Merek's eyes were glued to his brother, trailing him as he moved around the living room.

"What?" he asked, clearly distracted.

"Are you okay? Aren't you glad to see your brother again?"

"Of course I am," Merek responded, still not looking at her. But it was clear, no matter what he said, that he wasn't okay. He wasn't smirking or scowling or saying much of anything. As he watched his brother, Merek seemed to almost shrink in on himself.

Meanwhile, on the other side of the room, Cedric and Kat were still fighting without actually fighting.

"I am here for the same reason you are," Cedric said, his voice steadily rising. "To fix things in both our worlds."

"So long as you do not forget which world you belong in," Kat responded.

Cedric shook his head. "We do not have time for this argument now. We need to form a plan."

"Right. To rescue Liv. Again."

"Yeah, about that . . ." All heads swiveled to see Peter, who had reentered the room. This time, he carried a giant cardboard box that was looking a little worse for wear. The top edges were ripped and bent, and the bottom bowed out as though it were going to spill its contents any moment.

"We found this in the garage a while ago when we were looking for supplies," Peter continued. "They weren't useful. Until now."

Peter set the box on the floor and gently tipped it over. Out spilled a wide assortment of canisters of all shapes and sizes. Some were cardboard, some were plastic. They were bright yellow and orange and green, with polka dots and stripes and exclamation points. Lots and lots of exclamation points.

"Fireworks?" Shannon asked.

The others all looked confused as they examined the canisters on the floor. Peter pushed his glasses up his nose and grinned.

"Figured they'd make a pretty good distraction."

THE AVENGERS

In what felt like no time at all, they were pulling up to the front gates of Paramount Studios in Shannon's minivan with a solid plan in place.

Well, mostly solid.

Shannon's stomach flipped as she considered all the things that could go wrong. She couldn't stop touching her still-sensitive wrist, remembering how it had felt to hear those bones snap. But she'd already had this argument with herself, again and again. She knew the risks of coming back to LA to help her friends, and that was the choice she'd made. It was too late to back out now.

Plus, she didn't want to give any of these professional fighters the satisfaction of seeing her afraid.

Cedric, Kat, Rafe, and Merek filed out of Shannon's van. Peter, whose own injuries still made him slow on his feet, would wait behind to drive them off, should everything go according to plan. Back at the house, Peter had showed Cedric and the others how to set off the fireworks without blowing off their arms. They'd lit up a couple of practice fireworks from the beach. To Shannon, it looked strange to see the explosions burst apart over an entirely empty strip of sand and water, with no applause or collective oohs and ahhs as they fizzled red and gold and blue. It was even stranger to see their colors set against the eerie, oppressive sky. A familiar sight turned so, so wrong.

Now they were splitting the fireworks into five bags, some backpacks from the house and some canvas grocery bags they'd managed to find in the kitchen. Cedric and Kat walked through the studio's front gate first, weapons out.

"Keep your eyes out for guards," Rafe said from his position in the middle of the group. "And, Merek, do not forget to watch the rear."

Shannon waited for the smart-ass comeback from Merek, but instead he just nodded.

As they walked deeper into the lot, no guards appeared.

"Do you think we might have been wrong?" Shannon asked. "Or maybe we're right, but Malquin didn't expect us to find him?"

"Or maybe he already knows we are coming," Cedric said darkly.

The lot was huge, spanning out from them in all directions. They decided to walk straight. At the end of one giant parking lot was a large rectangle; it looked like a movie screen, although it was several times the size of any screen Shannon had ever seen. It was painted to look like the backdrop of a beautiful blue sky, meant to represent a regular, sunny Los Angeles day. But now, it stood out against the angry colors of the actual sky.

When Shannon looked at the backdrop, she got the disconcerting sense that *it* was real, and the world behind it was the painted, unnatural one.

"This place is . . . odd," Rafe said, staring at the blue backdrop.

"Shh," Cedric said. "We might be upon them any minute."

But they wandered for several more minutes, past giant, empty buildings and even a few abandoned catering trucks.

The knot in Shannon's stomach got tighter and tighter as she walked. She didn't know if she was afraid they wouldn't find Liv held captive here—or if she was afraid that they would. Finally, after walking past what looked like a brick apartment building—or at least, the front side of an apartment building propped up by wooden posts with nothing behind it—Cedric put one arm out to stop the others.

"Do you hear that?"

Shannon strained to listen, and finally she heard it. Voices. Talking. Arguing. Even laughing. Cedric led them slowly, single file, around the building facade. They crept across the street and bent low against another building, moving closer to the noises. Then, across the street, Shannon saw a group of men standing in front of a building labeled "Stage 18." To her, the men didn't even look out of place. In their jeans and T-shirts, they might have been a film crew taking a break.

"Are they . . . ?" Shannon whispered to Merek.

He nodded. "Wraths. And look."

Merek motioned to the shadows on the side of the building, where Shannon could just make out Joe's Jeep in the fading light. Her stomach dropped.

"So we were right," she said, adjusting the bag of fireworks on her back and trying to keep from collapsing in anxiety.

"There is a ladder to the roof, there," Cedric whispered back to them, pointing to the building. Shannon saw a ladder made of thin metal rods fixed to the building's exterior and leading up to the roof, where there was a door. "We have to take out all of those wraths before any can alert those inside. Then we go up the ladder. Everyone know what to do?"

Before anyone could respond, Rafe held up a hand. "Wait." He turned to Merek and Shannon. "Maybe you two should wait here."

Merek looked confused, so Shannon answered for him. "Excuse me?"

"This is a dangerous mission, and you are still recovering from your wounds," Rafe said. "I would hate to go home and have to tell Mother and Father that something happened to you."

"I . . . ," Merek started, his face turning alternating shades of red and white.

"We need Merek out there with us," Cedric said, a note of finality in his voice. "He is a strong fighter."

Rafe's eyebrows raised. "Is he? I haven't ever known that to be true."

Shannon scoffed, barely believing Rafe had the gall to say something like that. She waited for Merek to jump in and defend himself, the way he would if Cedric or Kat or anyone else in the world called him out. But instead, he was stony-faced and silent, his eyes on the ground.

So Shannon stepped forward. "Well, maybe you don't know him very well," she said.

Rafe looked at her, really looked at her, for the first time that night. His expression barely changed, but she knew he was sizing her up, and she refused to shrink under his gaze. Finally, he shrugged with one shoulder and looked to Merek.

"It is your decision, baby brother. Be it on your head."

He turned and faced the group of wraths standing by Stage 18, then slowly crept forward along the side of the building. Cedric and Kat each shot Merek sympathetic looks before following. Merek stood still for just a moment, his hand tightening on the strap of his backpack. Just as he was about to set off, Shannon reached out and grabbed his shoulder.

"He's wrong, you know. He might be your brother, but he clearly doesn't know you very well."

Merek turned to look at her. "He knows me better than anyone. He always has."

Shannon shook her head. "Maybe that used to be true, but it's not anymore."

"You don't understand," Merek said, his voice taking on a hard edge. "He was raised and trained to be a warrior and a duke, someone of importance. And I was not. He is right—I am not as strong a fighter as him, or Cedric, or Kat. I was nearly killed the last time we faced Malquin. Maybe I have only survived this far on luck."

Shannon felt a spike of anger. How could anyone make Merek feel that way, and how could he believe them? She gripped his shoulder tighter and spun him to face her head-on.

"Luck is for losers," she said, voice fierce. "And I don't make out with losers."

"Make out—?"

Shannon pushed herself up onto the tips of her toes until her face was level with Merek's, and then she kissed him. Hard. For a moment, he seemed more shocked than anything, and he stood very, very still with his hands at his sides. But after a few seconds, his lips pressed back against hers, and his hands met her waist and slid down along her lower back. Locks of his hair fell against Shannon's forehead, light and tickling and warm.

She kissed him until she felt dizzy, until she could hear the blood rushing from her head. She pulled back, her face just inches from his. This close, his eyes were blurry and indistinct, but she could see the intensity in them, the way they were focused on her and only her.

"Now go let's go kick some ass and save my friend," Shannon said. "And you better keep yourself in one piece, if you want what just happened to ever happen again."

Merek grinned. "One piece it is."

He grabbed her hand, and they moved together to face whatever the night would bring.

⊱⊰⊱⊰

Liv's arm was sore from being pressed against the concrete floor for so long. After the ground had stopped shaking, Malquin rambled on about all the ways they could change the world together through magic. Most sounded insane, but Liv's only plan was to keep Malquin talking long enough for her to try to slowly twist out of her bindings. Not that she was getting very far.

A wrath came up and whispered in Malquin's ear. His thin-lipped smile in response sent a shiver down Liv's back.

"It seems we have a guest," Malquin said. "And perfect timing, too, since I see you're going to need a bit more convincing. It's only fair you see what we can do together with your own eyes."

Liv cast a quick glance over to where Joe stood, staring down at her with black eyes.

"I've already seen it, thanks."

"No," Malquin said. "You really haven't." He tilted his head. "I got the idea from the Guardians, you know. After all, your little boyfriend's ancestors were the first men to ever ingest wrath blood for the purpose of gaining their power. Of course, magic on Earth was a little more . . . stable . . . back then, so the results weren't quite this dramatic."

Malquin smiled at Joe, who grinned hollowly in response. Liv felt like throwing up.

"But this better suits my purposes anyway," Malquin said. "All the power, none of the pesky personality. Joe's practically pure wrath now. And would you say he looks unhappy?"

Joe's mouth stretched across his teeth in a ghastly imitation of a smile. He didn't look unhappy. He looked . . . void.

Malquin put his good hand in the air and snapped his fingers. From around the fake wall of the castle, two wraths came forward, holding a gagged figure between them. One of the wraths was the fair-haired former Knight who'd thrown Liv against a wall in the OC house. It took Liv a moment to recognize the person he was dragging forward—it was a blond woman she'd only seen in pictures. The fair-haired man's wife.

It looked like she hadn't gotten away after all.

Malquin moved closer to the terrified blond woman, removing a sharp dagger from the belt at his side. The woman glanced at her husband—or what used to be her husband—and screamed for help against her gag. The fair-haired wrath was impassive. But Malquin didn't turn the dagger on the woman. Instead, he turned to another nearby wrath and ran the knife across the creature's forearm until black blood flowed from the surface.

Then, Malquin turned and handed the knife to Joe.

That's when Liv started to yell.

"Please, Malquin. You don't have to do this! You can leave her alone."

Malquin shook his head. "This woman sealed her fate when she joined her life with one of the Knights of Valere. She knew what he was, and she did nothing. She even *supported* him."

The woman thrashed against her captors, against her stone-faced husband, screaming into her gag. Liv again saw the pictures from the couple's living room. The fair-haired man might have belonged to the Knights of Valere, but he also had a family, a house, a sprinkler system. The couple had gotten married, had a dog, gone to Angels games. He was a Knight, but he'd also been a human being . . . and this woman hadn't done anything but marry him.

"Please!" Liv yelled. "Please! I'll do anything you want, just please don't!"

Malquin finally looked back at Liv. "Don't you get it? I

already have what I want. Two more scrolls, at my disposal. Enough to open up as many portals as I want. To let in as much magic as I want."

Liv thrashed against the ropes that held her. "That's insane. It'll destroy the world!"

"Destroy? The world isn't a worse place with magic, Liv. Whoever told you that was lying. We have the power now to make everything different. And I'll even give you the same choice I gave all of these Knights. You can agree to help me of your own free will, or . . ." Malquin nodded toward the wrath he'd cut, whose black blood was slowly running down the surface of his skin and landing in drops on the concrete floor.

"You can't just do this to people," Liv said. She took big lungfuls of air, trying to calm herself. If she couldn't yell Malquin down, maybe she could reason with him . . .

"I can, actually," Malquin responded. "The magic here has made it quite simple. I may not have the power the Knights did all those years ago, but I am a scroll, which means there's some magic already inside of me. And now there's magic in the very air. So as long as I have people around me who believe in the power of that magic, I can bend their belief to my will. I can make pretty much anything I want happen. Now watch."

Liv watched.

There was little else she could do. Even as she pulled against her ropes until the skin of her wrists cut open, even as she yelled until her throat was sore and scratchy, the only thing she could really do was watch.

She watched as the wraths forced the blond woman to the

floor and ripped the gag from her mouth. She watched as the bleeding wrath leaned over the woman, letting his blood pour into her mouth. Almost immediately, the woman started to choke.

She watched the woman try to spit it out, try to fight, try to thrash.

She watched as she went still.

"Now," Malquin said, his voice barely more than a whisper.

But the figures standing around the edges of the makeshift castle heard him. And they all started to speak. Or chant, really. Their various coarse voices slowly unified, growing louder and echoing off the set walls until Liv could finally make out what they were saying.

"Change. Change. Change."

"Please don't work," Liv whispered.

But as cracked and low as it was, her voice was still loud enough to be heard. Malquin turned to her, his own expression calm.

"It will work," he said. "I wouldn't have done this to my own brother if I wasn't sure of the success. Granted, it didn't work perfectly at first, and there were a few . . . unfortunate failures . . . but I finally figured out the secret."

Liv thought of the Knight they'd found in front of the Ralphs's parking lot, the one who'd died before them with black eyes and peeling skin. Had he been one of the "unfortunate failures"? Or was his fate what still awaited the woman who was writhing now on the ground? Was it what awaited Joe?

Behind Malquin and all around, the chants continued.

"All this time," Malquin said, "I thought the words mattered. But it turns out, they're just a means to an end. That spell I taught you to open a portal—someone *invented* that. Just made it up. Whether he was a Knight or a scholar or a sorcerer, it doesn't matter. He was just a man, like me. It wasn't the exact words that mattered, it was the *conviction*. The speakers have to believe in the magic, and in what they want it to accomplish. They have to *feel* it."

Malquin smiled serenely as he looked out over the circle of wraths, all still chanting, their voices running together and repeating so often that the word they were saying began to lose meaning to Liv's ears. But it didn't matter. She could see in their intense, focused expressions, in their fevered eyes, that they believed their words would work.

Liv's pulse started to race harder. The answer was here somewhere, the one she'd been looking for . . . but before she could concentrate, she saw the blond woman finally sit up across the room.

She moved slowly, deliberately. Her back was ramrod straight. She was faced away from Liv, so it was impossible to see her expression. Then, the woman swiveled slowly to her right, her head and shoulders inching in Liv's direction, her eyes taking in the room.

Her all-black, empty eyes.

It had worked.

Malquin turned to Liv. "So you've seen what I can do. Isn't it amazing? And now, my dear, it's time to make your choice. You will help me, but you can either do so willingly . . . or not."

She wanted to scream, and she wanted to cry. She wanted

to rip through her bindings and scratch Malquin's eyes out. She wanted Joe to snap to life and save her from this place. Malquin stared at her with his expectant eyes, and she did her best to square her shoulders from her position on the ground.

"I won't help you," she said.

Malquin gripped the knife once again, gesturing the bleeding wrath forward.

"Okay, then." Malquin shrugged, then turned to the wrath with the still-bleeding arm. "You're up again. Joe, restrain her."

Liv still stared at Joe, tears in her eyes. He had to be in there, somewhere. A part of him still had to hear her, had to care . . . *had* to . . .

"Joe? Look at me. Please, look at me."

He looked down at her and cocked his head. Was that recognition in his expression?

"Joe, you have to fight it. If you're still in there, just fight."

Without losing a beat, Joe kept walking across the room toward Liv. She strained backward, rolling over her bound arms and screaming as her hip bones pushed them into the concrete floor. She rolled over again, onto her stomach. But there was no getting away. Joe was halfway to her, his dead eyes barely taking in her struggle.

"Please, Joe. Please. I know you're still in there, I know it."

Joe put one foot on her back, pressing her to the floor.

"Joe . . ."

But the creature above her just pressed down harder, hurting her. Joe would never, could never, hurt her. And Liv knew—Joe was gone.

Joe was gone. Her eyes shut tight against hot tears.

And above her head, the room exploded.

That was the only way Liv could describe it. Lying on her stomach, she had a limited view of the room around her. But she could still hear as a giant, booming noise roared through the set, followed by a brilliant red glow.

The lights in the studio cut out, sending the room into darkness. Then came the second boom. This time, the entire room lit up blue, enough to see Malquin and some surrounding wraths looking up toward the ceiling with wonder and terror in their faces. After a few seconds, the blue light fizzled, and all was dark again.

That's when Liv smelled the smoke. Not just any smoke, but a particular, familiar kind of stench that only ever reminded her of . . .

The Fourth of July?

By the time the green explosion went off, Liv had enough of her wits about her to keep rolling again. Joe had removed his foot from her back. She could barely make out his outline in the dark, but at the next deafening boom, she saw his profile illuminated against flashes of red and gold. He was standing at attention next to Malquin, who was screaming out orders that no one could hear.

As she rolled again, Liv saw that the wraths were scattering, some climbing up to the rafters, toward the explosions, and others running out the door.

Darkness again. Then boom. The world turned brilliant purple, and Liv saw Malquin trying to keep the wraths in place.

Darkness, then boom.

In eerie green light, Liv saw a piece of scaffolding fall from the ceiling and collapse a corner of the Styrofoam castle.

Darkness. Boom.

A blue light that showed mostly smoke now. Coiling, thickening smoke that spread quickly through the room . . .

The smoke hit Liv's eyes and throat, and she started to cry and cough at the same time, nearly choking in the process. But most distressing was the ringing in her ears. She could still hear explosions going off, but the noises got dimmer and sounded farther away every time.

She didn't even hear the footsteps approach until they were right on top of her, until hands were grabbing her and lifting her up.

"No," Liv said, before her voice dissolved into a fit of coughs. She could barely see in front of her through the smoke.

"Liv?" The voice sound far away, like it was on the other side of a long tunnel. Still, Liv recognized it.

"Liv?" Cedric asked. His hands gripped her shoulders, and he held her steady as her bound arms and legs threatened to knock her off balance and cast her back to the floor.

"I've got you," Cedric said. He looked like he was yelling, but his voice sounded muffled and distant. "I've got you."

Liv could only cough in response.

Cedric looked around wildly. "Where's Malquin? Is he here?" They both scanned the billowing smoke, but Liv couldn't see anything beyond Cedric's face. He turned back to her, his eyes red and starting to tear. She could read the frustration and rage in them. Malquin had slipped away again.

"I don't know where—" she choked out.

He shook his head. "It does not matter. We have to get out of here. Where is Joe?"

When she heard Cedric say Joe's name, his voice so steady and unknowing, she felt a pain so intense she thought she'd split apart.

"He's gone," she finally managed to say as tears streamed down her face. "He's already gone."

THE DAY THE EARTH STOOD STILL

Liv vividly remembered the first time she saw an R-rated movie in the theater. She was eight years old, and she'd just been taken from the first set of foster parents who'd actually cared for her. Chuck and Marty hadn't just been kind to Liv, they'd treated her like a real person instead of some fragile orphan. And they'd introduced her to movies—lots and lots of movies. So when they had to move to Australia and leave Liv behind, she was heartbroken.

She remembered the day Joe came to pick her up from Chuck and Marty's place, a cozy bungalow in West Hollywood with a yellow front door. It was right after Christmas, and Chuck and Marty still had small, bright lights strung around the single palm tree in their front yard. When Liv passed it, she turned to wave good-bye to her now-former foster parents, who both cried as they watched her climb into the passenger seat of Joe's Jeep.

"We're going back to the big white building?" Liv had asked, thinking of the child services department located near the La

Brea Tar Pits. She'd already been through this twice before, once after her parents had died and again after Joe had taken her away from the Hannigans. She remembered driving past the small black pond with its statues of trapped and sinking animals as she waited to be delivered to another strange home.

Joe had grimaced, his hands on the wheel. "Not yet," he said.

"Then where are we going?"

"It's a surprise."

When Joe pulled up to Arclight Hollywood minutes later, Liv's stomach gave a happy flip-flop.

"We're going to the movies?" she asked, scared that Joe might realize his mistake, say no, and drive her straight to child services.

But Joe just grinned. "You like popcorn, right?"

And not only did he let Liv get popcorn, he'd let her pick the movie, too. Without hesitation, Liv pointed up to the lobby's giant screen listing movie times—the one that looked like it belonged in a grand train station rather than a movie theater—and pointed at *Pan's Labyrinth*.

Joe furrowed his eyebrows. "That's rated R. Might be a bit . . . much."

"I want to see that one."

"What about the one with the talking pig? That's still playing."

But Liv just shook her head, again pointing to *Pan's Labyrinth*. She'd read about it in one of Chuck and Marty's movie magazines, a dark and twisted fairy tale from a famous director.

She knew the movie was violent, and she doubted Joe would let her see it. Even Chuck and Marty had been a little hesitant to show her *The Godfather* trilogy a few months before.

Joe looked over for a poster of the movie, showing the silhouette of a little girl walking into a terrifying forest. He looked back at Liv, then nodded.

"Okay then."

The movie had scared the crap out of Liv. Its haunting visuals crawled inside her brain, seeming so real that she'd constantly had to look around the theater to make sure the monsters of Pan's Labyrinth weren't lying in wait at that moment, all around her . . . but as the images on the screen became more and more terrifying, Liv knew Joe was still by her side. His presence reminded her that the monsters on the screen weren't real. That she was safe.

Liv couldn't stop thinking of that movie now, as she lay in the backseat of Shannon's van, staring straight forward but not really seeing what was in front of her. Her ears were still ringing, and the smell of smoke lingered in her nose. She remembered in bits and pieces getting out of the soundstage, though most of them made no sense. The castle catching on fire, the fire spreading to the rest of the building. Cedric carrying her out. Kat and Rafe showing up out of nowhere to cut her hands free. She remembered asking what they were even doing there, though she didn't remember if they'd answered her. She remembered Shannon pulling her into a giant hug, and Peter looking at her with worry in his eyes when they reached the van.

They were all in the van now, silent as they drove through

morning with its skies turning slowly from rust-brown to lighter rust-orange. Liv was alone in the far backseat, the movement of the van gently rocking her back and forth. She wished it could lull her to sleep, the way it used to when she was a child. But she couldn't even shut her eyes.

Now that Liv's hands were free and she was relatively safe, the reality of the night began to sink in in sharp, jagged pieces. But her memories of the last few hours kept getting tangled up with older memories. She saw the black, soulless eyes set inexplicably in the middle of Joe's—her Joe's—face. She saw the creature from *Pan's Labyrinth*, its own eyes facing out from the middle of its black-tipped hands. She saw her own small hands covering her face as she sank lower into the movie theater seat (or was she now sinking down for real in the van seat?) She saw an orange sky passing by the window near her head. She saw Joe sitting next to her in a blue bucket seat as he leaned down and whispered, "Don't worry—it's not real."

His long-ago voice rang in her head along with the echoes of fireworks set off in a closed space. The movie had been fake, but it had felt real. What happened to Joe had really happened, but it felt unreal, like a dream. Movies and memories got tangled up inside Liv's head, and she couldn't pull herself out. She didn't want to pull herself out. Because there was that dread, at the bottom of her stomach, that seemed to know the truth.

Joe was now a monster who wanted to hurt her. Just like the monsters in the movie. But now there was no one sitting beside her to remind her that it was all fake, that even if it felt real, even if she was terrified for real—she was safe. She forced her eyes shut, trying to hear Joe's voice telling her she was okay, pulling her out of this nightmare world like he'd pulled her up from her belief in the movie monsters. . . .

Her strong, unwavering belief . . .

Liv shot straight up in a flash, the top of her head nearly colliding with the roof of the van. In front of her, both Rafe and Merek jumped. Merek put his hand over his heart as he scowled at Liv.

"Hell alive, Liv, I thought you were asleep back there."

"What is it?" Cedric asked, catching sight of Liv's white face in the rearview mirror. "What's wrong?"

Liv flinched, gutted by the question. Everything was wrong. Everything.

But she focused on Cedric's eyes in the rearview mirror. She steadied her voice.

"I know how to do it. I know how to fix the world."

Six heads swiveled back to face her, six sets of eyes looking at her as if she'd just grown an extra arm out of her neck. But Liv ignored their incredulity.

"We're going to make a movie."

A NEW HOPE

"Wait . . . what?" Shannon asked.

Liv had just finished laying out the basics of her plan, and now everyone in the Malibu house was staring at her blankly. Shannon, of course, was the first to speak what was on everyone else's mind.

"I mean . . . what?"

"It's our only option," Liv said. "Or at least, the only one I can think of. It's basically this or run and hide and wait for the world to slowly fall apart for good."

She looked around at everyone in the room—Cedric, with his eyebrows raised; Kat, skeptical with her arms crossed; Merek and Rafe, who were both covered in ash like they'd just stepped out of a forest fire; and Peter . . . poor Peter, who'd been quiet and withdrawn since Liv first explained, in a halting, breaking voice, why Joe wouldn't be coming back with them.

"Liv," Shannon continued. "Maybe we should just take a moment to recover from . . . what happened." Shannon's voice was gentle, filled with pity and something else . . . fear? Yes,

Liv thought, looking into her best friend's eyes—Shannon was definitely afraid. But of what? Her?

Liv glanced over at the mirror on the wall. She barely recognized the girl looking back at her. Soot covered her from head to toe, staining her pajamas a gray-brown. Tear tracks ran down the ash that covered her face, and her hair stuck out from her head at all angles. There were red marks on her wrists and ankles from where she'd struggled against the ropes. And her eyes looked . . . drained.

She looked shell-shocked. Crazy. Definitely not like someone anyone should be taking direction from.

Liv took a deep breath and looked back at her friends.

"We don't have time to recover. Malquin is building his army up more every day. Every minute we waste is another potential person he might turn into . . ." Her voice faltered, and she closed her eyes to compose herself.

"He will need some time to regroup," Cedric said. Liv opened her eyes to see him shaking his head. "The fire burned down his base, and the wraths scattered—"

"We have no idea how much the fire set Malquin back," Liv said, standing up straight and once again trying to gather a strength she didn't feel. "But we can't assume he's down for the count. Remember months ago, Cedric, when you said Malquin was one step ahead of us? That hasn't changed. He's looking to tear the wall between the worlds down even more. He wants magic to come here, wants the Earth to keep fighting it. He wants the destruction. He's building an army and using innocent people to do it."

"I thought you said he was only using Knights," Merek put in.

"Okay . . . mostly innocent. But what do you think will happen when he runs out of Knights and their families to turn? Do you think he's just gonna stop? We have to do something now."

Shannon cleared her throat. "If we do this—plan—will it bring Joe back? Will it make him . . . Joe again?"

Liv's breath caught in her throat. Once again she saw Not-Joe coming toward her, his eyes dark, bent on hurting her without a second thought. She wanted so badly to believe he could come back, but . . .

"I don't know," Liv said truthfully. "Even if the plan works, even if we restore magical balance to our worlds, Joe might be . . . gone."

Shannon cleared her throat. "About that . . . plan. Maybe you can run us through it one more time?"

"Yes, because not a single part of it makes even a bit of sense," Kat added.

Liv took another deep breath, looking around the room. It suddenly seemed like a huge feat to get everyone on board with her idea. Her plan had two key elements: moviemaking and magic. Half the people in the room had never even heard of movies before a few months ago, and the other half had never seen real magic *outside* of movies.

Liv took a deep breath, ready to plead her case.

"Henry Martin told us it's impossible to get rid of magic now that it's back on Earth. The only way to save our world—worlds—is to restore balance. To get our world to stop fighting this magic surge, right?"

"He said it was a theory," Cedric responded carefully.

"Well, let's just assume, because we have no better option, that his theory is true. That there's a way to allow magic to flow between our worlds for good in a way that doesn't burn up the whole sky or drain Caelum to nothing. To do that, we'd need power. The kind of power that hundreds of Knights had all those years ago when they opened the very first portal."

"Yeah, but—" Shannon started.

"But we don't have access to Knights anymore, I know. Even if Malquin wasn't killing and turning them, it would take us forever to track them all down. But remember, Mathilde told Cedric that the Knights weren't just important because they knew about magic, but because they *believed* in it. That's why their spell worked."

Liv moved her hands wildly as she talked, anxious to make them see. "That part's not just a theory. I saw it with my own eyes. Malquin needed a spell to turn humans into wraths, so he got his other wraths to do it. Not Knights, wraths. Believers. It didn't even matter what the words of the spell were—they just had to focus on what they wanted to happen. They just had to believe."

Cedric nodded. "I think I understand what you're trying to say, Liv. But it took hundreds of Knights to open that first portal. To get the whole world to stop fighting magic? It would take so many more of these . . . believers."

"Thousands, likely," Liv agreed. "Maybe more."

Everyone in the room looked crestfallen at this, but Liv felt like she was finally getting somewhere. "And what's the best way to reach thousands of people? Like, if you had a message you wanted to deliver?"

"The internet," Peter responded.

"Right!" Liv said. She actually clapped in response. The idea was so clear in her, if only she could make the others see . . .

Without even realizing it, she started talking faster. "But what if you didn't just want to deliver a message? What if you wanted people to really *believe* what you were saying? You wouldn't just tell them. You'd show them. You'd give them a story."

A collective pause fell over the room, just like it had the first time Liv had quickly explained her plan. But this time, instead of shaking her head, Shannon cocked it slightly—she was listening, thinking.

"That's how we can reach thousands of people. That's how we can get them to believe. Think about it, Shannon. When you watch a good movie, what does it feel like? What's it like when things are happening on screen and you get so caught up in them that you practically forget you even exist? Even if a part of your brain knows nothing you're seeing is real, you turn that part of your brain off. You imagine what you're watching is real because it *feels* real. You believe, even just for a moment, because you want to."

Shannon's eyes widened, and her mouth dropped open into a small O of understanding.

One, thought Liv. *I've got one of them.* She turned to her brother.

"Peter, remember when you were a kid, and your favorite movie was *Star Wars*?"

"Yeah, but what—"

"The whole movie is based on this completely imaginary concept, with intergalactic wars and light sabers and all these fantastic, non-real things. But when you're watching it, your emotions are real. You care when the characters get hurt, you feel tense when they're about to fight, and relieved when they live. You believe in them, and you *believe* in something like the Force, even if just for a little while."

Peter pursed his lips, thinking. "But that's not *real* believing. It wears off as soon as the movie's over."

"But what does 'real' believing even mean? Whether you believe in God, or your family, or yourself, or in a story . . . doesn't it all work the same? Belief is there for you when you need it, no matter how long it lasts, no matter what kind it is. If we can get enough people to believe in the magic in our story—even for just a few seconds—how is that any different from what some ancient knights believed in? Peter, isn't what you feel when you watch *Star Wars* sometimes just as strong as what you feel in real life?"

"Sometimes," Peter said, his voice soft. "Sometimes it seems even stronger."

Liv smiled, triumphant. "Exactly. So?" She looked anxiously around the room. She noticed both her hands were shaking, maybe from anxiety, from lack of sleep, from trauma. Or from just hoping, so hard, that the plan she'd come up with wasn't just a delusion from her smoke-addled mind.

"But how would it work, exactly?" Shannon asked.

"We tell a story with the spell inside," Liv responded. "It doesn't even matter what the spell is, we can make that part up. That's what Malquin did with the wraths. They chanted some random word, but as long as they believed what they were saying, it worked. In seconds, like . . . like magic."

"But to get that many people to really believe, it would have to be one hell of a movie," Peter said.

Liv grinned. "I know."

Kat looked incredulously between Cedric, Merek, and Rafe. "Does any of this make any sense to you?"

Cedric's expression was careful, watchful. "A bit."

Rafe shook his head. "Liar. That was all basically gibberish, and you know it."

"No, I think I understand, too," Merek said, looking directly at his brother. "Shannon exposed me to some of these movies—"

"The best of my collection," Shannon interrupted.

"And I understand what Liv is saying, how watching movies can make you feel . . . amused, sad, scared. I did not understand half of what I was seeing, but—"

"But you still cried during *Up*."

Merek's face went white. "I did not!"

"You did, I totally saw you. Don't worry, no one here is judging."

"I am, a little," Peter said, grinning. But he stopped smiling when he saw the furious look on Merek's face. "Let's get started, then."

Liv nodded enthusiastically. She turned to Cedric again,

and for a moment was confused to see him through what seemed like a strange, liquid veil in front of her eyes. Tears. She'd wanted so badly for them to understand her idea, and now they were on the verge of it, and for the first time in a long time, she felt something close to hope.

Cedric smiled. "What do you need us to do?"

Liv exhaled, feeling twenty pounds lighter. As if the hard part were done, and not still in front of them.

"Thank you," she whispered.

Kat nodded in Liv's direction. "I do not understand any of this, but it is not as though I have a better plan. I will help."

Kat looked to Merek, who nodded. "Me too."

Liv clapped her hands together, a director ready to start work. She looked around at her friends in the dim room, her mind already calculating what to do first. Standing across the room, Rafe raised his hand.

"Question. What exactly is a movie?"

THE LAST PICTURE SHOW

The first hurdle was finding electricity. They only needed enough to power their phones and a laptop. Shannon and Peter went about connecting the electronics to the house's small generator, which they'd agreed only to use when absolutely necessary.

Having little to do until the cameras started rolling, Kat, Merek, Cedric, and Rafe went through their combined selection of silver weapons and sparred on the hot sand below the house. Liv sat down in the living room to start writing her script, her hand flowing over the notebook in her lap.

"Hey, Liv?" Shannon asked from her position on the floor, where she was examining her own dead phone.

"Hmm?" Liv asked, still writing.

"So once we get this movie all made and everything . . . how are we going to get anyone to see it?"

Liv's hand stopped abruptly, and she looked up.

"Please tell me this isn't the first time you've thought of this?" Shannon asked, voice sharp.

"There's a lot on my mind!"

Shannon shook her head and crossed the room to sit by Liv on the couch. "Okay, well, where do you think we can put the movie where the most people will see it?"

"Um . . . YouTube?"

Shannon tilted her head and patted Liv on the shoulder. "Oh, Liv. Poor sweet, naive Liv. Do you know how many millions of videos are on YouTube?"

"She's right," Peter said. "Why would anyone watch ours? We have to direct people to it."

"With . . . Twitter?"

"Now you're just embarrassing yourself," Shannon replied.

"What?" Liv asked. "You're on Twitter."

"Yeah, and I only have 548 followers. All painstakingly added over the course of two years, by the way. And if it took that long for someone who looks this good to get followers, we're not going to be able to just add thousands more at the click of a button."

Liv's shoulders fell. Her brain whirred, trying to think up a solution. But it kept running up against dead ends.

"No need to look so depressed," Shannon said. "We'll think of something. And hey, we've got my 548 people, so that's a start!"

"I can post it to the D&D message boards, though it might take a while to build traction," Peter said.

"And I can start posting it to our school's Facebook page, and there's always Snapchat—" Shannon added.

"—I have access to the AFI film studies email list—"

"—can send it to all my cousins in Utah; there's like eighty of them. . . ."

They trailed off, trying desperately to think of more ideas.

"This is crazy," Shannon said. "I've been trying to be famous for, like, ever. If I knew a shortcut, I would have used it by now!"

"It's too bad you don't know any famous people who could help," Peter cut in. His eyes were still glued to his laptop screen.

"I've been saying that my whole life," Shannon said with a rueful shake of her head.

Peter shrugged. "A famous person would have a big following. A movie star would be ideal, since their fan base is already primed. . . ." He paused, looking up from the computer and around the room. "A movie star like . . . the ones that own this house."

Liv and Shannon both looked around at the Oscar statue and the framed red carpet photos. Then, at the same time, they yelled out, "Daisy!"

Shannon's eyes gleamed as she sat up straighter. "If she could just access her parents' Twitter—oh my God, she could reach millions!"

"Millions of movie lovers."

"We still need internet access," Peter said, but he was smiling. "In order to upload the video. And contact Daisy."

"Is there any way you could work a little magic . . . ?" Liv asked hopefully.

Peter shook his head. "If you're talking about technological magic, no. From what I can tell, most of the city's servers are down on the west side. And if you're talking about the other kind of magic . . . that's really more your department than mine."

"Okay, well, if the internet's down here, we'll just have to go someplace it's working again."

"On my way back to LA, my phone worked most of the way here," Shannon put in. "It was definitely working in the Valley, anyway."

"All right, that's not too far," Liv said. "Now there's nothing left to do but . . . start shooting."

She picked up her phone to carry it over to Peter, hesitating only when she saw her own reflection in its dead, black screen. Her hair was still an ash-covered mess, and she had definite bags under her eyes. But she no longer looked like the shell-shocked victim she'd been just an hour before. Her eyes were clear and full of energy. After months of confusion and fear and doing things completely out of her element, she was finally back in her own domain. She didn't have to wield a sword or tramp through woods or take protection during earthquakes. In order to save the world, she only had to do the one thing she loved best.

Direct.

‡+·+‡

"My name is Liv Phillips, and I know why the world is broken. I know, because it's kind of, sort of, partially my fault."

Liv once again stared at her phone, but this time it was on and running. She stood on the beach, and behind her the orange sky was spread out over the sea like an oppressive blanket.

Shannon held the phone, with Peter standing beside her. The others stood just off to the side, waiting for Liv to give them instructions. But for now, Liv just looked into the camera, ready to tell her story.

She figured the best thing to do would be to show anyone watching that magic was real, and that it was here in Los Angeles. That's why their group was standing so near to where Liv, Daisy, and Joe had opened their large portal in Malibu, the one that had caused the sky to turn orange in the first place. As soon as Liv made her quick introduction, she used Malquin's words to open the portal once again.

That would get any viewer's attention. Even if they thought it was all just special effects—which they probably would—hopefully some would be interested enough to keep watching. Interested enough to hear the rest of Liv's story. Interested enough to maybe even believe in what she was saying, if only for a second.

The portal opened, a black hole in the middle of the sky. Liv turned back to the camera phone. "Magic is real. I know it's crazy, but it's true. But this isn't where the story starts. It starts with him."

That was Cedric's cue to come before the camera screen. He looked nervous and unsure of where to look, even though they'd practiced this part three times. He had few enough lines, with Liv narrating most of how they met. Kat and Merek joined the screen to reenact their first trip through the portal. Kat's line delivery was as stiff as her shoulders, while Merek scowled every time he forgot what he was supposed to say. Not the best actors in the world, but they got the job done.

Liv left the camera rolling as an earthquake started up, just minutes after the portal opened, and she kept on filming when the portal closed back up after no one went through it. The group went through the main points of their story, using various parts of the beach and Malibu house as backdrops. Shannon was the only one really eager to be in front of the camera, so Liv made sure to give her as big a role as possible.

Then came the most important part. Liv once again stood with her back to the ocean, directing the others to help her fix the sky with a spell to bring balanced magic back to the world. When she spoke, though, her words were for the camera alone—or rather, the people beyond it. The ones who would watch. Liv figured the actual words of the spell didn't matter so much—Malquin had made his up, after all—but she didn't want to get this part wrong.

"Accept the magic," she said, over and over, asking the others to repeat after her. Their voices rose up higher and higher, and Peter swung the camera out to the roiling clouds in the sky. Liv and the others looked up at it, their faces filled with hope, their voices still mixing together in unison—

"Cut!" Liv said.

Peter hit a button on the camera screen, and everyone seemed to let out a collective breath. Peter had suggested using digital effects to make the sky turn blue again, but it had been Liv's idea to have the movie cut to black, just as people would wonder whether or not the spell worked. It would hopefully make anyone watching lean forward, interested to see what happens next, maybe repeating the words of the spell in their own minds, imagining what it would look like if it worked . . .

Liv turned to the others and grinned. "That's a wrap."

They headed back to the house so Peter could get a start on editing the footage on his laptop and the others could start to load up the van with any supplies they might need for the trip to find working internet.

Liv was alone in the kitchen, loading up a canvas bag with some snacks, when Cedric entered. He had a half smile on his face as he leaned against the counter top, and his hip bumped up against hers.

"So how did I do?"

"Pretty good," Liv said, smiling back. "I think you might have a future in this industry, kid," she joked.

He raised one disbelieving eyebrow.

"Well, you'd make a hell of a stuntman, anyway. Maybe not as good as an action star, but . . ."

Cedric looked quickly at a picture on the fridge of Daisy's parents—both of whom actually were action stars. "It is still difficult to believe that one could make a living playing pretend. Especially a living as nice as this." He gestured around the large kitchen.

"I know." Liv grinned. "Isn't it awesome? There's lots of ways you could make a living in this world . . . I mean, it would involve *staying* in this world . . ."

Cedric's expression suddenly turned serious. He shifted his position—just an inch or so—but enough so they were no longer touching.

Liv cleared her throat. "If this works, Cedric . . . if we can make it so the portals don't have to close forever . . ."

Cedric swallowed, and Liv continued in the heavy silence. "It's just . . . maybe you don't have to pick one place and stay in it forever. Maybe you could stay here just . . . for a while."

She reached impulsively for his hand, and when her fingers landed on his, she half expected him to pull away. But instead, he squeezed her hand. He looked pained, and a line deepened between his eyes. Liv suddenly didn't want to hear what he had to say. *Why'd I have to bring this up at all?* she wondered. *Why not just enjoy the time we have left?*

But she couldn't keep avoiding it. She had to know what was coming around the corner if she could. Even if the only thing in her future was hurt. So she didn't look away as Cedric moved closer once again, his face just inches from hers.

"It is so strange," he said, his voice low and clear. "When I first came to this realm, I felt like I had made the biggest mistake of my life. All I wanted to do was reverse what I had done, to go home as quickly as possible. But as time passed, as I spent more time here, those feelings changed. Everything I encountered was terrifying . . . but it was exciting. There was so much to do, so much to see and learn. And then, just as I started to get a handle on things, I had to return to my reality."

"To your home," Liv whispered.

Cedric squeezed Liv's fingers again. "Yes, to my home. Which no longer felt quite the same as it had before. And when I came back here, it was like I was struck with this sort of clarity. I could not shake the feeling that this is where I was meant to be. Maybe just until I could help you fix things and save our worlds, or maybe . . ."

"Maybe longer?" Liv couldn't keep the hope out of her voice. She held her breath, waiting on Cedric's answer. But he turned away from her finally, looking toward the floor.

"If it were up to me, I think I would very much like to stay longer."

Liv slowly nodded, her held breath escaping in a sigh. "But . . . it's not up to you."

Cedric shook his head. "If I were not a king—" He cut himself off, his eyebrows furrowing. Then his head tilted toward the window, and he straightened.

"Do you hear that?"

"What?" Liv asked, turning. She couldn't hear anything. But the front door of the house slammed open, and Kat came running into the kitchen.

"Something is coming, from up the road," she said.

Cedric and Liv both rushed outside, Kat close behind. Liv peered to the right, down the PCH toward Santa Monica. The road had been empty of everything but their own mopeds and vehicles for weeks. But now, in the distance, Liv heard something.

Engines. Lots of them.

Then she saw them, black dots moving down the roadway, growing bigger and bigger. An assortment of cars, trucks, and motorcycles.

Shannon skidded through the front door, her eyes going wide as she saw the train of vehicles moving closer.

"They found us," Cedric said, his voice tight. "How did they find us?"

The answer came to Liv quickly—and painfully, as she

smacked one hand against her forehead, unable to handle her own stupidity.

"Joe."

Joe-as-wrath knew where they were, knew everything—how could she not have thought of that? Because deep down, she still thought of him as the Joe she knew, the one who would do anything to protect her. Not this version, who would do anything Malquin told him to—even if it hurt her.

"Um, they're moving really fast," Shannon said.

"How many are there?" Kat asked, peering into the distance.

Liv remembered the circle of wraths lining the edges of the giant soundstage. "Too many to fight. We have to go."

Kat's forehead crinkled in confusion. "Run?"

"Drive," Liv said. She turned to Shannon. "Get the others. Tell Peter to bring his laptop, bring all our phones. We have to start this now."

Shannon dove back into the house as Liv looked for the van keys. Cedric and Kat quickly gathered up their weapons and were back outside, followed by Merek and Rafe. Peter stumbled outside quickly, still dragging his right leg a bit. He held his laptop in both hands.

"I'm not finished yet!"

"Finish in the car!" Liv yelled back.

They climbed into the van just as the first car reached the end of the driveway. Liv slammed the driver's side door shut and put her foot on the gas pedal. In the passenger seat, Cedric tightened his grip on his sword hilt and kept his eyes focused straight ahead.

"Can you get past them?" he asked Liv.

"I can try."

The van lurched forward, moving up the driveway. A small black car came toward them, head-on. A motorcycle was next to it, and behind both was a familiar, worn-down, boxy vehicle. Joe's Jeep.

Liv's stomach lurched. She drove straight on, getting close enough to the oncoming car to see the black eyes of the wrath behind the driver's wheel.

"Uh, Liv?" Shannon asked, leaning forward. "Please don't crash my mom's van and kill us all, okay?"

When the van was just feet away from the oncoming black car, Liv suddenly pulled hard on the steering wheel, whipping the van to the left side of the driveway and down onto the manicured lawn with a jolt, making everyone bounce in their seats. Liv kept her foot hard on the gas pedal, cutting a path across the grass, swerving around a pair of palm trees and coming out on the roadway.

The vehicles in pursuit on the driveway had to brake and swerve to try to follow Liv's van. She'd only bought herself maybe a thirty-second head start.

Liv kept her foot on the gas, racing up the deserted roadway, one eye on the rearview mirror. She saw the cars gaining on her, counting at least four of them immediately behind her. She was going to have to figure out a way to either outpace them or lose them, and neither seemed a likely option on this long, winding strip of road with the ocean on one side and steep hills on the other.

"Oh my God, oh my God," Shannon said, her head craned

back to see the cars speeding up in pursuit. "They're right behind us."

"Don't panic," Liv said, trying hard to calm her own racing pulse. "I can still lose them."

She pushed down again on the gas, as ocean and mountain alike sped by in a blur.

"Have you outdriven this many vehicles before?" Cedric asked, in a whisper only she could hear.

"Nope," Liv responded, her voice just as low. "But no need to tell everyone."

Cedric nodded, looking a bit green as the van hugged the side of a cliff.

"And, Cedric?"

"Yes?"

"Buckle up."

WHIPLASH

As Liv took another sharp turn up a narrow, steep road, Cedric's stomach lurched. He could barely look out the window at his side now, for fear of seeing how far the hillside to their right fell down toward the earth. If Liv were to turn the wheel of the car ever so slightly, they would all go pitching off the side to their deaths. Cedric did not know if smashing into the ground in this mountainous region would be better or worse than crashing into the ocean they'd left behind, but Liv had assured them that cutting through the hills that bordered Malibu would be the best way to get away from their pursuers. And, sure enough, the narrow roads here had forced the cars behind them to follow in a single file, which made it much less likely the van would be surrounded and overrun.

They also made it more likely that Cedric was about to see his lunch for a second time.

Cedric glanced quickly at Liv, whose jaw was clenched shut and whose knuckles were turning white. Her eyes continually went from the road in front of her to the rearview mirror, and her breaths were shallow.

"How are you doing?" Cedric asked, his voice low so only Liv would hear.

"Still alive," she replied, managing a grim smile.

They had been on the run for more than twenty minutes, and the mood inside the van was quiet and tense. The only noises were the sound of wind rushing by and Peter's fingers tapping over the thin device that sat in his lap.

In the far backseat, Rafe's face was glued to the window. As Liv followed another sharp turn in the road, Rafe put one hand up against the pane of glass, as if to keep himself from falling through it and tumbling down the side of the cliff below.

"Does anyone else think it is unnatural to move at this speed?" he asked in a tight voice.

Next to him, Merek smirked. "You can always close your eyes and wait until it's over."

Rafe scowled in response, but Merek looked smug.

Kat was ignoring both them both, her head turned around to face the line of cars pursuing them.

"We're almost out of the mountains," Liv said, taking another sharp turn. The cliffside dropped away, revealing a gentle slope covered in yellowed grass. Surprisingly, Cedric recognized a few of the shapes that blurred past the window. Horses—there were actual horses grazing behind fences. Cedric wondered why this world even had need of horses, when they had vehicles such as this one that could move so fast, but he sensed this was not the time to bring it up.

He wished he had more time here, to ask that question and a million more.

"They are not letting up behind us," Kat said from the backseat without even turning her head around.

Liv's eyes darted to the rearview mirror and back. "I know," she said. "I have an idea."

Cedric raised his eyebrows. "An idea?"

"It's kind of hard to explain."

The road smoothed out and became larger, and Liv pushed her foot down to make the van move faster once again. But the cars following them had the opportunity to go faster also—and to spread out behind them. Once they had all descended from the mountains, Kat set to counting how many were in pursuit.

"Thirteen," she said, her voice grim. "There are thirteen of those things behind us."

With a roaring noise, a vehicle that looked like the mopeds they'd used to find Henry Martin—only much larger—pulled up to the side of the van. Its owner looked to Cedric with narrowed, all-black eyes.

Cedric straightened, all attention, his sword at the ready. The wrath was so near to him, and he longed to jump out and fight it. It swerved quickly toward the van and away again, causing Liv to yelp and jerk on her steering wheel.

"Should we not stop here and fight them back?" Cedric asked.

Liv shook her head quickly, her hair slashing against her now bone-white cheeks. "I think I can thin them out first. We just have to hold on till Calabasas—"

"What's in Calabasas?" Shannon asked, but Liv didn't respond.

"I got it!" Peter suddenly yelled. "Cell phone service . . . and internet!"

"I'll call Daisy," Shannon said, whipping out her phone.

Peter's fingers click-clacked over the keys. "Uploading now."

Liv blew out a breath. This time, Cedric did reach out and briefly hold her hand. Her eyes slid over to his.

"This plan will work," he said, though he had no idea if that was true.

"If I keep us alive long enough to even give it a shot," she replied, just as another car pulled up alongside them and she revved the gas to move faster.

For the next few minutes, everyone in the car was racked with tension and anxiety. Well, everyone except for Shannon, who talked excitedly into her phone. Cedric heard snippets— "I'll send you the link . . ." and ". . . how would I know your parents' password?" and "Of course it's an emergency!"

"Linking to the video on other sites now," Peter said distractedly. "All our Facebook and Instagram profiles, Snapchat, my D&D forums . . ."

Shannon pulled her phone from her ear. "Daisy's in. She's on her mom's Twitter right now. As soon as she links the video, it'll go out to 2.1 million people. She's hashtagging it with the name of her dad's latest movie, so people will click on it."

"Sneaky," Liv breathed. "I can't believe we're actually doing it—we're saving the world through Twitter."

"If this works and we don't all die, you should definitely put that on your resume," Shannon replied.

Liv managed a smile, but it soon slipped from her face as another motorcycle moved up ahead of the van. It swerved, trying to cut the van off, and Liv had to slam on the brakes to avoid being driven off the road.

"Holy crap!" Shannon exclaimed, as Liv swerved to the right and hit the gas again. Behind them, the motorcycle moved in a fast circle and picked up pursuit. "If these guys are from another world, how is it they can drive like that?"

"Maybe they're not from another world," Liv said darkly.

"What do you mean?"

"Maybe Malquin has already turned more men into wraths than we thought. For all we know, his army might be mostly humans-turned-wraths at this point."

Shannon shuddered. "Can you imagine? Turning into a monster like that?"

Liv shook her head, her eyes flicking back to the rearview mirror. Cedric didn't have to guess who she was looking for in the crush of vehicles behind them.

A new thought struck him. "You said earlier that your ploy with the movie might not just fix the world—it could maybe fix the men Malquin has changed."

"Emphasis on the maybe," Liv said. "Malquin said that the only reasons the old Guardians didn't turn into monsters when they ingested wrath blood was because the magic on Earth was more stable then. If our plan works, if we can bring back balance . . . then maybe the wrath blood in these men will become stable. Or maybe not."

"If it does work," said Cedric, trying to be hopeful, "then would these men not regain control of their own minds? They might stop chasing us altogether."

Liv bit her lip, the way she sometimes did when concentrating hard.

"They might." She looked to Peter. "How's it coming?"

But Peter's face gave her an answer before he could. "It's only been a minute. These things take time."

"We don't have time," Kat said, her eyes carefully monitoring the two cars that were nearly at their bumper.

Peter bit his lip, and his eyes widened. "Shannon, give me your phone. I just thought of something."

"What?" Shannon asked, handing the phone over.

"Live streaming. Extra content to keep eyeballs on us, and maybe it makes the story even more believable."

"Couldn't hurt," Liv said. "Give it a shot."

As Peter clicked around on Shannon's phone, Liv took a hard right turn then, coming up to the intersection of two large roads.

"Uh, shouldn't we stick to the freeways?" Shannon said, gripping the seats in front of her to keep from being thrown sideways. "Not to challenge your driving or anything, Liv, but surface streets could get a bit . . . dicey."

"I know," Liv said as she hunched forward, eyes on the road ahead. She made another sharp turn.

In the backseat, Peter held his phone up, recording their drive. Cedric noted that the scenery passing by was now distinctly city-like, with darkened buildings and empty roadways.

In the distance, he saw a line of what looked like thin yellow paper stretched across the road in front of them. He recognized that paper—the police had lined it around the museum alleyway after he had battled wraths there.

Cedric leaned even closer to the large windshield, trying to see. Beyond the yellow barrier, objects appeared to be . . . floating in midair. A metal blue box with a cylindrical top, a green plant in a pot. An entire car. They all rotated a few feet above the ground, suspended in the air as if by . . . magic.

"What . . . ?" he started.

"Is that what I think it is?" Shannon asked, pushing herself between the driver's and passenger's seats again. "I saw those on TV, the Gravity Incidents? Liv, you're headed right for it. Liv? Liv?!"

But Liv wasn't slowing down. She sped right toward the floating objects, her eyes locked on the road straight ahead. Without thinking, Cedric gripped the sides of his seat, his fingers digging into the fabric there.

The nose of the van moved closer to what Shannon called the Gravity Incident, closer . . . closer . . .

Just as it was about to crash through the yellow tape, Liv suddenly pulled hard on the wheel, yanking it to the right. The van made a hard turn, screeching over the ground and throwing its occupants against the windows. It kept moving forward, nearly skidding into a metal sign that read "Donut Time" before Liv was able to pull the wheel again, righting it and directing it back onto the road.

Cedric turned his head to look behind him, and that's when he understood Liv's plan.

Several of the wraths' vehicles hadn't been able to make the turn in time to follow Liv, and instead had gone sailing straight into the Gravity Incident. Now four cars and two motorcycles hovered in the air, their wheels spinning uselessly as they floated through empty space. Many of the rest of the vehicles had stopped just before hitting the incident, and some wraths were getting out to try to help down their floating comrades.

Only one single car had managed to make the turn quick enough and was still following Liv, though as she made another turn, Cedric realized it might be easier for her to gain speed and lose it on these streets.

Liv grinned. "Calabasas Gravity Incident. One of the first."

"That," Cedric said, grinning in response, "was genius."

"Thanks, but I got the idea from the poor security guard who made the mistake of trying to chase me down in the Grove." She put one hand up toward the ceiling of the van. "I really owe you, random guard guy!"

Liv made another turn, her eyes on the rearview mirror.

"There is still one back there," Kat said from the backseat.

"Hey, I'll take one over thirteen," Liv said, but her smile slipped a bit. "I'll try to lose this one, too."

But as they drove on, turning down street after street, the vehicle behind them managed to keep up. It never pulled forward or beside them, but followed them at a safe distance. Kat counted three wraths in the car.

"Why's it staying back like that? What're they waiting for?" Shannon asked, her voice tinged with panic.

Liv shook her head, making turns and speeding up to try

to lose the vehicle. But it stayed stubbornly behind her as they passed gray, boxy buildings and empty lots filled with dirt. In the distance, a bolt of lightning forked to the ground.

Behind them, a second car joined the first one still chasing them. It pulled onto the road from a random side street and sped up quickly.

"They're regrouping," Kat said.

They were all quiet and tense, but Cedric noticed that Liv's shoulders grew straighter and straighter, her look of concentration pulled down in a frown. She looked down at the panel behind the steering wheel and bit her lip.

"Is something wrong?" he asked quietly. "I mean, more than usual?"

Liv swallowed and looked at him. "We're almost out of gas."

"What?" Shannon asked, leaning forward.

"That is bad, right?" Merek responded.

"It's pretty bad, yeah," Liv said.

Two more cars pulled into the road behind them, alongside the others. Liv pushed her foot down on the gas pedal, but the van seemed to be going as fast as possible already.

"On the plus side, the more cars that follow us, the more viewers we seem to keep on the stream," Peter said. "Almost eight hundred now."

Liv peered out at the still-orange sky. "Not enough."

"One more car just joined the group," Merek said from the backseat. "A Jeep."

No one said anything for a few moments, dread settling heavily over them.

"Maybe we should stop now and fight," Cedric finally said. As soon as the words were out of his mouth, the feeling of anxiety loosened from his stomach. It was much better to face the wraths and fight, swords out, than to sit in this chair and helplessly watch them get nearer and nearer.

"We need to give our plan more time to work," Liv said. "If you're right, Cedric, if this works and they turn back into men . . . I can't risk us killing any of them."

She looked at Cedric with pleading eyes, and he knew what she was saying—she didn't want him to kill Joe, even if he was in his new form. Even if he was one of the number of wraths pursuing them now.

"Nine hundred viewers," Peter said, angling the phone to catch the cars chasing them.

Liv's own eyes were on the glass panel behind the wheel, where Cedric saw a small red icon blink on. The word above it read "Empty."

They surged forward.

Cedric looked out his window to see one of the cars moving up on their right-hand side, pulling almost level with his window. It was close enough for Cedric to see the driver's black eyes through the window.

The wrath looked at Cedric and smiled, pulling its thin lips across its teeth. Then it jerked its hands hard to the left, sending its car smashing into the side of Cedric's door.

There was the sound of screeching metal, then a jolt. Liv swerved wildly to her left, but another car was on that side, boxing her in.

Shannon caught her breath first. "Holy sh—"

"Liv!" Peter interrupted, "Knock them back!"

"What?" Liv screamed.

"Try to knock them off the road before they can push you off."

Liv's eyes darted wildly between the two cars framing either side of the van. "Are you insane? I'm not Mad Max."

"Well, you're gonna have to be!"

Shannon stuck her head up near Liv's. "Do it!"

Liv's mouth fell open, her brows knitting together in concentration. The car on her side of the van swerved suddenly, smashing into her door and sending them all rocking in their seats again.

"Maybe I can help," Cedric added. He looked quickly at Liv, then pushed the button to roll his window down. He pulled himself partway up through the window and thrust his head and shoulders through—along with his sword.

The van was moving so fast that Cedric had to momentarily close his eyes against the wind, which blew his hair back and pressed his shirt against his skin. He balanced himself against the window frame and focused on the wrath driving in the car immediately to his right. The next time it swerved the car over to knock into the van, Cedric swung out with his sword arm, slashing its metal tip against the side of the car.

The sword didn't slow the car down, but it did leave a long scratch and a grating metal-on-metal noise that looked like it gave the wrath driver pause.

Next, Cedric swung for the window. He couldn't get enough

leverage on his sword to break through the glass entirely, but he swung out hard enough to send spiderweb cracks up the window surface, obscuring the face of the wrath driver.

Cedric heard another cracking noise and turned around—both Rafe and Kat were hanging partway out of their own windows, swinging their weapons at nearby cars as well. Merek kept an eye through the back windshield for new cars joining the chase.

Rafe made a solid hit against a car's wheel, and it went spinning off the roadway in a squealing cloud of dust. He turned to Cedric with a grin and shouted, "This is excellent!"

The wrath driver closest to Cedric pulled a few more feet away, though it still kept steady with the van. Cedric slipped back into his seat for a moment and looked to Liv. Her knuckles were still white on the steering wheel, and she gave him a wan smile.

"Seriously, stuntman is your calling." Her words were light, but she couldn't keep the strain from her voice. Her focus shifted to the red Empty light once again. Cedric turned back toward the window, ready to keep any advancing wraths at bay. But he counted eight cars behind them now—if all eight decided to rush their van at once . . . there was little his one sword could do.

"We're past a thousand. The comments are going nuts," Peter said. "People are confused, but they're loving it."

"Glad someone is," Liv muttered. Then she mumbled something else that sounded to Cedric like her made-up mantra, "Accept the magic." She kept her eyes focused ahead, where lightning still crashed down in the distance from the angry clouds.

Peter swung the phone around to aim it at the seat behind him, where Kat was still hanging half out a window, swinging her sword, while Merek held her legs down to the seat from inside. Cedric saw that Kat was engaged in an actual sword fight—one of the wraths sitting in the backseat of a large, boxy black vehicle was leaning out of his own window and trying his hardest to knock Kat from hers. Part of Kat's sleeve was torn and fluttering in the wind, and Cedric saw a thin trail of blood running down past her elbow.

"Liv! Move to the left—now!"

The van swerved suddenly, and Kat was given a moment's reprieve from the wrath in the other car. Unfortunately, Liv had swerved too far in the other direction, which nearly crushed Rafe between the van and the large vehicle on the other side. Rafe pushed himself flat against the window of the van, hugging its roof, as the wrath car nearest to him again swerved nearer. It grew closer and closer, too fast for Rafe to slip back inside the safety of the van—

And then it surged forward. The car moved quickly ahead, knocking into the front end of the van instead of Rafe's window and moving past them quickly. The black car next to Kat's window shot forward, too. Cedric whipped his head around, confused, and it took him a moment to realize—those cars weren't going any faster; the van was slowing down.

And getting slower every second. Several vehicles and motorcycles sailed past the van before putting on their brakes and turning around.

Cedric lowered himself back into the passenger seat. "What happened? Why aren't we going forward?

"The tank ran out." Liv's panicked eyes swiveled from the dashboard to him. "We're not going anywhere."

THE LAST STAND

Liv's foot pressed the gas pedal down to the floor, but the van refused to move.

The wraths in their cars and trucks and motorcycles were turning around, forming a large circle around the stalled-out van. A stucco apartment building sat in a wide lot on one side of the road, and on the other was a small building with "Sherman Oaks Burger Time" printed in faded red letters on a yellow roof. It looked abandoned, its lights off and its two patio tables empty in the daylight.

There was no one here to help them.

Liv turned to Cedric. His hair was wild from the wind, and his eyes were wide as they tracked the wraths that started to circle them.

"We're surrounded," Cedric said.

Liv turned around to see both Shannon and Peter staring out the windows at the wraths that circled nearer. They looked terrified, though Peter managed to keep the phone in his hand trained on the monsters outside so viewers could see.

"How are we doing, Peter?"

He turned to her, his face pale and stretched-looking, and in his eyes was pure panic. He didn't move.

"Peter," Liv prompted.

He jumped a bit, then looked at the screen shaking in his hands. "We're almost at two thousand," he whispered.

Liv half crawled out of her seat and grabbed the phone in his hands. "I'm Liv Phillips, and if you're watching this, you just saw the video we posted about what happened to Los Angeles. What's still happening, right now—"

Something large and heavy crashed into the front windshield. Liv and Cedric both jumped as cracks radiated outward from a small hole in the center of the window.

"Everyone close your windows!" Cedric yelled. "Lock the doors!"

"Say it with me, please!" Liv yelled into the screen. "Accept the magic, accept the magic . . ."

Two motorcyclists were circling the van now, exhaust pluming up in a ring of fumes. They were outnumbered, surrounded, and there was nowhere to go. The video wasn't working.

They'd lost.

"Oh my God, their eyes. What's wrong with their eyes?" Shannon asked, her voice high and sharp.

Liv followed Shannon's gaze out the window to two wraths who were getting out of a car and making their way over to the van. One held a sword while the other carried what looked like a Taser. The taller one had thin lips stretched back to reveal a mouthful of too many teeth, while the short one's mouth could almost pass as ordinary, if still terrifying. Both had pitch-black eyes that showed no whites at all.

"Their eyes always look like that," Liv responded.

"That's how you know they're wraths," Peter said, looking up from his typing.

Shannon shook her head, her own eyes still staring out the window. "Nuh-uh, I've never seen those before."

Liv looked back at the wraths, and then jumped in her seat, squirming around to face the others.

"It's working!"

They just stared at her.

"Shannon shouldn't be able to see their eyes," Liv said, excitement running her words together as she spoke. "Peter and I can because we're scrolls, and you guys can because you're Guardians, but Shannon's just a human—"

"*Just?*" Shannon interrupted.

"—so the Earth's quelling defenses protect her from seeing the wraths as monsters here . . . but if those defenses are breaking down . . ."

Peter's eyes widened with understanding. He looked down at the phone. "People are typing it in the comments. Accept the magic."

"Keep it going!" Liv said, throwing her hands up. She looked back out the window at the approaching wraths. They were only feet away now, but already they looked different, even to her eyes. The tall wrath looked even taller than he had a moment before, his head a fraction larger on his neck. His fingernails seemed longer, too, stretching out into claws . . . claws that swung out toward Shannon's window and connected with a thump.

Shannon screamed. "Um, do *they* know they're changing?"

The tall wrath punched the window again, and this time his fist left behind a small crack.

"We cannot stay in here," Kat said. "There are too many of them, and if they break those windows—we cannot fight from these chairs."

"We just have to wait it out," Liv said. "It's working—"

"Not fast enough," Cedric said. He looked out through the cracked windshield at the monsters bearing down on them. "We should run for cover."

"Cover?" Liv yelled. "Cover where?"

"There." Kat pointed toward the run-down, abandoned burger shack.

"How are we going to get there?" Liv asked, just as three wraths on Cedric's side of the van started pushing against it, rocking it up slightly.

"We're at three thousand views and even more currently streaming!" Peter yelled. The van rocked again.

"Oh, we're gonna die," Shannon moaned. "We're gonna die talking about YouTube views."

Merek reached over the seat and put a hand on her shoulder. "No," he said. "We're not." He looked up, his eyes meeting Cedric's. After a moment, they both nodded.

"Take this, then follow me," Cedric said, handing Liv a silver knife and turning away. One moment he was in the passenger seat, and the next he'd opened his window again and pulled himself out quickly in one fluid movement. First his head disappeared upward, then his body, then his feet, snaking past the window and landing with a thud on the roof.

A wrath lunged forward to the open passenger-side window, thrusting one arm inward toward Liv. She pushed herself backward from the hand—much larger than a human hand, and much grayer, too—and screamed. The clawed hand still reached outward, scrabbling at her neck, and then it fell abruptly down—into the passenger seat. The wrath at the window screamed, pulling back his arm—or what was left of it. Black blood spurted from where the creature's elbow used to be as Cedric wrenched his sword back again.

"I'm gonna throw up," Shannon said, her eyes frozen in horror on the grayish half arm resting on the van's seat.

Liv heard two more thuds moving across the top of the van, then saw Cedric land gracefully on the ground outside of her window. For a moment, the back of his head was just inches from hers. Then, he propelled himself forward, sword out, toward the group of wraths huddled outside.

Following Cedric's lead, Kat swung herself out of her own window, and Rafe and Merek did the same. Soon they were all outside the driver's side of the van, fighting back the growing number of wraths.

Another wrath reached in through the passenger-side window, scrambling for Liv. She pushed herself back through the door, calling out to Peter and Shannon, "Come on! We have to make a run for it!"

They pulled themselves out behind Liv, Peter keeping his

phone trained on the action in front of him. Cedric and the others had pushed the wraths back enough to create a small space just outside the van. It was big enough for Liv, Shannon, and Peter to stand in, but there was no room for them to move anywhere else. The sound of sword-on-sword fighting—one that had become all too familiar to Liv—rang out.

"We'll push them back to get you to that building," Cedric said, motioning toward the burger shack in between sword thrusts. "Take cover there."

Liv nodded. She reached for the knife in her boot and held it outward like Merek had showed her, but she still felt unarmed in the face of the wrath horde. Cedric and Kat fought on one side of her, and Merek and Rafe on the other. Liv kept her back to Shannon and Peter as they crept slowly away from the van and toward the abandoned building, the fight unfolding in a tight circle around them.

Rafe fought like Kat, both of them moving with quick, precise movements to block blows coming their way. Cedric was a little wilder, swinging out to hold off as many wraths as possible. They were all fighting on the defensive. Liv looked over the shoulders of the wraths—who seemed to grow taller every second—to see the burger shack looking impossibly far away. Something hard bumped into her shoulder, and she looked behind to see it was a horn—an actual horn—connected to the head of a stumbling wrath. Sickeningly, he still had the hair of a man, growing up around the horn. Liv slashed out with her knife, just nicking the wrath's shoulder. It turned to her and growled, its teeth seeming to elongate before Liv's very eyes.

Then the wrath was screaming. It dropped to the ground, and Liv saw Merek standing behind it, his sword covered in black blood. Merek just had time to look up at Liv before another wrath came up from behind and brought its own blade down on his right shoulder.

Merek yelled out; his eyes rolled back into his head, and his knees buckled. Before Liv could react, Shannon pushed past her, catching Merek before he fell. He leaned on Shannon's shoulder, backing away from the wrath just before Cedric whirled around to slice low into the creature's knees, knocking it to the ground.

Merek was still conscious, one hand tight on the blood stemming from his shoulder, as Shannon started moving him closer to the building.

"He needs help!" she screamed. But there was no one to help Merek. There was no one to help any of them.

"There's . . . too many . . . ," Rafe panted.

"Get to the building," Cedric yelled back. "Just get them there!"

They moved just an inch at a time, but eventually their circle reached the big picture window of Burger Time, next to a padlocked front door. Liv pushed her back up against a faded paper menu taped to the glass and took in the scene. Merek was on the ground now in front of the window, one hand over his shoulder to stop the flow of blood. And there was a lot of blood. Shannon dropped to her knees by him, bunching up the bottom of his shirt to put over the wound, while Peter leaned against the window, shoulder to shoulder with Liv.

"We have to get in there," he said, motioning to the empty diner behind them.

Liv looked around for something to break the window with . . . anything . . . but all she had was her knife. She banged the butt of it against the window, but barely even made a dent.

The wraths closed in, swinging and fighting all the way, until Liv could no longer see through them to the street beyond. The only things keeping her from the angry horde of quickly transforming monsters were the blades of Cedric, Kat, and Rafe, all of whom looked exhausted as they thrust back against blow after blow. Liv banged against the window again. It flexed a little under the weight of her fist, but it didn't break.

She closed her eyes, again repeating the lines she'd hoped would fix the world. "Accept the magic. Accept the magic. Accept the magic." She could barely hear her own voice over the sounds of fighting. But she tried to push every ounce of energy, of belief, that she could behind those words. When she opened her eyes again, she saw Cedric was being pushed back, closer and closer to her.

Then she saw the gun.

Cedric must have seen it, too, and known what it was, because he faltered in his step as the barrel of the gun pushed through the ranks of wraths. An arm followed it, then shoulders. And then a face, and Liv's mouth stopped working. Her lungs stopped working. Everything stopped working.

Joe held the gun firmly, a calm but determined expression on his face. Other than the black of his eyes, he still looked mostly human. Liv wondered briefly if he'd transform fully like the Caelum wraths. Could she handle seeing that? Could she even handle seeing this?

It didn't immediately occur to her that Joe would shoot

her—it went against every single idea and memory of him that she had—even when he leveled the gun at her.

It just wouldn't make sense.

But the gun was there, and so was Joe, and so was she.

"Not yet," a voice said beside Joe. Liv looked up to see Malquin sidle up beside Joe, his white hair blowing around his face in the breeze. "We need at least one of them alive."

Malquin looked between Liv and Peter, and she knew what he meant—he needed three scrolls to keep opening big portals and make the world even crazier than it already was. She moved instinctively toward Peter to protect him, and he did the same for her.

"Not going to happen," Cedric said, stepping in between Liv and Malquin.

But Malquin just narrowed his eyes and gestured to two wraths at his side, and they both lunged to Cedric, swords out. He blocked one blow and then the next, as the wraths pushed him farther and farther from where Liv stood.

The gun was just a few feet away now.

"Joe," Liv said, "please." She kept looking at him and him alone. Even though she wanted to tear her eyes away from his alien gaze, and that face that she both knew and did not know, she kept staring on.

"Accept the magic. Accept the magic. Accept the magic."

"What are you mumbling?" Malquin asked.

Liv kept saying the words, again and again. They were the only real weapon she had. Even if the knife in her hands were any match for the gun, she knew she couldn't use it—not on

Joe. The only shot she had was to use the power she'd apparently been born with—the magic curled up in the marking on her back.

"Accept the magic. Accept the magic. Please—"

"You know what? I don't actually care." Malquin turned to Joe. "Shoot her. Take the boy."

Joe nodded, almost imperceptibly, and his fingers moved against the trigger. The gun was just inches away now. Liv wanted to shut her eyes, but she couldn't. Her hand found Peter's, and they clutched at his fingers. But she stared in Joe's all-black eyes, forcing herself not to look away, not to flinch as he shot—

He faltered.

To Liv, it seemed to happen in slow-motion. In one half second, Joe blinked. Then blinked again. His hand slid just a fraction of an inch, then another. He blinked a third time.

"Do it!" Malquin yelled.

But Joe didn't nod. Instead, he shook his head, as if trying to clear it of a troublesome thought. He looked at Liv, narrowing his eyes. The hand holding the gun dropped even farther.

"Liv?" he asked, blinking. "What am I . . . where . . . ?"

Liv could vaguely tell the sounds of fighting around her were fading, but she couldn't piece together yet what that meant. All she saw was Joe's astonished face, the whites of his blinking eyes, and the sky, slowly turning blue, behind him.

THE PROPOSAL

It was easy enough to sort the new wraths from the old. The new wraths—most of them former Knights—stood around the dusty lot of Burger Time, blinking and staring at the weapons in their hands as if they'd never seen such things before. The old wraths fled quickly. Some took off as soon as half their army turned into regular, dazed-looking men, the others left as soon as their leader was escorted to the side of the diner at gunpoint. But Liv wasn't sure where these wraths would hide—nearly all of them now looked like themselves, full-blown monsters, the kind who'd seem conspicuous standing outside of a Burger Time in Sherman Oaks in broad daylight.

Joe had regained his faculties quickly enough, getting a firm grip on his gun and swiveling around to point it at his brother. But Malquin's own attention was on the sky. With every second, more and more orange faded away. At first it looked like nothing more than a particularly violent sunset, then the fading afterimage of one. Then complete blue—a blissful, calm blue—stretched wide across the sky.

"How?" Malquin murmured, alone and cowering near the diner wall, watching his army flee. Joe kept his gun trained on Malquin as Liv looked on from his side. Cedric and Kat, both heaving and worn-looking from their fight, came to join them as well.

"The important question is not how," Cedric said. "It is what to do with you."

"He deserves to die," Kat said, her voice flat. "In Caelum, he would be executed swiftly, not just for his crimes against our land, but for the murder of a king."

Joe swallowed hard, his eyes never leaving Malquin's face. After a moment, he spoke.

"I thought I could reach him, but . . ." He took two steps back, his eyes still trained on Malquin. He nodded in Cedric's direction.

"I understand what you have to do."

Cedric looked at Joe grimly before stepping in front of Malquin. He gripped the hilt of his sword and raised it over Malquin's neck.

"Please," Malquin said, his voice high. He scrambled back against the wall of the diner, his fingernails splayed against the fading wood. "I showed you mercy, Prince. At the first invasion, I could have had the wraths kill you, but I kept you alive. I kept your whole family alive—"

Cedric's eyes flashed, and Malquin stopped, seemingly realizing his mistake.

"I should not have killed the king, it's true. I was so angry, but—it's no excuse. I just wanted to get revenge on those who'd killed my brother, just like you're trying to get revenge now. You understand that, don't you?"

Cedric stared down at Malquin, his jaw tight. The muscles in his arm flexed and shook. Liv couldn't tell if he was fighting to keep the sword raised, or fighting to keep himself from smashing it down over Malquin's neck.

"Joe," Malquin said, shifting his gaze. "Please, you're my brother. My family. Don't let them do this, please."

Joe shut his eyes briefly, and sighed. "I am your brother, John. And you'll always be mine. But you're too far gone. Maybe you've been too far gone since the day Eric disappeared. I should have helped you then, and I couldn't. But that doesn't mean I'll help you now. Your fate is in Cedric's hands."

Malquin's eyes bounced wildly back to Cedric, then to the sword in his hand. "Please."

"Cedric," Kat said, her voice gentle but firm. "You can do this. For your father."

But Cedric didn't move. His feet stayed firmly in place, his sword raised high over Malquin's head. He turned to look at Liv. Their eyes met, and she cocked her head, trying to guess what he was thinking. His blue eyes squinted slightly, and it took Liv a second to realize why—the sun was shining down in them. The sun was back, bright in the sky.

Cedric lowered his sword.

"No."

"Cedric—" Kat started.

"In Caelum, this . . . man . . . would be executed immediately for his crimes. That is the way we have always done things, but it does not mean it is the best way. I've seen things work differently in this world." He paused, taking a breath. "We can be different, too."

Liv thought again about the professor in the woods of Caelum, of his death that had been lonely and brutal, whether or not it was justified. And though Malquin had caused much more pain and destruction than the professor ever had, she felt her insides swell at Cedric's decision. It was something more than just caring for him—it was pride.

Malquin's head shot up toward Cedric, his eyes filled with sudden hope. "You're . . . showing me mercy? Thank you, thank you—"

"I would not exactly call it mercy," Cedric said, his voice dripping with loathing. "There is still justice in your future, have no doubt about that."

"Just in case you're unclear, justice probably means dungeons," Liv added.

Malquin turned to look at her then, his hopeful expression shifting into a sneer. "Do you have any idea what you've done? He gestured to the blue sky. "You've brought magic back to this world—permanently. And now it's your responsibility to deal with it. Are you ready to do that? On your own?"

Liv stared him down, her eyes level with his. She tried to ignore how she didn't have an answer for his question. "Tie him up," she said.

⊱⊱⊰⊰

While Cedric and Kat guarded Malquin outside, the others had forced their way into the empty burger joint and started stuffing their faces on left-behind chips, pickles, and hamburger buns, too tired to even start thinking about their next move.

Liv looked across the room to where Shannon sat next to Merek in a booth, cleaning out his wound with wet paper towels. Rafe sat across from them, helping as well. The cut wasn't quite as deep as it had first appeared, and Shannon said she didn't think he'd need stitches. Then she had to explain to Rafe what stitches were, and his face turned white.

"Barbaric, isn't it?" Merek asked, grimacing. "You do not even want to see what they do with needles here."

Rafe adjusted in the hard plastic booth, and cleared his throat. "Cedric told me that you were injured here. It is impressive how quickly you recovered. And . . . how you fought today, that was also impressive."

"I know," Merek shot back. But looking at his brother, something in his face softened. "And thank you," he added.

The boys sat in silence for a moment, until Rafe looked away, clearly uncomfortable. He bit into a potato chip and made a face. "Interesting."

"You think that's interesting, try one of my Cheetos," Shannon said, pushing a crinkly orange bag across the table.

Liv smiled and turned back to Joe. "I think Merek will be okay," she said, her voice low. She and Joe sat at a tall two-top table near the Burger Time counter, under a large wall clock shaped like a pickle with a face. Its empty, cheerful eyes looked down over the bloody, exhausted group in the room.

Joe gave a small smile.

"Are *you* going to be okay?" Liv asked.

Joe ran a hand through his hair, a gesture so familiar to Liv that just seeing it made her heart twist inside her chest.

"I can't believe you're asking me that," Joe said. "I could have killed you, Liv. I was going to kill you."

"That wasn't you," Liv said quickly.

"No, not really. But none of this would have happened if it wasn't for me."

Liv shot him a confused look. "Hey, that's my line."

Another ghost of a smile. "I remember what Malquin said, back at Paramount . . . he was right about one thing. I did abandon him. If I had just talked John out of going through the portal, or if I'd been brave enough to go after him—"

"Then you never would have been around to protect me," Liv said. She reached out, putting her hand over where Joe's sat on the plastic table top. "And I wouldn't be around now to thank you for it. For watching over me, for being around when I needed you. For being like . . . family."

Joe looked down again, but this time Liv was sure it was to hide the tears in his eyes.

"Come on, now," Liv said lightly, fighting her own tears, "No crying in front of the pickle." She gestured up to the wall clock, and Joe smiled. Really smiled. But it fell fast.

"Are you really going to be okay?" Liv asked. "When Malquin put that stuff in you . . ." Liv trailed off, leaving the question unsaid.

"I was in there, somewhere, the whole time. But it was like that part of me—the part that makes me *me* was silenced. The new part of me that believed John and everything he was saying, that wanted to gain power, to hurt, to take things—that part was so loud, and I couldn't fight it."

"It sounds awful," Liv said.

Joe nodded. "But then, in an instant, that part went quiet. It was like my brain became at peace with what was happening in my body, and the real me was able to take control again."

"Just like with the sky," Liv said.

"That was a good trick you guys pulled," Joe said, his brown eyes warm, but serious. "But do you have any idea what the consequences will be?"

"A simple thank-you would work fine." Liv tore off a piece of hamburger bun and stuffed it in her mouth.

Joe rolled his eyes. "Of course I'm glad for what you did. But bringing magic back to this world forever—do you have any idea what that means? What it will do to the planet, to us?"

Liv shook her head. "No, but the sky's blue and we don't have a horde of monsters trying to kill us, so things are better than they were a half hour ago, right?"

Joe nodded, but his expression remained sober as he gazed out the window.

Liv bit off another chunk of her hamburger bun, pushing Joe's concern from her mind. Right now, they were alive and whole and together. She looked up at the pickle clock, something so ordinary, so much a part of this city and this world she loved, that she almost wanted to reach up and give it a hug.

Whatever new problems they'd unleashed on the world, they could deal with tomorrow.

}}··{{

After five minutes of his moaning and chatter, it became clear the easiest thing to do would be to knock Malquin out. Kat took the honor, using the blunt end of her sword hilt. After tying an unconscious Malquin to the front door of the building, Cedric and Kat moved a few feet away to the shade of a nearby palm tree.

"How much longer do you think you will stay?" Kat asked. Her question sounded innocent, but they both knew how loaded it was. She kept her gaze focused carefully on the street, and not on Cedric.

He looked at her with surprise. "How do you know I am staying?"

"Because I know you, and I am not an idiot."

Cedric smiled. "No, you are not."

Kat sighed. "I could tell you again how ridiculous it is to stay in another world for a girl—"

"But that is not why I am staying," Cedric said. The firmness in his voice seemed to surprise Kat, but she just narrowed her eyes at him.

"Or, not the only reason," Cedric added. "Kat . . . why is it that I am Caelum's king?"

Kat made a face like she couldn't even believe Cedric would ask something so stupid. "Because . . . because you are. Your father was king—"

"And his father before him, and his father before him, yes. But why does it work like that?"

"That is the way it has always worked," Kat said. Her tone was exasperated and a little disbelieving, as if he'd asked her why *A* comes before *B* in the alphabet.

"But why?" Cedric pressed. He gripped the end of his sword hilt, hoping the feel of it would help him keep going, help him say aloud the words he'd been wrestling with. "Our people came from this world hundreds of years ago. But look around, Kat. As this world changed, ours stayed the same. We stayed stuck in these old traditions without stopping to ask ourselves if they made sense anymore. Does it make sense that someone should be born to rule? That power and smarts would just be passed down by blood?"

He finished his words in a rush, eager to get them out, and Kat just blinked at him.

"How else would it work?" she finally said. But her tone was only half challenging—she seemed genuinely curious.

"Leadership should go to the person best suited for the job," Cedric said. "It's like Merek kept telling me, all those months ago when we first came to Los Angeles. The fact that I was born the son of King James does not automatically make me the best person to rule, to be in charge."

Kat rolled her eyes. "Merek was jealous—"

"Maybe, but there was truth to his words."

Kat shook her head. "You could be a great king, Cedric. I *know* it . . ."

"I could, maybe. But what if I do not *want* to be king? What if there was someone better for the position?"

"Who? How could we even decide such a thing?"

"The people would decide, of course," Cedric said. "But until then, there is someone much more capable who can step into my place."

Kat just stared at him.

"You, Kat. You should rule Caelum."

Kat's mouth fell open, and she took a step back. But behind her brown eyes, her brain was clearly working fast. She did not immediately refuse the proposition.

"Remember in Duoin, when we were at the inn and I was about to go after Liv—I asked you if you would give up Caelum if it meant saving me? I did not want to hear your answer then, because I knew what it was. Our homeland is *the most* important thing to you—more than any one person—and you are meant to be a leader in a way I never was."

"You led us, the whole time we were here—" Kat started, weakly.

"I can lead missions, yes," Cedric responded. "I am good at it, and that is what I enjoy. But leading an entire realm? Rebuilding Caelum, taking care of a whole population . . . Kat, you have already been ruling, the entire time since my father died. You are already queen."

Kat was silent as the words sank in. Cedric wanted to keep talking, but he knew he couldn't force this responsibility on her. Not the way it had been forced on him. For nearly a full minute, Kat's face was still, her eyes raking over the ground as she considered Cedric's words.

Then she lifted her head up, and she smiled. Cedric's heart lifted, but the smile quickly started to drop from Kat's face.

"And what about the other reason for you to return to Caelum?" Kat's voice lowered, but she kept her eyes on Cedric, displaying a strength he'd always envied. "Our betrothal? Is that a tradition you want to abandon as well?"

Kat's eyes remained fierce, but Cedric could see through them, could sense what it was costing her to ask this out loud. He was reminded of how she'd looked that day behind the pub, when he'd kissed her.

"You know I care for you, Kat, and always will, but . . . our lives could be different than we were raised to believe. They could be *more*."

A look of pain flashed quickly over Kat's face. "More?"

"I only mean . . . ," Cedric said quickly, swallowing hard. "Do you never wish you might have more control over who you might . . . be with? To choose for yourself?"

Kat looked confused. "I do not think I have ever . . . that is, I never . . ."

"Thought about it?"

"Of course I thought about it," Kat said, flustered. "But our future together was so sure. I never considered being with anyone else."

"But if you could?"

Kat looked down finally, and Cedric struggled to understand what she might be thinking.

"Kat," he continued gently. "I have never asked this before, but . . . do you really wish to marry me? Not for the benefit of Caelum, not to strengthen our kind, but to be with *me*. For always."

She reached for the necklace at her throat, the one with the betrothal ring hanging from its end. The one she'd worn every day since they were children.

"Cedric, you are my closest friend. My truest friend."

"And you are mine. But that is not exactly an answer to my question."

Kat shook her head slightly. "If you are not my always, then who—what—is?"

"I cannot say. But while these worlds are opening up to us . . . are you not at least a little curious to find out?"

Kat paused. "I do not know. I am not so enthralled with this new world as you are. But I *do* know . . . I will not force you to return. I do not want to spend forever with someone who does not want to spend forever with me."

Kat ran her fingers across the ring again before slowly and deliberately lifting the chain from her neck. She slipped it into her pocket, keeping her gaze steady on Cedric as she did so. For a moment, they stared at each other, both taking in how that one tiny gesture changed everything. Then, Kat gave a small smile.

"Does this mean I am going to have to start courting suitors?" she asked, wrinkling her nose.

Cedric laughed. "Not if you do not want to. Though I think Rafe would certainly be keen."

Kat made a face. Then her eyes slid to the sky, as though a new thought were occurring to her. "I think maybe he . . . is not my type." She gave a small half smile, one that felt private and that Cedric didn't really understand.

"And what will you do here?" Kat asked, finally looking at him again. "If you are no longer king, what will you be?"

Cedric turned her question over in his mind, the same question he'd asked himself hundreds of times in the past months.

He still did not know quite how to answer.

Finally, he shrugged. "I do not know. All I know is that I feel like myself here. It is difficult to explain, and even I am not entirely sure what it means yet, but I feel as though the life I should be living now is in this world. Maybe I will help these new men, with their wrath-infected blood. Or Liv says I could be a 'stuntman,' whatever that is. I suppose I really do not know." He grinned.

"It feels a bit terrifying," Kat said. "To not know exactly what the future holds."

"Yes," Cedric replied. "It does."

Kat smiled, and motioned her head toward the restaurant. "Shall we, then?"

"After you, my queen."

"Let us not get ahead of ourselves. If the people of Caelum *do* choose me as a leader, maybe I will go by something else."

Cedric smiled. "After you, Something Else."

Kat rolled her eyes. "This world is a terrible influence on you." She put her hand through the crook of his arm and led him back to where the others sat, waiting for them to return.

EDGE OF TOMORROW

Of course, the world didn't fix itself right away.

The sky remained a clear, determined blue one day after the showdown at a Burger Time in Sherman Oaks, but the city was still sweltering. The Gravity Incidents had ended, but the damage from the earthquakes and the lightning storms could not be as easily reversed. Stores were still looted; businesses were still closed. Cell and internet service were still knocked out for blocks.

Unfortunately for Shannon, that wasn't a good enough excuse to put off calling her parents. After the group had put gas in the van and driven back to Malibu, she'd taken off again in order to reach cell phone service and call them. She got more than an earful. Her parents had every right to be upset, of course, but Shannon wasn't looking forward to what would probably be a decades-long punishment.

Still feeling a bit bruised by the phone call, Shannon pushed open the door of Daisy's house to find Liv, Cedric, Peter, Merek, and Joe sitting around the living room talking and eating from cans of food and bags of Doritos. Shannon figured Kat and Rafe were still watching Malquin, who was tied up in the garage, waiting for his one-way ticket back to Caelum.

Everyone's voices stopped when they saw Shannon's face as she walked into the room. Merek jumped up from his chair in the living room and made his way quickly over to her.

"Well?"

"Well . . . there won't be a firing squad, at least."

"That bad, huh?" Liv asked from her spot next to Cedric on the couch.

"Oh yeah. I told them I'd drive back to Utah immediately, and we'd 'discuss' my future from there. As long as it doesn't involve military school, I'd say it's a win."

Shannon plopped down on a spare chair, and Merek took the one next to her. Looking around the room, she felt the tension in her shoulders loosen. They'd saved the world—both worlds—and figuring out what tomorrow would bring was a luxury now that she was sure there would *be* a tomorrow.

"You know," Joe said from his spot near the mantel, "I can talk to your parents if you want, Shannon. Explain things."

"Oh, trust me, I already tried. I even told them to look at our video online."

Their video was still trending, according to Peter, and he claimed more and more people were passing it around and wondering if there was any truth to it. Most said it was a hoax or a coincidence, and yet, the timing worked out. The sky turned blue just after the video gained around five thousand views.

But Shannon's parents weren't inclined to see it that way.

"What about you, Liv?" Shannon asked. "What will you do now?"

Liv took a moment, then shrugged. "Senior year? Who knows where I'll be living, though."

She looked down briefly, and Cedric took her hand.

"You know . . . ," Joe started, then cleared his throat. "That's something I've been thinking about. With the Knights scattered, there's no reason to really hide you guys anymore."

He looked between Liv and Peter, who exchanged a quick glance.

"There's no reason why you couldn't both . . . stay with me. In my apartment, of course, not that hotel room. It should be safe now. Peter, you're eighteen and can technically live with whoever you want, and Liv, for you there would be a process with paperwork and meetings, but if it's something the two of you think you might want . . ."

Liv's body went absolutely still, and for a moment it seemed like she hadn't heard Joe. But Shannon saw her lower lip shake, and knew Liv only blinked that hard when she was trying not to cry.

"It's entirely up to you," Joe added, stammering.

Peter grinned. "Promise to keep the house stocked with these?" he asked, holding up a bag of Doritos.

"I can do that," Joe said, smiling. But he turned to Liv, his eyes still questioning. "Liv, what do you think—"

"Of course!" Liv burst out. "I mean, yes. That . . . that would be . . ." She ran a quick hand over her eyes and smiled. "It would be great."

A happy warmth settled over the room, and for once it had nothing to do with the skyrocketing heat. As Liv and Joe continued to make plans, Merek leaned toward Shannon.

"Do you think your parents will make you stay in Utah?"

Shannon leaned over to meet him. "I hope not."

He reached out a hand, brushing the tops of her fingers with his.

"Me too."

≻+⋅+≺

The good-byes came later that afternoon. Merek's shoulder was well on its way to healing at that point, and Kat and Rafe were rested enough from their battle to make a return trip with Malquin, tied up and gagged, in tow.

The group of them walked down the Malibu beach, blinking from the glare of the sun. But not one of them complained about it. They reached the spot where Liv knew the portal would open, and she and Joe said the words to make it appear. The ritual was familiar to Liv—she had said these words often enough before—but it felt slightly different this time. The black hole that opened up in the sky didn't tear at her consciousness as it had before. Opening it up felt as easy as twisting a lid off a milk container.

Cedric and Kat embraced, and Kat whispered something into Cedric's ear that Liv could not hear. He smiled a sad smile as he watched her walk toward the portal with Malquin, and then he reached back to take Liv's hand. She squeezed his fingers with her own.

When it came time for Merek to say good-bye, he hesitated.

He looked between the portal and his brother, then took one hesitant step backward.

"I cannot go back," he said. "Not quite yet."

Rafe tilted his head in confusion. "What are you talking about? Of course you are coming back."

But Merek resolutely shook his head.

"You are a duke's son," Rafe said, his voice authoritative.

"A duke's second son," Merek corrected. "And you know, brother, that there is little need for me at home. I am staying here."

Merek and Rafe stared each other down for a moment, until Shannon stepped forward, her eyes blazing into Rafe's. "Are we gonna have a problem here? 'Cause it sounds like he's made up his mind."

"Merek has people at home waiting for him."

"He has people here, too," Shannon said, jutting her chin up to meet Rafe's eyes directly. Merek moved to stand nearer to her.

"Tell Mother and Father I am fine," Merek said.

Rafe took a few moments before finally nodding. "If that is your wish. I hope I will see you soon."

Rafe stuck out his hand, and Merek shook it with his free one. "I hope so, too," Merek said. "And in the meantime, Rafe? Try not to be such a dick."

Shannon and Liv both bit their lips to keep from laughing at the confused look on Rafe's face. He turned around to join Kat, and the two stood at the edge of the portal, looking back at the others.

"You know where I will be if you need me," Cedric said.

"Same to you," Kat responded with a smile.

She and Rafe raised their hands in farewell, then stepped into the black hole, taking their prisoner with them.

Liv, Cedric, Merek, Shannon, Peter, and Joe stood on the beach for a while, looking at the space where their friends had disappeared and waiting for the portal to close up after them.

It didn't.

Fifteen minutes passed, then thirty. The portal remained, a black tear in the sky. Without the Earth repressing magic, the portals were free to stay open and completely visible.

"Well," Liv said, after they realized the portal wasn't going anywhere. "This is going to be hard to explain to the neighbors."

A PLACE IN THE SUN

U p close, the letters of the Hollywood sign were large, the white paint on them fading in the sun. The sign had always felt important to Liv, like a symbol of everything she wanted to accomplish, everything she loved about her ambitious, dreaming city. Looking at it from a distance filled her with a sense of purpose, and being this close to it now seemed, fittingly, like something out of a movie.

Under normal circumstances, getting so close to the iconic letters wouldn't be possible. It was closed off with a chain-link fence, and anyone who jumped over to get close enough for a picture might find themselves being chased down the hillside by helicopters and the police.

But now the city was still empty of helicopters, and of people in general. Instead, it was spread out before Liv and Cedric like a sprawling, shining, slightly smog-covered blanket. Liv wanted to take this opportunity while she could. She wanted to share it with someone. And not just any someone.

Liv leaned her back up against the metal scaffolding of the

sign, her feet resting at a nearly ninety-degree angle on the steep hillside.

"You were right," Cedric said beside her, gazing out over the landscape. "This was worth the climb."

Liv smiled, her eyes also out over the city. Soon, the people would come back, with their cars and their big ideas and even bigger dreams. Meetings concerning millions of dollars would take place in the top floors of shiny buildings, while across town young hopefuls would keep their eyes glued to screens in darkened rooms, wondering when their own time would come. One of those hopefuls would be Liv.

Everything she'd always wanted was once again possible, now that they'd fixed what was broken. Of course, there were other, more immediate concerns. Even though Liv would be going to live with Joe—something that still seemed too good to even believe—she knew her social worker and friend still had some hard questions to face.

Joe would be forever changed by what happened to him, forever tainted with wrath blood. Whether he and the other Knights who'd been turned would become Guardians like Cedric or something else entirely was yet to be seen, but Cedric was keeping a close watch on Joe, and he'd vowed to keep close tabs on the others as well. If they'd gained strength from the wrath blood, they might also need training and guidance. They'd need someone who knew how to fight, and what things were worth fighting for. They'd need *him*.

Then, of course, there was the magic, and all of the unknowable shapes that it would take. That was the biggest question looming over Liv's head. The outside world had its own questions, some about Liv and her role in what had happened to the city. But Liv didn't want to think about any of that now, about the way they'd changed the world and how they'd have to answer for it. Right now, she was finally alone with Cedric, without fear of violence coming to tear them apart. Without fear that he might leave.

"See that whole big city out there?" Liv asked, gesturing at Los Angeles laid out before them like an uneven blanket stretching to the sea. "It's all yours now, for as long as you want it. What's the first thing you think you'll do?"

Cedric looked out over the hills and cocked his head. "Well, someone once told me I would make an excellent stuntman."

He grinned, pushing one shoulder up against Liv. Just feeling the warmth of his arm through her shirt sent a buzz through her skin.

"And you have no regrets?" she asked, pulling back a little. "About the things you're leaving behind? Your family?"

"I will miss my family, but it is not as though I will never see them again. The portals will no longer hurt our worlds, remember? And even if I do not see them every day, they are still my family. They always will be. Even those who are . . . gone."

"I think your father would be proud, you know? Of how you handled Malquin," she said.

"No," Cedric said, shaking his head. "I don't think he would. But it does not matter. *I* am proud."

Liv smiled. "Me too."

They sat in silence for a moment before she turned to him again.

"And you're absolutely, completely, totally sure you want to stay?"

Cedric shook his head and smiled. "Again, yes. I am sure. Completely, totally sure."

Liv felt a smile split across her face. "*Totally?* Careful now, you're beginning to sound like me."

"Maybe I *should* take care to sound more like you, now that I will be staying for a while."

"No," Liv protested. "Don't change too much—I like the way you talk."

Cedric smiled. "I like the way you talk, too. And the way you look."

"I like the way you look at me."

"I like the way you are."

Liv shook her head lightly, moving closer to Cedric. "We sound totally cheesy, just so you know."

"Totally. And I do not care."

He leaned closer, resting the tip of his forehead against hers. Beyond him, the city landscape became fuzzy, and Liv's eyes focused automatically on his features—his nose, his mouth, his eyes that were looking only at her.

"Good. I don't care either."

Cedric leaned forward and kissed her then, first her jaw, then the edge of her lips.

"I never really thought I could have this," he whispered, his words nearly getting swallowed up against her skin. "Something as strange and wonderful as getting to be here in this world, with you."

Liv pulled back a fraction, smiling. "Cedric, don't you know the first thing about LA? It's where happy endings are made."

He cupped the side of her face with one hand. "Endings? I do not like the sound of that."

"Good." Liv smiled. "Because that's the other thing about LA—there's always a sequel."

She kissed him again, and this time neither of them pulled away for a very long time.

⟫⟪

They drove back at sunset, up the PCH with the ocean on one side and the city on the other. They passed the Santa Monica Pier, and Liv remembered another day, only a few months earlier, when she had first truly opened her heart up to someone else. How terrifying and full of risk that moment had been. It seemed like so long ago.

As Liv drove Joe's Jeep down the two-lane highway, she passed two other cars coming in the opposite direction. Already, people were starting to return to the city. She slowed a bit as a convertible passed on her left, and Cedric eyed the Jeep's steering wheel, a glint in his eye.

"Don't even ask," she said, grinning.

"I have driven before," he said. "And I was fairly competent. Good even."

Liv snorted. "That's not the way Kat told it."

Cedric made a face, but he wasn't mad, not really. There was time for Liv to teach him how to properly drive. There was time, now, to do anything they wanted.

Liv followed a twist in the road, and the bright orange

sunlight lit up the car. She flipped the sun visor down. "You realize how cliché this is, that we're literally driving off into the sunset?"

"Are you making another movie reference that I could have no possible way of understanding?"

"Man, we have so much work to do," she said, looking over at him with a smile. "I mean, the Western genre alone will take us weeks."

"That sounds good to me," Cedric said, returning her smile.

Liv looked back to the road, feeling as though she were light enough to float up through the windshield. Without even looking at Cedric, she knew he was feeling the same thing. Because they were driving through her city—no, *their* city—side by side, both knowing, beyond a doubt, that this was exactly where they were supposed to be at this exact moment.

And if that wasn't the feeling of being at home—finally, finally at home—then what was?

But even though they were literally driving off into the sunset, Liv didn't feel like it was time to roll credits. Because now that they knew what home was, they wouldn't have to waste any more time looking for it. They could just live in this moment and look forward to the moment to come. Because in that moment, anything could happen.

Anything at all.

ACKNOWLEDGMENTS

For having only four letters, *home* is a pretty big, important word. I've been incredibly lucky in my life to have found home in a few wonderful places, one of which, Los Angeles, played a big hand in shaping this series. Just like Liv, I love this city of dreams come to life, and nothing has been a bigger inspiration to me during this process than the beaches, mountains, freeways, hidden castles, movie sets, and, yes, ridiculous juice bars that exist here.

But home isn't just about the places we love, but also the people who populate them. I am forever thankful to my Los Angeles friends who have provided unrelenting enthusiasm and support (and wine) during the past few years I've been working on this sequel. I don't know what I did to be lucky enough to end up in this place with these people, and all I can do is be grateful that I'm here, and that they exist.

I am of course thankful to everyone in my first home, too. To my parents, my sisters, my friends, and family old and new in Michigan and scattered beyond, thank you so much for your unwavering confidence in me and in this series. Your support has made me cry on more than one occasion (in a good way, I promise).

Just like me, this book was fortunate enough to find its perfect home. Thank you so much to Jess MacLeish and the whole HarperTeen team for bringing this sequel to life and making it better than I ever imagined. Many thanks also to Kate Klimowicz for the gorgeous cover design of this series. And hundreds of thanks to Reiko Davis, dream agent.

I've also been enormously grateful these past few years for the support and encouragement of the Sweet Sixteens; a girl couldn't ask for a better, funnier or smarter group of fellow authors to share this experience with. And many thanks to everyone who helped me make a cool-as-hell trailer to celebrate this series—Christine Riccio, Jesse George, Kat O'Keeffe, Tillery Johnson, Sam Kimbrell, Julie Park, Mike Costantini, and Kimtsy Gomez-Sanchez.

And thanks to Phil, as always, for everything.

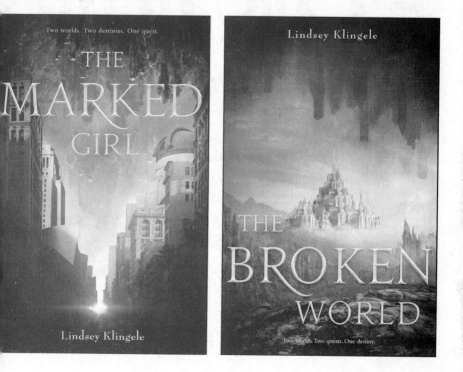

JOIN THE

Epic Reads

COMMUNITY

THE ULTIMATE YA DESTINATION

◀ **DISCOVER** ▶
your next favorite read

◀ **MEET** ▶
new authors to love

◀ **WIN** ▶
free books

◀ **SHARE** ▶
infographics, playlists, quizzes, and more

◀ **WATCH** ▶
the latest videos

www.epicreads.com